To Mike –

THE DECISION TO KILL

A True Crime Story Of A Teenage Killer And The Mother Who Loved Him

LESLIE GHIGLIERI

Leslie Ghiglieri

WILDBLUE
P R E S S

WildBluePress.com

Grief is the price we pay for love

THE DECISION TO KILL published by:
WILDBLUE PRESS
P.O. Box 102440
Denver, Colorado 80250

WILDBLUE PRESS is registered at the U.S. Patent and Trademark Offices.

ISBN 978-1-957288-34-5 Hardcover
ISBN 978-1-957288-33-8 Trade Paperback
ISBN 978-1-957288-32-1 eBook

Cover Design / Interior Formatting by Elijah Toten
www.totencreative.com

THE DECISION TO KILL

ACKNOWLEDGEMENTS

Thank you to my beta readers who generously gave of their time to read my manuscript and offer suggestions. I am grateful to each of you.

Sherri Beeler, Allyson Elmore, Debi Hassler, Sarah Hyman, Gina Jones, Nancy Lee Lane, Mel Neilitz, Karissa Quant, Erica Schwam

To those who edited my work. Vickie Reierson who got me on track in the beginning and encouraged me to stay the course. Suzanne Ray who edited and re-edited many pages. Your persistence reassured me that someone was by my side to the end. Nancy Lee Lane who offered helpful editing suggestions and held my hand through computer frustrations. You are a good friend.

And to my husband, Andy Ghiglieri, from the beginning you supported my commitment to do this project for Cherie. You read chapters and offered ideas for improvement. Most of all, you reassured me to keep going when I felt discouraged. I couldn't have completed the book without you.

Thank you Donette for your patience with my incessant questions at all hours of the day. You welcomed me into your home and always treated me with respect for my mission with your mom and were friendly to me. I appreciate your willingness to open the door to events that were traumatic for you and answer questions with candor. You are an exceptional woman.

DEDICATION

To Cherie

*A woman I admired for doing what she believed
was right despite her own feelings. Thank you
for the privilege of documenting your story.*

TABLE OF CONTENTS

PROLOGUE

In February of 1986, my then future husband Andy and I attended a sweetheart banquet in a quaint brick restaurant in the Southern Oregon town of Grants Pass. The small church we went to had organized the event and, soon after we entered the bistro, we were seated at a table with a couple neither of us knew. Their names were Don and Cherie Wier. I wish now that I would have known then how our lives would intersect over the next thirty-five years. I would have paid closer attention to the conversation Andy and I had with Don and Cherie that night. My recollection is of an enjoyable evening shared with a warm and friendly couple who caused us to laugh and made us feel as if we'd always been friends. I remember leaving that night thinking how glad I was that we'd been seated with them. I cannot help but wonder, when looking back, if they'd mentioned trouble with their sixteen-year-old son and I hadn't paid attention. Probably not. I never could have imagined that these many years later, I would be writing a book sharing intensely private details of Don and Cherie's lives.

Andy and I married in 1987 and moved thirty miles away to Jackson County in 1989. I remember seeing Cherie several times over the years, but it wasn't until October of 2016 that our reunion would take a very special turn.

That fall afternoon, I was looking forward to attending the women's get-together Cherie was hosting outdoors on her picturesque property along the Applegate River. An invitation to visit the grounds was a treat in itself, the surroundings breathtaking and the atmosphere serene.

We would sit outside, of course, and the opportunity to reconnect with friends would be a bonus. I sat near my dear friend Sharon, and we talked about old times and mutual acquaintances. The discussion drifted to comments about the almost magical quality of Cherie's property and then to the subject of Cherie herself. As we marveled at all that Cherie had overcome in her life, Sharon commented that Cherie's personal story would make a fascinating book. Something stirred in me at that moment and I felt drawn to act on my friend's observation.

That same day, after everyone had left, Cherie and I stood in her kitchen discussing the story of her life. For more than twenty years, she'd been passionate about the idea of a book chronicling her experiences that might bring hope to others going through struggles similar to hers. I told Cherie I would document her life story if she would let me, but I admitted I had no experience writing professionally. I'd always wanted to write a book, I told her, remembering I'd first had the desire when I was in the fifth grade. Cherie was seventy-six and I think she realized, after waiting so many years, that this might be her last chance to see her vision become reality. She said she would trust me to do it. That afternoon, Cherie and I entered into an agreement that would bind me to her and consume me with her story for the next five years. I was naïve about the scope of the task but prayed that my diligence would compensate for my lack of experience.

Over the next three years, I visited Cherie as often as I could. For months at a time, we would meet weekly, having lunch at her home, talking about her life. I recorded our interviews and took notes, knowing I couldn't rely on my memory to recall the volumes of information we covered. When she became sick with an unknown illness, I visited her in hospitals in Grants Pass and Medford and when the need for emergency surgery sent Cherie to Portland transported by Mercy Flights, I rode along. For the duration of the flight, I watched with amusement as Cherie flirted with the handsome young paramedic in charge of her care. We traveled in a Lear jet with two paramedics and two pilots to the Oregon Health and Science University, where we stayed for five days. Everywhere we went, she introduced me to people and told them we were writing a book together. I wish I'd made a list of the names of those individuals who requested a copy when the book was finished. I sat in the background, wanting only to keep her company and let her know she wasn't going through this journey alone. I couldn't help but be awed at how naturally she spoke with people she met and how quickly she engaged others in conversation. She had a gift for connecting with strangers.

I considered my promise to complete this book an irrevocable commitment to someone I loved and admired. I can say with confidence that these pages tell a true story. The content comes from personal interviews I conducted, newspaper articles, police interviews and reports, psychiatrist reports, and other official documents. Where letters are incorporated, I have quoted portions verbatim without correcting grammar, spelling, or punctuation errors. I deliberately avoided drawing conclusions and simply presented the facts, allowing readers to form their own opinions. I read 350 letters and extracted the sections I found pertinent. There are gaps in time when letters weren't exchanged. I cannot account for what went on during those periods. There was no documentation of telephone conversations, though there was reference to them in a few letters. Several early readers of the book asked for more information about Donette. Out of respect for her privacy, I have included only those incidents she felt comfortable sharing with me.

Prior to writing this book, I worked in the criminal justice field for over twelve years, employed by the 911 Center in Santa Cruz County, California; by the Josephine County Sheriff's Office in their records, warrants, and dispatch services; and by a company providing a computer system (RAIN) that delivered networking capabilities to more than half of Oregon's law enforcement agencies. My criminal justice work aided me in sifting through the various court papers and police reports necessary for compiling significant portions of this book. My intention is to donate a portion of each book sale to the ROC Recovery Center, a local faith-based program that provides help for those addicted to substances and their families.

Cherie Wier's story demonstrates how the seduction of addictive substances can tear apart and devastate a family, ruining not only the life of the reckless drug abuser but also the lives of loved ones impacted by the drug user's irrevocable decisions. Her account covers a forty-year period from 1970 to 2010, but today, in 2022, substance abuse has escalated. More than at any other time and affecting every demographic, substance abuse runs rampant, and a story such as this one needs to be shared to encourage those struggling with destructive behaviors and those who love them. Cherie Wier's story is about hope—the hope she kept and the hope she shares to encourage parents in the midst of the battle. She discloses her personal hardships and her path through them in an effort to show others that in the darkness of life's hardest times there is hope, even if change is excruciatingly slow in coming.

CHAPTER I — OCTOBER I 7, I 986

The day that changes his life begins like any other. He wakes at 7:30 and pops two Valium he got from a friend at school who had pilfered them from his mother's medicine cabinet. At age sixteen he doesn't care where the drugs come from. He traded some of his weed for the pills, and both he and the kid with the Valium were happy with the arrangement. After downing the Valium, he grinds up some bud and packs a fresh bowl. As he lights up, he inhales and watches the vapor disappear from the bong. The smoke from the bubbling water enters his mouth and lungs. Shoving open the window in his room, he makes a meager attempt to conceal the smell. His mother and father have caught him with weed several times, so he half-heartedly covers his tracks to avoid a hassle. He lies back in a daze and slowly exhales. Last spring, the rehab doctor warned his parents that he suspected their son had a severe amphetamine addiction, and there was the incident six months ago when his folks found him having a bad trip from hallucinogens. But his parents are lost in their manufactured hope for his recovery, neither of them aware how hopelessly devoted he is to any substance that will get him high.

At 8:30, his father drives him to school. Fridays are early release days, so at noon his father usually picked him up and would take him home; however, he had gotten into trouble. As a consequence, he's required to go to work with his father after school. A mechanic for a logging company, his father is often called to work in the woods. Today's early morning rain has created muddy conditions on a forest service road, causing a truck to slip off the roadway into a ditch. His father is needed at the accident site.

It's torture for him to be stuck in a pickup for hours while his father repairs logging trucks in the remote Southern Oregon forests. Antsy, he climbs out of the truck and walks around the front of the rig. Leaning against the truck's hood, he watches the small group of loggers scramble around the disabled truck. Situations like this always make him uneasy. He isn't sure why, but he feels awkward and incompetent.

Bored, he crawls back into the truck, itching to go home and play his music. His stash of little yellow pills and weed serve to assuage his resentment as he restlessly sits in the cab. A cigarette laced with bud is a bonus. He lights the joint, impatiently fidgeting, and takes a drag while surveying the cab's interior. The floor is littered with grease rags and random machine parts—the tools of his father's trade. Maybe the cluttered cab will yield some forgotten coins or even dollar bills under the seats or in the glove box. He rummages around only to find small change. *What a joke*, he thinks, slumping against the passenger-side window.

Turning, he looks back into the truck's bed littered with bulky engine parts and toolboxes. "Not worth the effort to hunt through that mess," he mutters to himself. He straightens in the seat and his eyes return to view his father, whom he calculates is twenty-five yards directly in front of the truck talking with two other men from the logging company. His gaze again drifts toward the bed of the pickup, and he takes note of his father's rifle mounted in the rear window rack. Surprised that he hadn't spotted it before, he studies the weapon carefully. His eyes narrow. He takes stock of the gun's caliber and wonders about its accuracy. He considers just how close the target would have to be for a shot to be lethal. His father looks toward the truck; they briefly make eye contact. He thinks he reads disapproval in his father's eyes. Perhaps his father is disappointed that he isn't down in the ditch offering help to the exhausted men. But why should he care? It isn't his problem. He again examines the gun in the truck's rack. Looking at the rifle gets him thinking; it's time to make a plan and take some action. It's 8:30 or 9:00 p.m. and he's fed up with waiting in the truck. The autumn light has long since faded, and he can see the full moon between the evergreen boughs of the forest canopy. The excruciating wait finally ends as his father climbs into the cab and starts the truck. Over an hour passes before the father and son near home. At long last, the truck turns onto the gravel drive leading to the house. His jaw tightens. Through clenched teeth he scowls and mutters beneath his breath, "It's about time!" His father doesn't pick up on the comment.

Around 12:30 a.m., he hears his father talking on the phone in the kitchen. He guesses the call is from his mother, who is out of town at a school reunion. The two of them talk every night when she's away. Since it's late, he knows the conversation won't be long, so he needs to execute his plan quickly. He slips into his parents' room and takes a 30-30 rifle and some ammunition out of their closet where the hunting rifles are stored and moves them into his own room. Quietly, he loads the weapon and carries it into the bathroom off the front room. He engages the safety, dropping the hammer down to half-cock. In order to keep the weapon hidden from his father, he lays it in the bathtub and quietly closes the shower door.

He returns to the hall satisfied that he has acquired the weapon and ammunition without detection. Hearing his father in continued conversation with his mother, he casually walks into the kitchen and takes a cold beer out of the refrigerator. His father, immersed in the phone call, doesn't react as his son pops the top and takes a drink from the can before returning to his room. Unruffled, he'll bide his time until his father is asleep. Meanwhile, he props himself up with pillows and stretches out on his bed. He hears his father retire shortly afterward and waits until the house is quiet.

Recalling the events that wasted his day, he lifts the unfinished beer and pours what remains down his throat. He savors the coolness then pitches the empty to the floor, adding to the growing pile of cans.

He finds the waiting difficult and fumbles through the empties until he finds an unopened can. Slowly popping the aluminum ring, he uses one hand to muffle the familiar hiss as the top breaks free. He chugs the warm beer while fixating on the source of his irritation.

He dredges up the hot anger he felt when his father required him to go to the woods after school instead of allowing him to return home to practice his music. His passion is his guitar and his song writing. Seething, he thinks about the numerous times his parents have interfered with his music. They don't get it. His idols are KISS and hard rock. He believes those guys have "made it" and he longs to play just like them. Self-taught, he works hard at his music and considers himself an accomplished musician. With increasing resentment, he thinks about how his parents don't support his dream of musical success and constantly push him to consider a career in computers. He knows better. He'll make it big someday. He'll show them. He's tired of being treated like a child, unfairly punished for pilfering money from his mother's purse. After all, he does chores and his parents refuse to give him an allowance. What he finds around the place is rightfully his, so what's the big deal? Why can't he just take what he wants?

Still thirsty, he slips into the dark hallway and heads toward the kitchen. He opens the refrigerator door and searches for any remaining beer inside. Startled by the bright light as the door opens, he quickly grabs the two six packs from the back of the fridge and pushes the door closed. Noiselessly, he returns to his room. The cans under his arm lie ice cold against his ribs. Aware of fuzziness in his head and a sour stomach, he supposes the cause is his substance intake over the last few hours. He reasons that more beer and weed will make him feel better. For him, it's all about feeling good. Besides, he tells himself, it will help steady his nerves. He ingests more Valium. He has lost track of how many he has taken. Was it four or five or as many as eight?

While trapped in the truck's cab for hours, isolated in the remote woods, he fumed and formulated his plans—and consumed drugs as he endured his captivity. Certain of one thing, he's sick to death of his parents meddling in his life and is resolved to do whatever the hell he wants to do with his future. No one is going to stop him.

CHAPTER 2 – THE ADOPTED SON

Sixteen years earlier…

Railene Coleman had resigned herself to living in a home for unwed mothers in the Lincoln Heights area of Los Angeles County. The year was 1969 and Railene, a high school sophomore with an oval face and dainty features, was pregnant after a two-month association with an eighteen-year-old boy she'd met at the drag races. Heartbroken when he dumped her after she disclosed the pregnancy, Railene was persuaded to give her baby up for adoption. Railene's relationship with her own mother was so strained that she'd run away from home three times, so the expectant mother would live in the maternity house until her baby was born. On January 11, 1970, shortly after the new year, Railene gave birth to a hefty baby boy of almost eleven pounds. The young mother saw her infant several times while she was in the hospital. Her decision to relinquish him for adoption didn't seem to waver, though she was "weepy" the day she signed the final papers. Afterwards, she was able to say she was happy that her baby would soon be in a "whole" family.

***

On February 3, 1970, Don and Cherie Wier, a young couple who had longed for a child for eight years, tenderly held their soon-to-be adopted three-week-old baby boy. In 1970, adoption laws were stringent, and the names of parties on both sides were legally protected. As Don and Cherie looked at the infant's curiously dark brown eyes and sandy blond hair, they brushed aside concerns about the limited background information they'd been given by the adoption agency. The elated couple thought of the child as a clean slate and were confident that the two of them would ensure that the boy grew up loved and secure.

The final ceremony for the adoption took place in the Los Angeles County courtroom, when the new parents placed their left hands on the Bible, solemnly swearing they would care for this infant to the best of their ability until he reached the age of eighteen. No matter what lay ahead, Don and Cherie considered their promise a sacred responsibility, to God and to the helpless child in their arms.

The new mother and father adjusted easily to the changes that came with caring for a newborn. Don operated heavy equipment at the nearby Castaic Dam project and, with a son to support, he readily opted to work extra hours whenever he was offered overtime. Next to her role as a wife, Cherie had craved being a mother. Content with an infant to care for, she settled comfortably into her role. The couple named the child Dwayne Dean Wier.

Dwayne had just turned three months old when Cherie spotted large, painful-looking welts on his skin whenever he was wet or cold. Adding to the upset, Dwayne started having breathing difficulties that led to a diagnosis of asthma. Visits to the doctor's office or the hospital's emergency room became commonplace, and both parents were distressed to see their baby plagued with ailments. They tried not to worry.

Having started their family, Cherie and Don were determined to leave California and find a home in the Pacific Northwest that would be perfect for raising children. Imagining a life away from the city and full of boating and camping opportunities, they saw no reason Dwayne's mysterious medical conditions should deter them from pursing their dream.

So, eight months after Dwayne's adoption, the family travelled to Oregon. They easily found a real estate agent in the Southern Oregon town of Grants Pass willing to show them rural property near the neighboring community of Murphy. The agent drove them to a listing located in the beautiful Applegate Valley, where a popular fishing waterway meandered along acres of rich farmland. The valley's scenery surpassed the couple's imaginings as they drove past horse ranches, including the home of the famous Thoroughbred stallion Flying Lark, and acres of irrigated hay pastures and lavender fields. The flatlands were edged by mountains that created a sheltered feel, as though the valley were separated from the rest of the world.

Arriving at the listing's location, the group exited the vehicle and surveyed the heavily overgrown land. Even though the couple took note of the work involved to clear the property and ultimately prepare it for a homesite, they discussed the listing's possibilities and enthusiastically submitted an offer the following day. By December of 1970, the Wiers owned a small portion of the Applegate Valley. In spite of their eagerness to live in Oregon, for the next two years Don and Cherie put their dreams on hold, continuing to live in California and trying to save every penny.

The prospect of moving to the Pacific Northwest motivated the couple to think optimistically about their future, yet Cherie found that her worries over Dwayne's continued poor health dampened her spirits. At twenty-one months old, Dwayne was admitted to the hospital "due to reoccurring unresolved conditions," presumably referring to the blood in his urine and mysterious skin welts. He underwent a variety of tests during his two-day admission, which only confirmed the existence of the symptoms that had brought him to the hospital in the first place and didn't provide insight as to the underlying cause or a direction for specific future treatment. On the discharge forms, typed in bold-face, were the words: "PROGNOSIS: Probably good."

Witnessing the toddler's misery, Cherie couldn't help but be alarmed watching him suffer with persistent pain and itchiness from conditions that didn't respond to treatment. The young mother cared for Dwayne as his doctor directed and prayed that her son's year and a half of repeated medical visits didn't indicate the likelihood of bad health in years to come.

CHAPTER 3 – MOVE TO THE APPLEGATE VALLEY

Exhausted after hours on the road, Don pulled the trailer onto the overgrown dirt driveway of their Applegate property. Their two years of life in California had passed, and the Wiers' long-awaited aspiration of moving to the Northwest had finally become a reality. Within a month of arriving in Oregon, Don landed a job working for the Army Corps of Engineers on the construction of the nearby Applegate Dam. On weekends, and during the week when Don could squeeze out an hour or two, he and Cherie took on the task of reclaiming their land from the wilds of Oregon. The acreage was covered with scrubby bushes, oak and madrone trees, and tall evergreens. The couple imagined that with enough work, they could transform the dense brambles and poison oak bushes into a lush, park-like setting. They had no idea the metamorphosis they pictured would take years.

One winter afternoon, when the fishing season was at its peak, the young couple slipped under the old wire fencing near their homesite and followed the weedy trail down the steep bank to the river that bordered the property on its west side.

January 1972. Don smiles proudly holding his first steelhead pulled out of the Applegate River. He caught the 6-pound fish while sitting on the rock just behind the house.

They came armed with fishing gear, prepared to test the waters. Cherie caught sight of a gray boulder just off the river's edge and, soon after, Don had perched himself on the rock and caught his first steelhead. That cold January day in 1972, the rock took on a special significance to Don and Cherie because it was the place where Don caught his first steelhead on their own property.

While Cherie and Don continued to improve their property, Dwayne grew from a toddler into an active small boy, running, jumping, climbing, and exploring the world. Outdoor living for the family included deer and elk hunting, in addition to fishing, when the seasons came around. Don couldn't wait to share these outdoor adventures with his son.

At daybreak one Saturday morning, Cherie was awakened by a muffled sound from outside. Groggy, she strained to listen for whatever noise had roused her but heard nothing more. A minute or two passed before she perceived what sounded like a whimper, maybe a child's voice.

Cherie slipped out of bed and looked out the window. Standing at the edge of the lawn in his pajamas, soaked from head to toe, shivering and crying softly, stood Dwayne. Cherie gasped and wakened Don, who leapt from bed, pulled on his jeans, and ran out the side door. What was their four-year-old doing in the yard this early, and soaking wet besides? When Don reached Dwayne and looked him over, he discovered scratches on his arms and hands, some of them sprinkled with bright red flecks of blood. By the time Don scooped the boy up and brought him inside, Dwayne had turned a bluish color, and the all-too-familiar welts were beginning to appear on his skin. He shook violently.

Four-year-old Dwayne took this path to get to the bridge where he tossed the kittens into the creek and where he too, fell in. The footbridge was quite a distance from the house.

Twenty minutes later, when the initial shock was over and Dwayne's coloring had returned to normal, Don and Cherie questioned the boy, frantic to discover what had happened. Dwayne said little, only mumbling something about kittens. Their cat had delivered a litter of kittens several weeks earlier, and Don went out to look for them. Maybe finding the cats would lead him to answers as to why Dwayne was wet and cold. He headed to the creek down the road, just past where Cherie had first seen Dwayne. A wooden foot bridge connected the Wiers' property and that of the neighbors. When Don reached the creek, he found the mama cat and her litter curled up in the grass near the blackberries several feet from the water. All were as wet as Dwayne. Unmistakably, they'd also landed in the creek. Don knew the kittens wouldn't have willingly gone into the water, but why, he wondered, would his son toss the helpless kittens into the cold stream? Not knowing what to make of the situation, he hurried back to the trailer for answers.

Don told Dwayne about seeing the cats near the creek. Dwayne blurted out that the mama cat scratched him and pulled him into the creek as he stood on the bridge holding her. After several moments, Dwayne said he wanted to see if the kittens could swim, but quickly changed his story, explaining that the kittens wanted a drink of water. As the parents pressed Dwayne, trying to learn the truth of the events that had taken place, he told them he threw the kittens into the creek because they'd scratched him. Ultimately, Don and Cherie never got a clear story about what had really happened and were troubled to consider that Dwayne might have tried to drown the helpless animals.

What Don and Cherie knew was that Dwayne had fallen into the creek from the foot bridge, and the cold water was so deep that he could have drowned. They surmised that he must have managed to pull himself from the creek by grabbing the blackberry vines that grew alongside the banks, because he had thorn scratches on his hands as well as feline claw marks on his arms. Uncertain why Dwayne had cast the kittens and mother into the water, they knew they had to fortify their home to prevent him from going outside undetected. That very day, they devised foolproof safety locks for all of the doors and committed to keep closer watch over him.

Despite Cherie and Don's resolve to keep their son safe, Dwayne's odd behavior manifested in another troubling incident later that summer. Cherie arranged for a babysitter to come to the house before Dwayne woke up so she could enjoy some fishing from the bank. After about an hour, she walked back up to the house to check on Dwayne. As Cherie approached the residence, she smelled smoke and saw black clouds rolling out the kitchen's screen door. She panicked at spotting Dwayne inside, standing on a chair he'd pulled up to the front of the stove. He'd started a fire by filling a small pan with papers, somehow managing to ignite the contents, and was stirring the flames with a spoon. In a frenzy, Cherie grabbed the pan's lid to cover the flames, removing the pan from the burner. She rushed Dwayne outside to the fresh air and, after ensuring the fire was out and Dwayne was no longer in danger, she turned her attention to finding the babysitter. The girl had fallen asleep on the living room couch, not waking until Cherie shook her. Livid, Cherie sent the teenager home after telling her that her carelessness had nearly cost Dwayne his life and the Wiers their home. The rest of the afternoon, Cherie couldn't help but think of how much worse the day could have turned out. Six weeks later Dwayne would start kindergarten, and the anxious mother was relieved to begin a new routine.

Soon after the school year began, Dwayne's teacher called Cherie, concerned that occasionally Dwayne didn't respond when spoken to. At the teacher's suggestion, Cherie consulted a hearing specialist who diagnosed Dwayne with a hearing impairment, though he couldn't pinpoint the reason for it. The audiologist fitted Dwayne with hearing aids at the substantial cost of a thousand dollars. When Dwayne returned home after his first day wearing the hearing aids, he was excited and told his mom he'd never before "heard the birdies singing in the trees" as he walked down the gravel driveway to the bus stop. Even though the hearing aids were expensive, she and Don were grateful that there was a solution to their son's hearing condition and Dwayne seemed pleased with his newfound hearing.

When Dwayne spoke favorably about the hearing aids, Cherie thought it showed his willingness to wear them. Unfortunately, that wasn't the case. Soon after Dwayne acquired the devises, Cherie found out from the school staff that he would pull the aids off and keep them in his pocket when he went to school. He was evasive when Don and Cherie talked to him about his reluctance to keep them on. His aversion to the devices didn't change even after adjustments at the audiologist's office. Their son seemed to need the devices to hear properly, but Don and Cherie didn't want to force him to wear them, believing if Dwayne was helped by using the hearing aids, he would do so on his own.

Considering that their son's medical and behavioral issues were a part of the inevitable trials of parenthood, Don and Cherie weren't dissuaded from wanting more children. Oregon had exceeded their expectations and seemed the perfect place to grow their family. Dwayne had turned five and Cherie hadn't yet become pregnant. The couple decided it was time to take steps toward another adoption.

CHAPTER 4 – A NEW ARRIVAL

Cherie needed to pass her pre-adoption physical, the last step in completing the adoption process. Feeling out of sorts all morning, she considered postponing her exam but feared rescheduling might delay their adoption. Dwayne was five, and Don and Cherie agreed they wanted their children to be close in age.

At the appointment, Cherie mentioned her morning wooziness to the doctor and asked him whether he thought she might be pregnant. The doctor knew her history of infertility and told her that although pregnancy was doubtful, he was willing to do a test to be certain. He phoned the following morning and wasted no time in telling Cherie that she was, in fact, pregnant.

Thirteen years of infertility had gravely diminished her expectation that she would ever bear her own child, yet she'd never completely given up hope. She was joyous with the thought that she was carrying a new life. Don had stayed home from work that morning anticipating word from the doctor's office. The two embraced, celebrating the miraculous news.

***

During the pregnancy, Cherie and Don, concerned that Dwayne might feel uneasy about how this new baby would change his life, looked for ways to reassure him of their love and his place in the family. In the midst of baby showers and transforming the bedroom into a nursery, the parents were attentive to Dwayne's moods and included him as much as possible. The nine months passed quickly and, on October 21, 1975, a healthy, beautiful baby girl was born to Don and Cherie. The parents named their daughter Donette. As soon as they were permitted by the hospital to do so, Don brought Dwayne to see his mother and new sister. A week later, when Cherie and Donette were discharged, Don took Dwayne with him to the hospital, wanting them all to come home together as a family.

Donette is only a few weeks old. Dwayne is five.

During Donette's first weeks at home, Dwayne eagerly brought Cherie things she needed for the baby. He helped Cherie when asked, but soon the novelty wore off, and he seemed to grow bored with the baby who slept a lot and cried often. After all of the hype, perhaps Dwayne was disappointed his sister wasn't the playmate he'd expected.

The new family routine made Don and Cherie happy, but Don found himself increasingly disgruntled with his job and longed for a career change. For fifteen years, he'd operated heavy equipment. The work was gratifying and paid well but he wanted to try something new, so in 1976, he was open to an offer made by his friend Bill.

Bill and Dixie Mendenhall operated the E & I Market for 23 years until it closed in 1994. Their customers were their neighbors and friends. Don was a regular visitor at the market, stopping almost nightly to visit with the couple.

Bill and Dixie Mendenhall owned the E & I Market, a deli and convenience store on the outskirts of Grants Pass. Don stopped by the market most nights to visit on his way home, and Cherie shopped there often enough that the two couples had become friends. Bill also owned a stick mill in Murphy and asked Don if he might be interested in becoming a partner. Don had never owned a business, but he reasoned that since the Mendenhalls had run a successful market for years, they understood how to operate an enterprise. With Cherie in agreement, Don accepted the offer, but by the beginning of the third month he discovered the downside of being the boss. Small business ownership afforded him a certain independence and flexibility, but it demanded long hours, and Don felt the burden starting to wear on him. He resented the time away from his family, and the income from the business wasn't enough for them to start the construction on a home on their property as they'd planned. Despite Don's drop in wages, the dream of a new home again became feasible when Cherie's grandfather passed away and left her $20,000. The generous inheritance gave the couple what they needed to begin construction on the house after all and, in 1977, $20,000 went a long way.

Don could fix anything with moving parts, but he wasn't a carpenter; in fact, he knew little about building anything. Cherie also lacked construction knowledge and skills, but she was determined to help her husband build their home and took on the task of drawing house plans. Don worked on the construction whenever he wasn't at his job. Cherie provided labor for the building project. What the two lacked in experience and training, they made up for in hard work, ingenuity, and trial and error. They jokingly nicknamed the residence "the crooked little house that Don built."

The couple spent $50,000 constructing the modest, single-story home with attached garage. Pleased with the simple floor plan that suited their needs, they added extensive decking with seating for barbecues overlooking the river. Cherie cultivated a garden of seasonal flowers around the front of the house. By now, Cherie's mother Lois and Lois's husband Arnie had moved to Grants Pass from Southern California. In November of 1977, Lois and Arnie joined in celebrating the Wiers' first Thanksgiving in the mostly completed home. Don and Cherie never tired of their beautiful property and named it "Our Little Bit of Heaven."

Work on incomplete house projects was ongoing and didn't deter Cherie from signing Dwayne up for Boy Scouts when she learned he was old enough to join. She hoped he would be fond of the outdoor learning activities and group projects. Wanting to do her part for the troop and share in her son's pursuits, Cherie agreed to be an assistant den mother. Every week, Dwayne looked forward to dressing in his Cub Scout uniform. At one of the meetings, the boys received a myrtle wood seedling to take home, and Cherie was pleased that Dwayne wanted to pick out the spot on their property where they would plant the baby tree.

*Dwayne receiving his Boy Scout Wolf badge
with Don and Cherie looking on.*

Cherie committed to helping with the troop for three years. She watched Dwayne with boys his age and couldn't help noticing he often needed extra help in doing craft projects. Cherie realized that children develop skills at different rates, but Dwayne had trouble sequencing steps to complete every task, and his finished projects were noticeably messier than those of the other boys. She was certain Dwayne couldn't help but see the difference too. When activities required involvement with others, Dwayne participated but given a choice, he was a loner. She reasoned that because he'd been an only child for six years, he was accustomed to playing alone, but she feared that the behaviors she witnessed were symptomatic of something inherently different in her son.

Months rolled by and, while Cherie attended Scout meetings, Don's responsibilities at the mill kept him away from home. The allure of owning his own business had faded, and he longed for fewer demands at work. He needed a break. Wanting to let off steam, he found an outlet in going to friends' houses for a beer or two or stopping at a bar on his way home. Busy with kids aged eight and two and incomplete painting projects in the new home, Cherie waited with growing aggravation for Don's arrival from work each night, hoping for a break of her own.

The property makeover, childrearing, and house construction consumed all Don and Cherie's time. Before they realized it, they'd lost sight of each other. Both short on sleep and grouchy, Don and Cherie unwittingly let an irritating tone creep into their conversations, leading to heated quarrels over simple differences. When they'd moved to Oregon and begun clearing the land and building their home, they'd been enthusiastic about the work. Lately, both were weary, and they found themselves taking out their frustrations on each other. Their marriage was in trouble.

CHAPTER 5 – TROUBLE IN PARADISE

The tension that they'd allowed to grow didn't lend itself to an easy resolution. While Cherie and Don knew there was discord, they were each too busy and irritable to do anything to make the situation better. Instead of resolving their differences, they ignored the warning signs, pretending all was well.

Life went on as usual with friends and unexpected visitors frequently dropping in to say hello. Often, someone brought a vehicle with a problem the owner hoped Don would fix. It wasn't uncommon for the occasional individual to pull up to the Wier house just as the family sat down to eat dinner on the deck outside. Don would get up from the table and find out what the visitor wanted, telling them he was going to finish his dinner before looking at their car. One weekend afternoon as Don fiddled on his truck and Cherie worked in the yard, an unfamiliar car came up the drive. Don recognized the pretty young woman who got out of the vehicle and introduced her to Cherie, explaining that she was an employee at the mill. The woman asked Don if she could watch him work on his truck. Don didn't see why not, so she walked with him to the garage and leaned against the truck while Don tinkered on the vehicle's engine. Cherie couldn't help but spot the woman's flirtatious manner and she noticed that Don responded to her with friendly smiles.

Annoyed with the visitor's intrusion into their family's weekend, which by now had lasted over an hour, Cherie pulled Don aside and asked him, "Is she a little weird or what?" She was bothered that the woman, who had no legitimate reason for coming to their home, continued to linger on the property watching Don work on his truck. Fed up with witnessing the unabashed exchange between her husband and a pretty girl, Cherie told the visitor she would have to leave because she and Don had errands to take care of in town.

After the woman left, Don told Cherie the girl was only nineteen and never had a father. He thought she saw him as a father figure and then admitted she'd baked him cookies and left small gifts on the seat of his truck. Don may have rationalized that he was a father figure to the girl, but Cherie believed the girl saw him as a prospective boyfriend. She harbored insecurities about herself, secretly wondering how SHE ever got so lucky to end up with Don Wier. Usually happy to welcome visitors, Cherie had been put off by the unexpected guest.

With growing tension between them, Cherie hadn't been on the receiving side of Don's friendly smile for some time. A few weeks after the woman's visit, Cherie stopped at the mill after dropping Dwayne off at school. She'd made Don lunch and intended to surprise him. Walking into Don's office unannounced, Cherie not only caught him unawares by her arrival, but she was shocked at the sight before her. The pretty female employee who had been at their property two weeks earlier was sitting comfortably on Don's lap. Mortified, the young woman jumped up, making a useless attempt to look as though all was proper. Humiliated, she quickly exited the office. Don knew there was no way to hide the impropriety of the situation. He and Cherie glared at each other, emotions raging. Cherie tossed the prepared lunch onto Don's desk and stormed out of the room. Trouble had been brewing at home and without efforts from both of them to remedy the cause, it had only gotten worse. It was no longer possible to pretend that ignoring the emotional distance between them could magically lead to marital harmony.

The icy wall of silence took effort to maintain, and both Don and Cherie knew it was stubbornness that kept them angry and withdrawn. They'd neglected addressing their problems partly because they couldn't clearly identify them or, if they could, they didn't see a solution. Not wanting the tension to continue, one evening after the children were asleep, Cherie and Don decided to talk seriously. Tired and fearful of the distance between them, they agreed that each of them needed to make changes.

Don admitted that he'd chosen to seek solace in drinking to manage the money worries and job demands that plagued him. He knew it wasn't a good solution, but the reality was that the beer momentarily took off the edge. He could push his worries an arm's length away. Drinking gave him a break from negative thoughts that he couldn't resolve. He admitted he should be home with the family in the evenings and not leave Cherie to do all of the disciplining and care of the children. He talked about the female employee, how his friendliness had encouraged her flirtatiousness and then how he'd been flattered by it and hadn't put a stop to it early on.

Cherie acknowledged that she resented the incomplete house projects and the fact that Don's work demanded extra time. She'd also been indifferent to her own self-care. Having turned to food as a consolation, she'd gained 100 pounds. But most importantly, both Don and Cherie admitted that they'd overlooked their individual and family spiritual well-being. Don recognized that if he wanted a happy marriage, he needed to extract himself from the partnership at the mill and find a church the family could attend regularly. That night in 1978 was a turning point in their relationship as the couple stepped back from the brink of separation, deciding that they both wanted to salvage their marriage.

Determined to act on their plan to stabilize their relationship, the couple found a non-denominational church to attend in the nearby community of Ruch. Don returned to work on the Applegate Dam and, as the years passed, he found himself enjoying life more. He regretted that his long workdays often meant he didn't get home until after the children were in bed, and he devised a plan he hoped would partially compensate for his absence. He made a habit of stopping at the E & I Market on his way home and picking up treats that Cherie normally wouldn't allow the children to have. Frequently, when he arrived in the evenings, Don was outfitted with candy bars, bubble gum, small bags of chips, and soda. While Cherie was less than enthused with his methods, she appreciated the excitement the routine brought out in the kids. As usual, Don found ways to put gaiety in life for the kids and for her.

Donette, especially, responded to her dad's renewed focus on his family; she was Daddy's little girl. Shadowing Don when he worked on car engines, she was quick to squirm under a vehicle or retrieve tools from the bench for him. By the time they were finished working, both had grease smudges on their hands and faces. Disappointed that Dwayne didn't show an interest in learning about cars even when invited, Don happily shared his hobby with Donette.

If troubleshooting engine problems was a hobby that Don desired to share with his children, fishing was a passion. As Dwayne and Donette grew, Don and Cherie taught the kids to fish and swim in the river, but Dwayne felt awkward at fishing. He couldn't seem to get the hang of it, and the water was too cold for him to enjoy swimming, causing him to break out in the familiar welts. As a result, when invited to go fishing, he opted to stay home.

The Wier property was a perfect place for a young person to get lost in his or her imagination, but Dwayne seldom wandered outside. Cherie longed to find a pastime that caught his attention and got him out of his room. She noticed that he seemed interested in music, so she encouraged his enthusiasm by purchasing a boom box and buying him a selection of CDs.

Dwayne prized the treasured boom box, and music could be heard nonstop coming from his room. But despite successfully connecting with Dwayne through music, Cherie couldn't shake the feeling that there was something inexplicably different about him. There was an indefinable something in his manner that "didn't fit." She considered his hearing impairment and suspected that not hearing normally might affect his self-confidence and his ability to interact socially. Dwayne often wore his hearing aids at home but according to his teachers, he seldom put them on at school. When asked about wearing them, Dwayne claimed that the aids were ugly and noticeable, suggesting that he was very self-conscious when wearing them. There was nothing to be done about the appearance of Dwayne's hearing aids. Cherie could only take him to the audiologist to be sure they were working correctly when Dwayne did wear them. She speculated that Dwayne's hearing impairment might be fueling his feelings of inadequacy, leading to his preference for solitude. But she still thought there was something else about Dwayne that wasn't right.

Worrying her too was the awareness that Dwayne had begun to steal. The first occasion that she knew of was when he'd pocketed an ink pen at a local convenience store. The owner called Cherie, telling her that as long as she came and got Dwayne from the store, he wouldn't report the incident to the police. When Cherie questioned Dwayne about why he'd stolen a pen when they had plenty at the house, he only shrugged. Recently, Dwayne's performance at school had been slipping. His teacher reported that he wasn't participating in class and wouldn't do assignments although he was capable. Cherie wasn't disturbed by a single major incident, but a string of small, curious behaviors. She sought mental health counseling through the county system for her fifth-grade son, and answers for herself in understanding his behavior. Cherie and Dwayne saw three different counselors from the Josephine County Mental Health program, but Cherie didn't get the answers or help she was seeking, and Dwayne refused to keep going. Dwayne had exhibited little impulse control at a young age, appearing to act without thought. Witnessing this inclination, Cherie wondered whether he chose his actions without understanding consequences, or simply wanted to disobey the rules. One afternoon, an event took place that added to Cherie's fears about her son's disregard for the possessions of others.

Cherie owned a ring given to her by her grandmother Hazel, who had received it as an engagement ring in the late 1880s. The couple had decided to break off the engagement and the spurned lover told Hazel to keep the ring as a remembrance. Hazel had never worn it and had given it to Cherie when Cherie turned sixteen. The lovely ring featured a reconstructed ruby secured in an old-fashioned, white gold setting. One afternoon, twelve-year-old Dwayne brought his girlfriend Sandy home with him after school.

Cherie was working in her yard, happy whenever she managed to carve out time to garden. She'd noticed the myrtle wood seedling that Dwayne had brought home from Boy Scouts had taken on little growth since they'd planted it four years earlier, and she decided to transplant it to a sunnier location. She was in the middle of the task when she saw Dwayne and Sandy approaching the house. Cherie noticed Sandy was wearing her keepsake ring. When Cherie asked Sandy where she'd gotten the ring, the girl looked at Dwayne and said he'd given it to her. Cherie explained to Sandy that Dwayne didn't have the right to give the ring to anyone because it belonged to her, and she went on to say that, although she was sorry, Sandy would have to give it back. While Sandy was taking the ring off, Cherie told her that it had belonged to her grandmother. After Sandy left, Cherie told Dwayne that if he wanted to give one of her rings to Sandy, he should have asked her, and she cautioned him not to assume he could take anything that belonged to someone else in the house.

The theft of her vintage ring by Dwayne upset Cherie, but several weeks later she was even more disturbed by the realization that Dwayne was being beaten up by an older student at school who had his own set of problems. She discovered the awful truth one afternoon when Dwayne came home from school and pulled off his tee shirt, exposing bruises all over his torso. He told his mom that a kid at school had used him as a punching bag. Cherie was sickened at what she saw. She told Dwayne that behavior like that was inexcusable and that they were going to the school right then to talk with the principal.

Cherie and Dwayne met with the head administrator, who took a dim view of students treating others with aggression. The boy who had beaten Dwayne was an eighth grader whose behavior had come to the attention of the school authorities on multiple occasions. The student had been suspended several times throughout the school year and recent disciplinary reports had caused him to be permanently expelled from the junior high. The principal said that the boy's dad treated the boy the same way he was now treating his fellow students. He'd learned that physical violence was normal behavior. The administrator made it clear that the school tried to keep students safe on campus. Cherie left the meeting relieved that the incident had been dealt with, but inwardly she couldn't ignore a sense of restlessness, a distinct harbinger of doom. She wondered why this bully had singled Dwayne out and worried about how the brutal beatings would affect her son, who already showed a disinclination to associate with others.

As Dwayne continued his junior high years, problems increased at home and in school. He neglected his class work and made the situation worse by lying to his parents when asked about assignments. When Donette overheard conversations about Dwayne getting into trouble, she would ignore the discussion, thinking, *That's his problem and not mine.* She was six and oblivious to the seriousness of Dwayne's actions, preferring instead to play with her dolls. As time went on and Dwayne's conduct worsened, Don and Cherie tried to keep his defiant behavior secret, not wanting the problems with their son to concern their young daughter. Eventually, Dwayne's actions did affect Donette personally, because she began to notice her saved allowance money was missing from her room. Dwayne had begun to steal from his sister. When he was confronted by his parents, he flippantly responded, "I'll pay her back."

Don and Cherie tried to curb Dwayne's habitual stealing, telling him that if he needed cash, he could borrow from either of them. They reminded him that they frequently gave him money for items he wanted. Don preferred to give him a little at a time because he was suspicious about Dwayne's purchases. He and Cherie noticed that any money they gave to Dwayne quickly disappeared. Despite their talk with him, the stealing from his sister persisted.

On weekends, when Don wasn't tinkering with a vehicle or confronted with another complication involving Dwayne, the couple welcomed friends and their families over for barbeques. The get togethers were a favorite pastime for Don and Cherie. These social gatherings were less exciting to Dwayne who, at almost thirteen, preferred the company of his own friends. At one of these events, Dwayne wandered to the grill where Don was cooking and watched as his dad opened a can of Budweiser. Dwayne asked if he could have a sip of Don's beer. Don said it was fine with him. It was a hot day and Dwayne was waiting for the burgers to be done. Besides, maybe sharing a sip or two of beer with Dwayne once in a while might be a way Don could connect with him. Dwayne took a drink and stood near his dad, talking with Don as he watched the patties cook.

Despite Don's efforts to relate to him, complications with Dwayne didn't let up. Instead, like ocean waves, one difficulty rolled in after another. There had been trouble at school, and Don and Cherie were summoned to the school's office. Dwayne would be suspended, the administrator told them. Dwayne had sold what he'd represented as a drug to a female student. Upon further investigation, the pill was determined to be an over-the-counter medication, but Dwayne's passing himself off as a dealer of illicit drugs was a serious matter. He wasn't allowed at school for three days and ordered to attend a drug counseling program.

The escalation of Dwayne's incorrigible conduct distressed his parents. They needed help, the help Cherie hadn't been able to find when Dwayne was in the fifth grade. Maybe a drug counseling program would provide answers.

In the midst of an upside-down emotional world dealing with Dwayne, Don and Cherie looked to their church in Ruch for stability and hope that life with Dwayne could somehow improve. The fellowship provided them a place to gather with other Christians for support at this difficult time. But circumstances with Dwayne were about to change, altering their involvement with the Applegate Fellowship. Dwayne had made several friends at school who attended a Foursquare church in Grants Pass, and he asked if he could go to that church instead. The question created a dilemma. The churches were sixty minutes apart and in opposite directions from the Wier home. Cherie and Don wouldn't be able to continue at their present church if they were shuttling Dwayne into Grants Pass. The couple wanted Dwayne to enjoy going to church and hoped that if he had friends at the Foursquare, Dwayne might be more inclined to attend services.

Cherie visited the Foursquare church and didn't find the teaching and worship style to her liking, but if Dwayne wanted to attend the church, the family would drop him off there and go to services at the Calvary Chapel nearby. Unlike the large fellowship the Wiers had attended in Ruch, Calvary was small enough that the family was recognized as newcomers and greeted with genuine friendliness. The impetus to move to a church in Grants Pass had been to accommodate Dwayne, but the family benefitted from the smaller congregation where they soon developed close friendships. It was while attending Calvary Chapel that their faith grew. As they listened to teaching from the Bible, they learned that every person has value and purpose, and that God is near no matter what the circumstances. They couldn't have foreseen, in 1983, how the people in this caring church would help them through the nightmare to come.

CHAPTER 6 – HEAVY METAL MUSIC, DRUGS, AND ALCOHOL

Cherie's purchase of a boom box fueled Dwayne's preoccupation with music and, wanting to be supportive, she and Don decided to buy him a guitar. After all, they reasoned, if Dwayne was going to sequester himself in his room, learning to play an instrument would be a valuable activity. Perhaps he would one day be good enough to play in the church's band. Dwayne's attraction to music grew, and playing his guitar became his favorite pastime. The purchase of a guitar was followed by the acquisition of a used drum set, which he played in the garage. He would put on a CD and accompany the music with his guitar or drums. Performing music and writing song lyrics turned into a passion for Dwayne. Playing his guitar loudly, especially when company visited, Dwayne acted as though he were on stage in front of an audience, and the volume was so deafening that he regularly needed to be told to turn his music down.

If Cherie was busy in the kitchen, Donette found herself in the middle of dealing with Dwayne's blasting music. Cherie would ask Donette to tell Dwayne to turn the volume down. Donette would open the door to Dwayne's room, shouting above the sound for him to turn it down. Although Dwayne complied for a moment, by the time Donette walked back to the kitchen the music was blaring again. The volume was a reoccurring problem since Dwayne thought himself a proficient player to whom people would want to listen, and he wanted to be heard.

Dwayne gets a guitar for Christmas. The following month he turned thirteen.

At 12 years old Dwayne joined a band made up of guys he knew from middle school. The group practiced at a house on nearby Humbug Creek Road. Don and Cherie did not realize that letting him go would turn out to be a mistake.

When Dwayne turned thirteen, he was invited by three boys at school to play drums in their band, Black Diamond. The group met at a member's house on Humbug Creek Road, not far from the Wiers' place. The prospect fired Dwayne up, and he asked his mom for permission. Not knowing the boys or their parents, Cherie refused to consent until she could speak to the band member's mother and find out details regarding the practices. Even after a phone call from the parent reassuring her that the jam sessions would be well-supervised, Cherie had misgivings. Her mother's intuition set off an uneasiness about the arrangement, but she wished to encourage Dwayne's interest in music. She rationalized that it was good he had friends he wanted to hang out with. Reluctantly, Cherie consented and transported her son and his drums to the teen's house for the band's first practice. What Cherie and Don didn't know was that the group of band members were pot smokers who got high on the weed grown by the parents on their Humbug property.

Dwayne had been playing with the band for about three months when Don found a bag of marijuana stashed between the car seats when he transported Dwayne home from practice. Once inside the house, Don took Dwayne into the bathroom and confronted him with the dope. He told him the dangers of drug use and let Dwayne know how worried and angry it made him to see Dwayne was using.

His parents hadn't told Dwayne that when Don was twenty, he'd been arrested for possession of marijuana. In the late 1950s, that conviction led to a two-year sentence in a California state prison. The grim incarceration had subdued Don's behavior, which up until then had been characterized by a generally reckless approach to living. The last path Don wanted for Dwayne was a life behind bars, so he became emotional as he tried to convince Dwayne of the danger of drug use.

Dwayne only looked at Don, obviously not caring in the least.

When Cherie saw Don come out of the bathroom with tears running down his face, she was shaken and asked him what was wrong.

"He's going down the wrong road, Cherie; he's going down the wrong road. I can't do anything about it. I can't turn him around." Overcome by emotion and fear, Don could barely speak.

Cherie went to Dwayne's room. "What's going on, Dwayne? Something bad must have happened because Dad doesn't get upset like that. He wouldn't be crying unless it's something really serious."

"Dad didn't tell you?"

"Tell me what?"

He responded with, "Well, if he didn't tell you, I'm not going to tell you either. You'll have to get it from Dad. I'm not telling you anything."

Cherie went back into the room where Don sat. "It's all right. We'll figure it out," she told him. "But you've got to tell me, Don. You can't keep it from me, whatever it is."

Silence followed as Don took time to absorb the disturbing news of Dwayne's drug use. Then he told Cherie, "I found some pot. Dwayne has been getting high with his friends. I had a feeling that something like this was happening." Letting Dwayne go to the house on Humbug Creek when he and Cherie didn't know the parents or the kids was their mistake, he thought. Now, after the fact, he and Cherie would require Dwayne to sever his ties with the band, but it was too late. Dwayne had been introduced to marijuana and liked the sensation of getting high.

Later that same evening, Dwayne appeared from his room and announced to his parents that the band had promised to play for a party at the Humbug Creek house on the upcoming Friday. Feeling confident asking for permission, Dwayne knew Don and Cherie stressed the importance of following through with his commitments. He was right. The couple grudgingly gave in to Dwayne's request but strictly stated the time they would be picking him up and reminded him that the Friday night performance was the end of his involvement with the group.

The band members' parents had been told that the music portion of the party was to finish at 11 p.m., so Don and

Cherie arrived at 11:15. Turning down the driveway, the couple was baffled to see the open field near the house void of cars, and no evidence of a party or partygoers. Don got out of the pickup and walked into the back yard of the property, catching sight of a garden where pot plants had recently been harvested. He circled back to the front of the house and went inside through a door that was ajar. The sweet stench of burning marijuana was unmistakable, and the parents were nowhere to be seen. By now, Cherie was also out of the pickup and following Don inside. They found the teens in one of the back rooms and confronted them about the dope. Not surprisingly, the boys denied knowledge of the marijuana.

Don told them, "You guys knew the rules, and the rules were that there would be no drug use. The pot party and band gigs are over."

Don and Cherie had no idea of the extent of Dwayne's use of marijuana. Cherie upped her scrutiny of Dwayne's behavior at home and did her best to monitor his whereabouts when he was gone but generally, Dwayne seemed himself at home and so, infrequently, his parents would have him watch Donette on a Friday night.

Believing Dwayne to be capable of keeping an eye on his nine-year-old sister, Don and Cherie would tell her, "We're just going to go out and go dancing for a few hours. Dwayne's going to watch you." But Donette would hang out in her parents' room while they were getting ready to go, wishing they would stay home instead of leaving her with Dwayne.

On the nights when her parents went out and darkness fell, Donette would turn on all of the lights in the house. She wasn't afraid of strangers lurking outside, but the lights made her feel less alone. One Friday night when she and Dwayne were watching television, Dwayne on the couch and her on the floor, Donette laughed at something funny and turned around to see if Dwayne was laughing too.

To her surprise, the couch was empty. Wondering where Dwayne could possibly have gone, she searched the house, closets and all, without success. She stepped out on the deck and yelled his name into the darkness. There was no response. Bewildered, she went back inside, searching each room again only to find the house empty. As she rechecked Dwayne's room, she turned back toward the hall and found him standing in the doorway. The sight of him made her jump because she hadn't heard him come back in the house.

She confronted him, "Where were you?"

"What are you talking about? What do you mean?" he asked.

Looking straight at him, Donette said, "You weren't here. I looked for you. You weren't in the house."

Dwayne said, "Oh, I just went down to the river…"

Donette didn't let up. "But I called for you and you didn't answer."

Dwayne would repeat his disappearing acts whenever he was supposed to be watching Donette. Donette never shared the occurrence of Dwayne's strange behavior with her parents, having been convinced by Dwayne it was just her imagination. As far as they knew, the Friday evenings were uneventful—until the night Dwayne left the property after stealing Cherie's car.

Dwayne was fourteen when he sneaked out of the house and drove Cherie's car the two miles to Ray's Sentry Market in Murphy, where he pocketed a can of chewing tobacco. The store's manager caught him red-handed, detained him in the office, and called the sheriff's department. Charges were pressed against Dwayne and he was ordered to perform community service. It wasn't until after this incident that Donette told Don and Cherie about Dwayne habitually disappearing from home during their date nights. Unauthorized use of Cherie's car, shoplifting, and especially leaving Donette alone in the house at night added to the increasing mistrust the couple had toward Dwayne, who never seemed to think about the consequences of his actions.

Belonging to the band had provided an opportunity for Dwayne to add the use of marijuana to his troubling behavior. His drug use and the car theft prompted Cherie to search once again for competent counseling. Substance abuse was a behavior she wasn't equipped to handle. She knew too that without intervention, problems with Dwayne would inevitably worsen. The disappointment she'd experienced when she'd sought help from mental health counselors during Dwayne's fifth grade year had given her a reason not to want to return to therapy. Time had moved forward and nothing had changed except that the hurdles were more serious and frequent. She and Don had tried all of the methods they knew for raising children and had sought insight from Christian and secular books on effective parenting. All of their attempts to help Dwayne develop positive interests had failed. Cherie supposed it couldn't hurt to try counseling again. Maybe a different therapist would have answers.

Cherie went alone to her first visit with the new counselor. She began by sharing Dwayne's consuming interest in music. Although she and Don were supportive of his pursuit, Dwayne was now a devoted fan of heavy metal and in particular idolized the band KISS. Disturbed by the group's lyrics and image, she and Don were concerned about negative influences on Dwayne. Of course, trouble with Dwayne was about more than his choices in music. Cherie told the counselor they'd caught Dwayne lying and stealing, and that his demeanor suggested he was getting high and doing so with increasing regularity. Dwayne had run away twice and at fourteen, he'd been arrested for shoplifting and sentenced to community service. When Dwayne arrived home from school that afternoon, Cherie told him she'd gone to counseling.

He looked at her, uninterested. "What for?"

"Maybe the counselor will have some ideas how Dad and I can better understand how you're thinking," Cherie offered. What she didn't say but thought, was, *We need to know what to do with you because you're getting into trouble and doing stupid things.*

Dwayne acquiesced to his mother's repetitive pleas and did go to the counselor a few times. He never said it was helpful. He never wanted to go, and there was no indication he ever made an attempt to see value in the appointments. Cherie accompanied him for two visits, hoping she could prompt dialogue with the counselor. Dwayne didn't cooperate; instead, he sat silent or answered questions with a few words. The fifty-dollar visits were a sacrifice. Don allowed Dwayne, who had just turned sixteen, to get his license and drive Don's pickup so that he could go to counseling appointments. But when Dwayne drove the truck, he got in an accident and wrecked the rig's front end. Although the collision wasn't Dwayne's fault, until the truck was repaired, he didn't have transportation.

Dwayne wrote on the back of this photo that was taken in the Wier living room. "Mark is on the guitar, Nick on drums, and me on bass. Lovecraft was our title. One of my last bands. We were about ten years ahead of our time."

Dealing with Dwayne's behavioral problems didn't interfere with Don and Cherie inviting friends over for barbecues, considering the get togethers a reprieve from their weekly obligations. Guests, grateful to have an opportunity to come out to the Wiers' property, contributed to the meal preparations by bringing food and beverages to share. Sometimes, Dwayne asked friends to come over and the teenagers hung out in the garage playing music.

By early afternoon on one such weekend, Dwayne was hungry when he smelled his dad barbecuing and walked out toward the grill. The family's dog, Snooks, was keeping a vigil near Don's feet, hoping to score a dropped piece of chicken or burger. Snooks, a smallish cross between a chihuahua and a cockapoo, wagged his tail when he saw Dwayne approach. Dwayne patted the dog and then spotted his dad's open can of beer sitting near the barbecue. Without hesitation, he picked up the can and took a sip. Preoccupied with cooking, Don glanced at Dwayne and told him he didn't want Dwayne finishing his beer, but if he wanted a can of his own, he could get a beer from the cooler, but only one. Dwayne loaded his plate with food and moseyed to the ice chest, pulled out a cold one for himself, and headed back to the garage. Don, focused on grilling, broke off a small portion of an overcooked burger and tossed the piece to a grateful Snooks.

With the weekend over, Cherie returned to her search for professional help. During her contact with the Mental Health Department, there had only been one male counselor who had insight regarding Dwayne's disposition. He told Cherie he suspected that Dwayne had a personality disorder, but there was no follow-up counseling to delve further into that diagnosis or establish a plan to help the parents. Between Dwayne's unwillingness to continue, difficulty with transportation, and the lack of value in the appointments, the efforts to find answers through counseling stopped. Don and Cherie had spent a lot of time and a large amount of money, there were no answers, and nothing had changed.

Unable to find help, Cherie did her best to tackle issues with Dwayne on her own. Donette was nine when she began to notice that Dwayne seemed to be getting in trouble a lot. Frequently, when Donette came home from school, Dwayne would be slumped in a chair sitting silently across the kitchen table from his mom while she droned on. There were lots and lots of lectures, as Cherie called them, efforts on her part to change Dwayne's behavior. Cherie confided to Donette that she felt her words to Dwayne "went in one ear and out the other." Like many parents of teenagers, Cherie suspected that Dwayne wasn't listening to her advice but hoped that he was.

At sixteen Dwayne was given use of Don's truck.

While Cherie searched for a good counselor, Don changed jobs. The Applegate Dam project was completed, and he now worked for Jantzer and Sons Logging Company as a mechanic, keeping trucks and support vehicles running. Because Don's new position required him to drive to remote logging roads to help disabled rigs back into operation, he decided to purchase a truck more suited to the needs of a mechanic, one that would include storage compartments and space for welding tanks. He would give his yellow 1971 Ford pickup to Dwayne to use, but only under very specific conditions. Don had longed to find common ground with his son and now that Dwayne would be driving, Don hoped the two of them would have an opportunity to work on the pickup's engine together. Don responded enthusiastically when necessity prompted Dwayne to come to him with questions about basic maintenance and repair. He and Cherie hoped that if Dwayne had his own transportation, he would be able to do errands for them and get himself to his job at the Chevron station in Grants Pass. Don's trips to the back woods resulted in extra-long hours, leaving Cherie responsible as the primary parent to Dwayne and Donette. Scheduling activities, assigning chores, and monitoring Dwayne fell mostly on her. A change in Don's routine one morning created a different dynamic.

Don usually left for work before sunrise, but this morning he was heading out later, and the kids were getting ready for school. Normally calm, Don's temperament was put to the test when he overheard Dwayne arguing with Cherie in the kitchen.

Whatever the topic, Dwayne responded, "I don't know why you're so upset. What difference does it make?"

Dwayne's tone sparked a reaction from Don as he listened to the intensity of the quarrel increase. He strode into the kitchen, his posturing clearly authoritarian, and exclaimed in a raised voice, "Listen, if you want to fight with somebody you just come on and fight with your old dad here. You don't need to be fighting with your mom over every little thing. That's all you ever do is argue and fight with your mom. You always want to prove a point, and you always think you're right." Then he taunted, "Come on, fight with Dad. If you really want to fight, fight with Dad." He shoved Dwayne against the wall.

Suddenly subdued, Dwayne said, "No, I don't want to fight with you." Reacting to the escalating exchange, he put his hands up to protect his face. As quickly as the confrontation had started, it was over.

Don sank into a kitchen chair, shaken that he'd allowed his anger to result in aggression toward his son. "Dwayne," he said, "why do you cause me to get so angry with you? You know how much your mother and I love you. We care about you and we want you to do things right."

Dwayne sat at the table, looking down. He wouldn't answer. After Don left for work, he told Cherie, "You know, I could have Dad arrested for child abuse."

"Dwayne, come on. What are you thinking? Child abuse?" She continued, "Your dad could have hurt you if he really wanted to. He's trying to make you understand that what you're doing is wrong, but you can't see it, Dwayne." Other than his surly threat to report the behavior to the authorities, there was no indication that Dwayne was affected one way or another by his father's harsh discipline.

In 1985, Dwayne made contact with the stoner crowd at his high school. It was an association that would introduce him to the world of even more dangerous and illegal drugs. As his participation in this lifestyle persisted, Don and Cherie responded with more boundaries. When Dwayne arrived home later than expected, he was given an earlier curfew, and broken curfews were met with tougher restrictions. Still, his behavior didn't change.

A particularly disturbing episode occurred one night when Cherie found Dwayne huddled in the corner of his bedroom, terrified. Wild-eyed and paranoid, he chewed on his arm and cheek, screaming that the walls were breathing and spiders were crawling all over him. Apparently, he'd upped his game to acid and was having horrifying hallucinations.

Watching Dwayne in his drugged state reminded Cherie of her last year in high school when she found her mother unconscious on the bedroom floor. An empty pill bottle nearby indicated that Lois had attempted suicide using her prescription drugs. Cherie had called the hospital that night too, and the recommendation had been similar: get her up, keep her walking until the drugs wear off. Cherie remembered how she and her three siblings had taken turns walking the floor with their mother until early dawn. Here she sat, twenty-nine years later, awake all night in Dwayne's room keeping a vigil, watching her son's crazed behavior and wondering how it could get any worse.

The experience of a bad trip on acid didn't cause Dwayne to rethink his behavior or his use of hard drugs. Two nights later, he left the house knowing he was supposed to be home at 10:30 and, although the curfew came and went, he didn't return. The hours ticked by and at 1:30 a.m., Don rolled in from work. Cherie was awake, sitting on the couch keeping watch for Dwayne's return. She informed Don that Dwayne was still not home and suggested that Don go look for him.

Exhausted from the long workday, Don balked at the idea. "I can't go, Cherie. I'm too tired."

Cherie, fired up from the hours of sitting and brooding over Dwayne, announced that she would go.

Not wanting her to go out alone so late at night, Don shook his head, irritated. "No, I'll go. That's all right, I'll go."

He put his shirt back on, climbed wearily into Cherie's car, and drove off. The constant tension with Dwayne had put both parents on edge and lately, Don and Cherie had found themselves taking their frustrations out on each other.

Don had been gone about forty-five minutes when Dwayne came home. Having gone to bed, Cherie heard her son come in but decided it would be better for her not to get up. She suspected she would only make matters worse by confronting Dwayne and decided to leave the situation to Don.

Don returned a half hour later and by then Dwayne was in his bathroom. Don pounded on the door and told him to open up. Cherie didn't see what happened but heard quarreling. It sounded as though there was a clash between the two; then Don shouted that he was "sick and tired of this bullshit. You just keep blowing it every time. What am I going to do? How am I going to show you how to make good choices? I've done everything in my power to influence your behavior and you keep acting recklessly."

Violating his curfew was reflective of Dwayne's disregard for his parents' rules. His drug use expanded as he experimented with whatever hard drugs he could find. He started to abuse methamphetamines. Finally, with a doctor's counsel, Dwayne was admitted to a drug detox/rehab program in Medford, about an hour's drive from Murphy. He agreed to comply with the program after being told that he would receive medication to help ease the effects of withdrawal. Two days later, realizing the drugs they were giving him weren't as good as drugs off the street, Dwayne contacted friends to pick him up. It wasn't a lockdown program, so Dwayne freely walked out of the facility. His buddies must have dropped him off several blocks from the hospital because he was later found by the local police, eating lettuce out of a dumpster. When questioned, he claimed the medicine the recovery program gave him was worse than the illegal drugs he took. At this point, he was lodged in the hospital's psychiatric unit on a seventy-two-hour hold and assessment. When he was released, the attending physician said Dwayne didn't appear to have any psychological problems. Several attempts were made by Cherie to enroll Dwayne in one of the two residential rehab programs available in Southern Oregon, but Dwayne refused to go, contending that he could and would manage his drug problem himself.

With few options left to turn around Dwayne's increasing drug use, Don and Cherie decided to enroll him in a Christian school that would support their values. They hoped this change would outweigh the disadvantage of him being in town where he could easily skip school or frequent unsavory places.

By February of 1986, Dwayne had given in to his drug addiction and routinely lied and stole to cover his tracks. The Wiers hoped that the stricter expectations and the Christian environment of the school would provide Dwayne more structure and accountability. When they met with the principal, they were candid about their troubles with Dwayne. The administrator assured Don and Cherie that he and the staff would do all they could to support them in an effort to encourage Dwayne to follow rules and apply himself to his schoolwork. His parents hoped that a positive change in Dwayne's environment would affect the quality of his friends, but Dwayne's choice of friends didn't vary. He quickly found two classmates anxious to trade the Valium they stole from their mother's medicine cabinet for his weed. Sadly, the woman was undergoing cancer treatment and was the wife of the principal of the Christian school. By now, the Wiers were no longer naïve about Dwayne's drug use, having witnessed him high on multiple occasions, but Dwayne had masterfully concealed the degree of his dependence so that Don and Cherie had no way of knowing just how far out of control his addiction had gone.

***

Liberty Weekend lit up New York City with spectacular fireworks, concerts, and parades. July 3, 1986, was the beginning of a four-day celebration in recognition of the restoration of the Statue of Liberty.

The Wier family was at their neighbors', John and Sam's, marking the holiday by having a barbecue, and John had turned on the television broadcasting the festivities. When Cherie overheard a comment on the program stating that the Statue of Liberty had been dedicated to the United States on October 28, 1886, mention of the historic date reminded her that she had an old silver certificate that had belonged to her grandfather. Cherie had stored the rare bill in her bedroom, and she suddenly had an urge to find it and show it to her neighbors. She walked back to her house and looked for the small cedar box she knew contained the certificate as well as the silver coins she and Don had collected.

Cherie located the box, but when she picked it up, she was startled by how light it felt. She lifted the lid, confirming the box was empty. The all too familiar sickening feeling swept over her as she suspected the obvious, another episode of Dwayne stealing. Her stomach cramped as the ire inside her caused her to shake.

Dwayne was in the house and Cherie ordered him into her room. There was no mistaking her tone; Dwayne knew she was mad. She pointed toward the floor by the dresser, directing him to sit down. He stood firmly in place, refusing to submit.

She repeated, "Sit down." As he grumpily acquiesced, she flooded him with claims of wrongdoing. "Where is my money, Dwayne? Where is my silver certificate? What have you done with it? Don't tell me you don't have it. I want to know where it is!" Her anger grew, fueled by all of the other times they'd had to confront him about missing money and items, causing shrillness in her voice.

"Mom," he said, "I don't know nothing about it. I don't have it. I don't know where it is. I haven't seen it."

Cherie continued with her onslaught. "Dwayne, you're lying to me and I know it. I've had it! I want my money. I'm sick and tired of you stealing from us. This time, you've gone too far." She grabbed him by the hair and pulled. She started to kick him, and he gripped her wrists, holding her.

"Calm down," he told her.

Enraged, she replied, "I won't calm down. I'm upset. I'm mad. I can't believe that you'd do this, Dwayne."

She was unraveling and couldn't stop yelling and screaming at him. She swore at him, using words she never said, and as she swore, she realized she was no better than he was, yelling and completely losing control.

Dwayne released his hold on her and went out the back door to John and Sam's house, where the barbecue was still going on. Cherie followed him to the door and yelled across the yard for Don to come back home and bring Dwayne with him. Recognizing the urgency in her voice, Don returned to the house with Dwayne in tow.

When Don and Dwayne came in, Cherie told Don what had happened. Highly agitated, she reached for Dwayne, intending to strike him. She was in the worst state she'd been in since the family began dealing with Dwayne's deceptive behavior. She felt horrible, upset with herself for losing control and for the awful words she'd said. After half an hour, she finally began to recover from her feverish state. She couldn't return to the neighbors' place; she told Don she just wanted to go to bed.

Exhausted and sighing deeply, Cherie curled up in the sheets and blankets, seeking comfort. All she could do was pray.

The next morning, when Cherie got up, Don was already awake. "Did you look in the strongbox for the silver certificate?" he asked her.

Confused by the question, she answered, "No, why would I?"

"Something tells me we put it in there. I know you used to have it in that box with all your silver, but didn't you move it to the strongbox?"

She thought about it, feeling certain that she'd always kept it where she'd put it at first, but wanting to be absolutely certain, she got out the strongbox and was surprised to find the silver certificate secured inside.

Still raw from the turbulence the night before, Cherie faced another twist to the situation. Dwayne had stolen the coins, she knew that, but he hadn't taken the certificate, and she'd blamed him for that as well. She felt terrible for accusing him of something he hadn't done. Cherie knew she needed to admit that she'd been wrong about the certificate.

Right away that morning, Cherie apologized to Dwayne for her error and told him she didn't want to blame him for something he hadn't done. She explained that because Dwayne had stolen items and lied to her and Don in the past, he'd eroded the trust between them. Although he wasn't at fault for the misplaced silver certificate, he'd stolen the coins and for that he would be restricted.

As usual, Dwayne showed little reaction.

The situation in the Wier home had become dire, and Don and Cherie responded with increased consequences for Dwayne's defiant behavior. "Dwayne, you're not going to be doing a whole lot of things until we can see a change," Cherie said. "You'll come home from school, do your homework, do your chores, go to your room, and go to bed."

The day after Dwayne had been grounded to the house and his truck taken away, the Wiers decided to go over to a friend's house. Don asked Dwayne if he wanted to go too. Dwayne said he would rather stay home and play his music. Cherie privately told Don that maybe they should have taken Dwayne's music away. Maybe restricting his access to his beloved music would be the incentive he needed to change.

Don disagreed. "Let him play his music. We won't be home. We don't have to listen to it."

The sun had set long before Don, Cherie, and Donette got home. Surprised to see no lights on in the house, they walked inside to discover that Dwayne was gone and with him two amplifiers, guitars, the ghetto blaster, clothes, and cassette tapes. After talking over their options, Don and Cherie loaded Donette back into the car, deciding to drive to town to look for him. An hour of aimless searching proved unsuccessful and the worn-out family returned home.

The next morning, having no idea where to find Dwayne, Don and Cherie decided to check out an address on Lawnridge in Grants Pass. Ever since Cherie suspected Dwayne was using drugs, she would eavesdrop on his phone conversations, listening with the intention of finding out about his illicit activities, names of suspicious friends, or unsavory places where he might hang out. The address on Lawnridge was a recent location she'd heard mentioned and Cherie thought it might be a drug house. Before heading into town, Don and Cherie dropped Donette at a friend's house, then drove directly to the suspect house on Lawnridge. As they approached the residence, Cherie saw a shadowy figure standing in the doorway. She recalled, from the overheard conversation, that several girls were supposed to live there and one of them was a girlfriend of Dwayne's. Agreeing that Cherie going to the door would be less threatening to the occupants, Don waited in the car, parking the vehicle across the street and a few doors down.

Nonchalantly walking up the steps to the house, Cherie noticed that the front door was slightly open. An unkempt, middle-aged woman met her on the landing. Skipping the small talk, Cherie asked if Dwayne was there and told the woman he hadn't been home the previous night. The woman said he wasn't at the house and she didn't know his whereabouts. Bluffing, Cherie insisted that Dwayne had told her he would be in town at this address. The woman swore she hadn't seen him. After the brief exchange, Cherie fabricated a story to get inside the house, asking the woman if she could use her phone because her young daughter was home alone and she wanted to let her know she would be back soon. The woman shrugged, opening the door wider and pointing toward the phone on the table in the front room. The unmistakable odor of tobacco mixed with marijuana smoke greeted Cherie as she stepped inside. Taking the opportunity to scan the area, she searched for any indication that her son was hiding in the residence. Right away, she caught sight of his shoes against one wall, and next to them was the familiar boom box. Cherie saw the house was occupied by another woman, this one shorter and painfully thin, with sharp features and unbrushed hair. Though the room was dimly lit, she caught sight of two men in the back corner of the room, barely visible in the shadows. All of the occupants smelled of foul body odor that, combined with the scent of smoke and that of a nearby overflowing trash can, caused the acid in Cherie's stomach to burn in her throat. She didn't see any children or teens. Hastily glancing over the space, probing for any information she could get, Cherie detected the reason for the room's dimness. A sheet had been draped across the doorway separating the room from the adjoining one. Cherie knew the woman had girls Dwayne's age and wondered where they were. Pretending to have called her home, Cherie put the phone back on the cradle. She turned and faced the woman who was still standing in the doorway. "My daughter must be outside because she didn't answer the phone," Cherie told her. Considering her next move, she recalled a recent conversation she'd overheard.

When Cherie had eavesdropped on Dwayne talking with a male who made a reference to his house on Lawnridge, Dwayne and the caller were discussing an eight ball. She knew by the conversation that it was an illicit substance, but she had no idea that the term referred to an eighth of an ounce of a drug, usually cocaine, but could also be a mix of crack-cocaine and heroin. She decided to use the information to flush Dwayne out of hiding.

Turning, she faced the two uncouth males, noticing their long, dirty hair, and in an accusatory tone asked, "Which one of you was talking to Dwayne about an eight ball?"

Her allegation sparked a quick response from one of the men, and a stream of cussing came out of his mouth. The other man joined the exchange, and the woman at the door interrupted by ordering Cherie to immediately get out of the house, claiming that no one there knew anything about that kind of stuff.

Cherie wasn't intimidated. "If you know where my son is, you need to know this. I'm going to find out where he is, and if he's here, if he's hiding behind that sheet or wherever, you need to tell him he better get his butt home right now. And this ghetto blaster is his and so are these shoes. I'm taking the ghetto blaster with me."

The woman argued, stepping between Cherie and the boom box, adamant that the ghetto blaster was going to stay, that her daughter had bought it from Dwayne. Undaunted, Cherie pushed past the woman, grabbing the boom box from the floor, telling the woman the ghetto blaster belonged to her and Dwayne had no right to sell it to anyone.

The escalating noise from the commotion reached Don, who was waiting in the car, and he bounded up the few steps to the landing. As he shoved by the woman in the doorway, he caught sight of Cherie arguing with the two men. Cherie knew that Don would stop at nothing to protect her, so she grabbed her husband by the arm and, with the ghetto blaster in hand, told him they needed to leave. She nearly dragged Don to the car, not wanting to see the situation worsen. When they got in their vehicle, she told Don she'd seen

Dwayne's shoes and socks inside, and she told him about the boom box.

The two drove up the street a short distance, parked, and watched the house to see if Dwayne would come out. He didn't have a vehicle, so if he was going to head home, he would have to rely on someone to drive him. They waited about ten minutes without seeing Dwayne. Then, slowly passing by the drug house again, they could see that people were watching them from the window.

Cherie was agitated. The Lawnridge residence was undeniably a drug house peddling substances to teenagers, and she felt compelled to do something about it. Don, appreciating her justified concern, cautioned her that there was nothing she could do. He told her she could get herself killed meddling in the illicit business and that the people living there weren't fooling around. They were dangerous.

Don suggested they notify the city police. Cherie agreed and the two drove straight to the police department where Ron Dague, a neighbor of the Wiers and a Reserve Grants Pass Police officer, was on duty and happened to be working in the office. Cherie told Ron what had happened and asked him if he would go by the Lawnridge house in a patrol car. She wanted the residents to know she was serious about reporting their suspicious activities and that Dwayne better get himself back to his house. With Ron's assurance that he would follow up at the address, Don and Cherie headed home.

It was late when the couple arrived at their little bit of heaven. The calm and quiet of the beautiful property soothed their senses, but they knew their respite would be brief. Dwayne would be home soon and with him would come more unrelenting troubles and bad news.

When Dwayne finally did show up, he was obviously high and mumbled indiscernible words as he walked straight to his bedroom and closed the door. Don and Cherie looked at each other, both sensing a need to talk with Dwayne in an effort to find a resolution to the never-ending series of conflicts, yet tired out from the late night followed by the bizarre visit to the Lawnridge house. Neither one saw much point in trying to pull information out of Dwayne or give him another one-sided lecture while he was stoned.

Years later, Dwayne told Cherie that she'd almost been shot that afternoon in the house in town. He told her he couldn't believe she'd come inside and started an argument with the people living there. He explained that there had been a guy in the kitchen holding a .357 magnum behind the draped curtain and he had it pointed at her. According to Dwayne, the man had been waiting for the slightest provocation to pull the trigger.

A month passed and it was the middle of August. Cherie had read that the 1986 World's Fair was being hosted in Vancouver, British Columbia and would be open until mid-October. With the school year around the corner, Cherie's mind was working. She was determined to figure out something to do with the family, some activity that would get them all out of town for some fun. A trip to the World's Fair would mean a seventeen-hour drive through Oregon and Washington. Cherie reasoned that going to the fair would be an adventure and time for the family to interact away from routine pressures. Besides the entertainers, the fair was packed with exhibits and rides, as well as food samples from the participant countries. She was excited by the prospect and felt it would be a unique opportunity for the family.

When she approached Don with the idea, she was disappointed that he didn't share her enthusiasm. He was worried about the loss of income from his time off work. Knowing how important a break was to their family life, however, Cherie urged Don to agree to the trip. She told him the family needed to do this, to have the time away together. She confessed that she had special hopes for Dwayne. She believed that getting him away from his friends and easy access to drugs and alcohol would give them all a reprieve. Despite Don's reservations, he had to concur. A change of scenery and an adventure would do them all good.

Old school friends of Cherie's from California had come up to Oregon. They were on board with a trek north to the World's Fair, so the two families decided to caravan to Canada. The group arranged for lodging with mutual friends from high school who lived in Vancouver within walking distance of town. It was a perfect set up, since the family the group was staying with had a teenage daughter who was willing to babysit the younger children. It wasn't long after the Wiers arrived at their lodging that Dwayne and the teenage girl hit it off. Whenever the families weren't at the fair, Dwayne and the girl were together.

One afternoon, Dwayne was nowhere to be found. Ever since the discovery of weed in Dwayne's possession four years before, Cherie had felt the need to be aware of his activities, so she decided to look for him in town. Wandering along the sidewalks in an area of small shops, she happened to pass a bar and glanced through the window, catching sight of Dwayne sitting at a table with a drink in his hand. She'd hoped the trip would mean freedom from dealing with Dwayne's bad choices. But the familiar gnawing in her stomach, the kind that always accompanied troubles with Dwayne, confirmed her fears that even on vacation he would find trouble. Hesitant to approach Dwayne in the tavern and feeling she didn't have the energy to face him, she opted to defer the management of this situation to Don. She hurried back to the house to talk with her husband, her mind reeling.

Don headed to town after Cherie's report. Locating Dwayne drinking in the tavern, Don sat next to him and told him that he needed to leave before he got himself or the business owner in trouble. Don paid for the drink and Dwayne responded by following his father out of the bar.

As the two walked back to the house, Don told him, "You know they can put you in jail here, in Canada. They might shut down the tavern because the business served an underage person. You're not using your head, Dwayne, not at all. You could get into more trouble than you can imagine doing something like this in another country."

Dwayne responded as he always did. There was no indication of regret, only disappointment that he'd been caught.

The bar incident set Cherie off. She wondered if Dwayne had been taking drugs. She thought she'd checked everything, made sure he hadn't hidden away marijuana or prescription drugs in his suitcase. Maybe he'd found a place to get drugs near where they were staying. There seemed no escape, no break from the allure and consumption of addictive substances. Had she been too optimistic that they could find relief, if only for a short time?

Despite her worries, the bar incident was the only glitch of the vacation. Cherie had wanted Dwayne to see how life could be without drugs, the fun, making memories with family, the activities that didn't involve playing music alone in his room or smoking dope with his friends. In many regards, the trip was a success.

Clothes and souvenirs from the vacation hadn't yet been unpacked when three carloads of company arrived at the Wier house. Without prior notice, Cherie's sister Vonnie, her older brother Denny, and all of their children had decided to take advantage of the Labor Day weekend and surprise Cherie and Don with a visit. Vonnie's two boys were within a year of Dwayne, but despite the closeness in age, Dwayne mostly kept to himself over the weekend. Don thought of Dwayne in his room with his music and wished he was interested in hanging out with his cousins.

Don barbecued for the visitors and, in typical Wier family style, there was no shortage of food at the table. The families packed the weekend full of good memories.

Cherie didn't wish to cast negativity on the visit, but she took Vonnie and Denny aside and confided that she and Don continued to struggle with managing their son's drug addiction. The siblings knew that for years Don and Cherie had dealt with episodes of Dwayne's stealing and dishonesty. They expressed their concern for the family and offered to be of help if there was some way either of them could make a difference. Looking back, it was a good decision for Cherie's siblings to make the spontaneous trip to Oregon that Labor Day weekend. None of them knew it would be the last time they would see Don alive.

CHAPTER 7 – STOLEN MONEY
THE LAST STRAW

With the Labor Day weekend over and the visitors gone, Cherie readjusted her schedule to life with her kids back in school. Dwayne was finishing the first two weeks of his junior year at the Christian high school in Grants Pass. Cherie stood in her kitchen, thumbing through the stack of mail she'd retrieved earlier and noticed an embellished envelope among the bills. The packet held an invitation from Mar Vista High School notifying alumni that the thirty-year reunion celebration would be held on October 18. News of the reunion wasn't totally unexpected, as Cherie regularly kept in contact with her former classmates, but realizing the date was imminent renewed her excitement at the prospect of seeing close friends. When Don came home that evening, she showed him the invitation, and without hesitation he insisted that Cherie start making plans for the trip. She protested, citing difficulties with Dwayne had worsened, and she feared her absence would give him more opportunity to get into trouble. Don wouldn't take no for an answer, knowing that the time away from family strife would do her good.

Don told Cherie the kids would be fine and reminded her that if something happened and he had to work overtime, Donette could go to the neighbors' place for a few hours. The Wiers already had an arrangement with neighbors Jon and Sam; Donette was welcome at their home if she found herself alone or needed help of any sort. Recalling this plan, Cherie relaxed a little, confident that Donette would be okay, and she redirected her efforts to preparing for her trip, trying to keep her mind from traveling to fabricated problems with Dwayne. Cherie would be staying in San Diego for a week with Don's mother, Carrol. In fact, after the reunion, Carrol would be flying back to Oregon with her for an extended stay, perhaps even until Christmas.

The weekend before Cherie left, Don surprised her with an extra sixty dollars, wanting her to have spare cash for an unexpected purchase. Smiling and appreciative, she took the money and secured it immediately in her wallet, which she then placed in her purse.

The night before Cherie was to fly to San Diego, she found herself packing and repacking her suitcase, second guessing her choices. She picked up her purse, checking to make sure she had her driver's license and wallet. On a whim, she opened the billfold to confirm that the sixty dollars was still tucked safely inside. The bill compartment was empty, and the familiar sinking feeling crept over her. Cherie had lived through a variation of this event many times before. Initially, she would be surprised that something of value was missing and would search her mind, considering what could have happened to it. After thoroughly investigating other logical places for the item, she would resign herself to the fact that Dwayne had once again helped himself to something that didn't belong to him. The subsequent events were equally predicable. She and Don would ask Dwayne if he knew where the missing item had gone, and he would emphatically deny any involvement. They felt as though they were fighting shadows.

Cherie had tired of greeting Don at the door with news of Dwayne's latest tricks, and she was sure Don was weary of it too. She was even more hesitant now because she wanted the night before her trip to be a pleasant one. The missing money couldn't be ignored, however, and when she told Don of the discovery, they discussed the predicament and, as expected, when they asked Dwayne about the money, he denied any involvement. Dwayne looked bewildered by the accusation, refusing to confess. He contended that Cherie must have misplaced the money and argued that he hadn't been in their room. Don and Cherie had long since stopped giving Dwayne the benefit of the doubt. They didn't trust him, and Dwayne knew it. The three had reached an impasse. Cherie pulled Don aside, telling him that she'd read that taking away something of value to a teenager could be an effective method of discipline. Until now, they'd taken away everything they could think of except Dwayne's sound equipment. After a brief exchange, they turned to face Dwayne. This time, they announced that they were taking possession of his music gear, all of it: the guitar, drums, amps, and boom box. The equipment would be locked in the trailer outside. Dwayne wouldn't get it back for at least a week or until he admitted to stealing the money. Hopes for an agreeable evening had failed miserably. Dwayne leaned against the wall in his bedroom and sullenly watched as his dad hauled the equipment piece by piece to the trailer outdoors and locked it up.

Neither Don nor Cherie slept well that night. Cherie's scheduled flight to San Diego departed before sunrise Monday morning. The two crawled out of bed at 2:30 a.m. in order to reach the airport by 4:00. Don dropped her off at the terminal, then headed the forty miles north to Jantzer's shop. He mulled over the extra tasks he would need to take care of that usually fell on Cherie's shoulders. He knew that taking her place would be a challenge.

Don didn't have long to wait before complications set in. His friend Larry had been laid off from work and had appealed to Don for financial help. Empathic to Larry's situation, Don offered to pay him if Larry could help out during Cherie's absence. An opportunity to call on Larry arose when Don was called into the field at the last minute to repair a broken-down tractor rig. Calculating the time the job would take him, Don knew he wouldn't be back until after dark, and Dwayne needed to be picked up from school. Don and Cherie had agreed it was necessary to drive Dwayne to and from school to keep an eye on him. Don called Larry and arranged for him to pick Dwayne up and take him home. Darkness had set in long before Don drove back into the valley. As he entered Grants Pass, Don was notified by Jantzer's dispatch service that Larry hadn't picked Dwayne up; he'd forgotten. It was 9:00 before Don drove onto the dimly lit school grounds, finding Dwayne upset that he'd been abandoned. Deciding to take the blame, Don didn't tell Dwayne that he'd asked Larry to pick him up. As far as Dwayne knew, his father was responsible for leaving him stranded at the school for hours.

Cherie's trip to San Diego provided a welcome break from the conflicts with Dwayne. She missed Don but didn't let that prevent her from filling her time with amusement. Saturday was the official reunion party but in the meantime, she got together with friends, shopped, went to the beach, and enjoyed the company of her mother-in-law and brothers Denny and Gary.

When Cherie called Don Thursday night, she filled him in on her outings and he got her up to date on his day's work. He told her that Donette said Dwayne had come home that afternoon carrying a brown paper bag she suspected contained beer. Don knew he would have to talk with him. Cherie agreed but doubted Don would get a straight answer from Dwayne.

After Don hung up, he decided to question Dwayne about the alleged beer purchase. After all, he thought, there was no reason to delay the discussion. When Don asked Dwayne if he'd brought home beer, Dwayne reacted with indignant denial. "Why do you always blame me for everything? You and Mom always think the worst." Dwayne looked steadily at his dad, his voice rising slightly.

In an effort to give Dwayne a chance to come clean, Don asked him again, almost pleading, "Dwayne, we don't trust you because you've proved you lie to us when we ask you questions. I want to know if you bought beer at the market. I want to trust you, Dwayne, but I keep finding out I can't. I want to know if you bought some beer."

Still looking at Don, Dwayne began to cry, then tearfully asked, "Why do I always get blamed for everything?"

Don struggled to fight being manipulated by Dwayne, but he could feel himself swayed by irrational hope and misplaced parental guilt. He gave in, deciding to take a softer line. "I'm sorry, Dwayne. Mom and I don't want to blame you for things you haven't done. We've caught you stealing from us, and from Donette, too, and you refuse to admit it, even if we catch you. Try to see it from our position. We want to trust you. We want to believe you are doing what you say you are. But we've caught you in so many lies, Dwayne. You have to understand. It's hard for us to trust you."

Desperately wanting to connect with his son, Don considered the quarrel over and put his arm around Dwayne. "I'm sorry I blamed you, Dwayne. I love you, son." Relieved, he sensed a new-found closeness to Dwayne, trusting that their talk had been candid and the incident resolved.

However, Don soon learned that the discussion with Dwayne the night before hadn't been the heartfelt conversation he'd believed it was. After dropping Dwayne off at school Friday morning, Don stopped at the E & I Market. Because of the longtime friendship the Wiers had with the Mendenhalls, the Wiers had a charge account set up at the store. Bill was behind the counter, and Don asked him if anyone working in the store could have sold beer to Dwayne earlier in the week. Bill checked the Wiers' account and saw that Dwayne had purchased (and signed for) two six packs. A new employee who didn't know Dwayne had taken Dwayne's word for it that he was over twenty-one. Embarrassed, Bill apologized to Don for providing alcohol to Dwayne. Don brushed off the apology and said that Dwayne should be the one asking for forgiveness since he'd lied to the employee and put the store at risk of having their liquor license revoked for selling alcohol to a minor. Don thought back to Dwayne's weepy denial the night before and realized he'd been duped again.

At 6:00 p.m. that same day, Cherie received a call from Donette. Donette told her that Dwayne wasn't home from school. The bus had dropped her off at 3:15, and now it was dark and she was alone. Cherie started to ask why she hadn't gone to the neighbors' house, when her daughter launched into the real reason for her call. She wanted to know if she could go to a skating party with her girlfriend Jennifer. Jennifer's mother would take them to the rink from 6:30 to 8:30. Cherie gave her permission and told Donette to leave a note on the table for her dad. She also instructed Donette that if her dad still wasn't home when Mrs. Locke brought her back, she should ask Jennifer's mom if she could spend the night with them. Satisfied that her daughter was safe and that Don would know where Donette had gone, Cherie hung up, suspecting it would be late before she talked to Don that night.

While Cherie and Donette finalized plans for Donette to attend the skating party, Don and Dwayne remained stuck on a remote logging road where they'd been since mid-afternoon. The recovery of the disabled log truck was arduous and the retrieval more difficult in the dark. Light from the strategically set up flood lamps around the accident site cast eerie shadows as the men moved in and out of the ditch. Bored and edgy, Dwayne sat in the cab of his dad's work truck or wandered around nearby. Even though he was bored stiff, he saw no reason to be of assistance to men doing a job that wasn't his. All he wanted was a diversion from watching this ox-like, plodding work.

His attention had been redirected. He'd caught sight of the rifle in the truck's gun rack. Idle hours and the consumption of substances had fueled his temper. Being imprisoned in the cab of his father's truck as discipline for the purchase of beer was crap. His parents treated him like a ten-year-old. He couldn't take it anymore; he wouldn't take it anymore. Whatever he needed to do to end the hell he lived in, he would do it. Then and there he devised a plan, a permanent solution to his troubles. He would show them all. At 9:00 p.m., he began taking Valium. Half an hour later, Don, sweaty and covered with dirt, climbed into the cab of the pickup. The tractor rig had been up-righted and the men freed to go home.

Dwayne's own words, during a subsequent police interview, recount their actions after leaving the woods:

"At approximately 9:30 p.m. Beaner, a truck driver employed at Jantzer Logging, my dad, and myself left the woods to go get something to eat. Beaner drove his log truck and my dad and I went in Dad's truck. There was no problem of any sort with my dad. Everything was fine; we were having a simple conversation about an engine he built. We've always talked about that sort of thing together.

"We arrived at the restaurant at about 10:00 or 10:15. Beaner and my dad ate ham and eggs. I had a cheeseburger. We were all talking and flirting with the waitresses as usual. I don't remember what restaurant it was, but I believe it was about an hour's drive from Grants Pass. At 10:50 p.m., I went out to the truck to wait for him. At that time, I took four #10 Valium and smoked about half a gram of bud, which I laced in several cigarettes. I'd fallen asleep on the way home, but when we got there, I woke up and it was about 11:30 p.m."

After the late-night drive from the restaurant, Don was relieved to be home. Coming back to the empty house made him miss Cherie. He didn't have long to wait before the phone rang. It was quarter to twelve. Don sat down at the kitchen table, happy to finally be talking to his wife.

He reported that Donette was staying the night with a friend and Dwayne was in his room getting ready for bed. He reassured Cherie that even though Dwayne had requested access to his sound equipment several times during the week, Don had told him no. He filled Cherie in on the day's activities, explaining that he'd taken Dwayne to school that morning and picked him up at noon. Initially, he'd considered bringing Dwayne home before going to work, but after the revelation at the market he'd known he had to talk with Dwayne about the beer purchase and the lying. What he didn't tell her was that he'd naively fostered hope that Dwayne might be of help to him in the field. In any case, having Dwayne accompany him at work had given Don a chance to have a conversation with him about his drinking habits, resulting in Dwayne's reassurances that he had his drinking under control.

Don had been right that Dwayne was in his room, but he wasn't getting ready for bed. Instead, Dwayne had walked into the hall and taken several steps toward the kitchen until he had full view of Don sitting at the table on the phone. Confident that his dad was immersed in conversation with his mom, Dwayne seized the opportunity to begin to carry out the detailed plan he'd formulated earlier while sitting in his father's work truck. He retreated down the hall to his parents' room and removed three rifles from their closet. After carefully assessing the qualities of each weapon, he decided to put two of the rifles in the cab of his truck. He stashed the 30-30, the most powerful of the three, in his bedroom. From the closet shelf, he took nine rounds for the 22 and six rounds for the 30-30. He loaded the 30-30 in his bedroom and carried it into his parents' bathroom near the master bedroom. Carefully, Dwayne pushed the shower door open with one hand while he held the rifle in his other. He put the safety on by letting the hammer down to half-cock and laid the weapon in the bathtub, purposing to keep it hidden. Just as cautiously, he slid the shower door closed. The drugs he'd ingested earlier in the evening fed Dwayne's self-absorption and resentment, aiding in his justification for what he was about to do.

Oblivious to Dwayne's activity, Don continued his conversation with Cherie. "You know, we've tried everything with Dwayne, and nothing seems to be working. We both know he has a serious problem."

Cherie agreed and asked him what had happened when he confronted Dwayne.

"Well, I talked to him as much as I could when I had the time. We really didn't come to any conclusions, but I told him that you and I would talk when you got home. We need to make some decisions as far as getting him help in a rehabilitation place. Dwayne thought he could help himself and we see that he's not, either because he can't or he won't. The situation isn't getting better like he assured us it would."

Don brought up the outpatient center that Dwayne had walked out of after two days. After that failed stay, Don and Cherie had agreed that he needed to be confined in a locked residential facility until his system was free of substances and his mind clear enough to make better decisions. But these programs were terribly expensive. Cherie said she'd heard fees ran between $2,000 and $5,000 a month. Where would they get that kind of money? They would have to take out a loan somehow, but then what? What if Dwayne refused to go? They couldn't allow the stealing or lying to continue. They also recognized that they were legally responsible for Dwayne and his actions.

Meanwhile, Dwayne walked back into his parents' room and opened the dresser drawer where keys were kept for his truck and the trailer. He grabbed the keys, anxious to possess his treasured music gear. Yes, his parents had paid for it, but what good was it to them? The equipment would help him avoid becoming the person his dad expected him to be. He was a musician, an artist, not a person who worked on computers and certainly not a mechanic. He stowed away the two rifles in the cab of his truck and moved the vehicle so that it faced away from the house and toward the driveway.

Don was lost in conversation with Cherie as they talked about treatments for Dwayne.

"Finding an effective program for Dwayne's addiction is one thing," Cherie told Don, "but getting Dwayne to cooperate is another. Remember when he agreed to go to Program 180 and then just walked out of the place? I don't think he'll agree to go to rehab."

In desperation, Don suggested, "I don't know, Cherie. If he won't go willingly, maybe we could trick him somehow into going. Maybe once he's in a good program and he begins to experience the effects of being drug free, he might settle in and go along with the treatment?" Don's tone reflected his words were more of a question than a statement.

Cherie admitted it might come to trickery. "Dwayne keeps saying he has drugs and alcohol under control; that we shouldn't worry about it. But Don, we both know Dwayne doesn't have any of this under control. If we trick him to get him into a lockdown facility, what little trust we have between the three of us would be gone."

Don sighed. Problems with Dwayne were complicated, and this time was no different. "You know, Cherie," he said, "if Dwayne isn't willing to go, he won't cooperate or benefit from any treatment, no matter how expensive the program."

Don and Cherie knew that Dwayne wanted to keep using and getting high. They understood the seriousness of the situation but recognized that this wasn't the time to make a major decision.

Don continued, "It's late and we're both tired. We can't resolve this over the phone anyway. We'll talk about it and come up with a plan when you get home."

Confident that his dad was consumed in conversation, Dwayne returned to the house, walked into the kitchen, and grabbed a beer from the back of the refrigerator. He popped the lid and drank deeply, enjoying the coolness and flavor rush down his throat. His dad barely gave him a look as he heard Dwayne open the beer. Dwayne knew that Don believed his problems were serious where drugs, stealing, and lying were concerned, but when it came to him smoking cigarettes and having a beer once in a while, he thought those habits were pretty minor. Dwayne sauntered back to his room at the end of the hall.

Cherie asked Don, "Is everything okay now?"

He reassured Cherie that everything was fine. He'd told Dwayne that the three of them would talk about his drug use and alcohol when she got home and they would figure out what they could do to help him.

Then conversation between the couple took a personal turn. Don desperately missed his wife. He told her he'd watched a romantic movie on television, and all he could think about while watching it was how it reminded him of her and the rare love they shared. His voice choked, full of emotion, as he told her how very lonely he was without her.

Cherie, moved by his tender words of devotion, no longer thought of the expensive long-distance call but hung on his every word and thought how wonderful it was that he was talking to her about his love and longing for her. She'd been enjoying her time in San Diego, but hearing his voice now brought an intense feeling of closeness to him. She was anxious to see him and hold him close.

Don told her Donette was supposed to be home in the morning and promised Cherie that between the three of them, they would make sure that the house was in order. With the reunion celebration beginning the next morning,

Don and Cherie decided that they should probably say good night. Then telling each other how much they loved one another, they reluctantly said goodbye.

CHAPTER 8 – MURDER AND
THE HOURS AFTER

Just after midnight, on October 18, Dwayne heard Don finish his phone call to Cherie. There was muffled noise as his dad prepared for bed and then silence. Dwayne bided his time until 1:15, when he sneaked into the kitchen and grabbed the remaining Hamm's beer from the fridge, careful to make no sound. He was pleased to see there was still a half case left.

"I got my bong, my bud, my pills, my chew, my cigarettes, and the beer and went into the bathroom and drank six of the beers in a row. I smoked the rest of the pot I had (about 2 ¾ grams) and threw up. I then took the rest of my pills."

Between 1:30 and 2:30 a.m., Dwayne drank two more cans of beer. The time ticked by on the clock. He proceeded to get totally screwed up.

At 3:00 a.m., Dwayne was done waiting. *Just watch me*, he thought. *I'll prove I can be successful my way.* He shut off the bathroom light and opened the door. With purpose and cool calculation, he headed into the other bathroom where he'd hidden the gun. With no thought of turning back, he slid the door open with one hand and reached into the shower with the other, retrieving the weapon from the bathtub.

It was pitch black in the house. Even the illumination of the night's full moon didn't penetrate the home's partially drawn curtains. The teen realized he would have to turn on the bathroom light to get a good shot. He stood in the doorway of the bathroom and briefly considered his options. He flicked the switch on the wall and the light cast a wide beam through the hall into the master bedroom. The sudden brightness caused him to blink. He paused, wanting to be sure his dad was still asleep, and took a few moments to let his eyes adjust. As he'd hoped, his dad was sleeping heavily and didn't stir.

Calmly, Dwayne stepped toward the doorway of his parents' room, ensuring his shadow wouldn't obstruct his vision. Without hesitation, he took careful aim. The thought, *KILL,* dominated his mind. He pulled the gun tightly against his shoulder and squeezed off the deadly round. A deafening bang rang out from the single shot, causing the house to shake. Dwayne stumbled backward, briefly caught off balance. He wavered, then regained his composure. Calmly, almost meticulously, he surveyed the final scene. He crouched down and retrieved the lone spent casing, pushing the brass shell deep into the front pocket of his jeans.

In one statement, Dwayne later reported, "I seen blood all over his sheets and under his pillow." But in other interviews, he claimed not to have walked around the bed to look closely at his father. In all accounts, it's certain that Dwayne didn't linger in the bedroom. His mind was fixated on loading up his stuff and leaving.

Kneeling on the carpeted floor, he grabbed his dad's suitcase from under the bed and crossed the hall into his own room. Before packing, he went outside to start up his truck, wanting to be sure it was ready to go.

He went back inside the house and tossed his personal belongings into the suitcase. Walking into the kitchen, he spotted his dad's paycheck on the counter. The $2,100 could fund his trip to Canada. He had plans to join up with the girl he'd met while vacationing in British Columbia. The two had hit it off, and Canada sounded like a good place to escape to. He scrawled his dad's name on the back of the check and purposed to stash it with his other personal property. He returned outside to the now unlocked camp trailer where his music equipment had been stored. After locating every amp, guitar, boom box, and peripheral component, he loaded each one in his pickup, hopped in the driver's seat, and lost no time heading out. He didn't realize that behind him was the folded payroll check lying in the gravel driveway, the money he'd hoped would fund his getaway.

At 4:00 a.m., two residents of 480 Murphy Creek Road were awakened by knocking on the sliding glass door of their trailer. Initially believing the knocking to be a meaningless noise, Blair "Scooter" Moen ignored the sound, but when it continued, he got up and walked to the slider. He recognized Dwayne Wier standing at the door. Since his release from jail two weeks earlier, Scooter had been staying at the Allen place on Murphy Creek. Smelling alcohol on Dwayne's breath, Scooter thought he appeared quite intoxicated and noticed that Dwayne was carrying part of a twelve pack of Hamm's beer.

Dwayne stepped inside. Scooter noticed the silhouette of Dwayne's Ford pickup parked in the driveway near the trailer. Seeing Dwayne's level of intoxication, Scooter thought it better to keep him at the trailer for a while. Dwayne stayed for about an hour talking with Scooter, feeling comfortable at the residence.

The two were engaged in conversation about music and instruments when without warning, Dwayne announced, "I killed my father."

Scooter, certain Dwayne was drunk, didn't take the comment seriously. Dwayne continued the report saying he'd been near the bathroom by his dad's bedroom and had aimed the 30-30 at him and shot him. Convinced Dwayne's claim was a drunken rant, Scooter dismissed the information. About an hour of aimless conversation took place before Dwayne said he needed to leave. Scooter told Dwayne he didn't want him to drive in a drunken state and was afraid that if he went out, he might be nabbed for a DUII. Dwayne assured Scooter he was fine and would be back in about an hour. He walked out of the trailer, climbed into his pickup, and sped away.

***

Helen Havens and her boyfriend Michael Sharp had spent the night at a friend's house watching movies. They headed home around 4:30 a.m., but they were fighting. The friend's house was in Grants Pass, but they resided several miles away toward Murphy. Both were tired and irritable. Michael called for a taxi and Helen decided to walk home.

Helen's feet hurt. Walking the day before she'd developed blisters, and this unexpected trek didn't help. Now her feet were swollen. She stopped often, hoping that taking breaks would allow her to make the distance home. Besides, she didn't have her glasses and could barely see without them. She wore a floppy brimmed hat and studied the ground as she shuffled painfully along. When she'd set out it had still been dark, but now dawn was beginning to break.

Helen reached the E & I Market, longing to rest her feet. The store wasn't open yet, but there was a two-toned pickup parked out front by the market's gas pumps. She saw a man standing near the truck. She stared at him, trying to make out his features. He said hi to her and she responded in kind. Anxious to have a reason to stop walking, Helen didn't resist the opportunity to strike up a conversation. She and the young man discussed music, and he showed her his amplifiers that were covered by blankets in the back of his truck. Helen told him she used to sing in a band and admired the sound equipment. Flattered by her comments, he told her if she ever wanted to join a band again to look him up as he planned to start a new one soon.

Although this photo shows snow, it was not snowing in the early hours of October 18, 1986. During the breaking dawn of that day, while parked at these gas pumps, Dwayne met Helen Havens.

Helen looked at him closely and thought he appeared kind of young. She asked him if his parents knew he was out and about.

He told her that he and his dad had been "fighting all week."

Helen said, "Parents and kids fight all the time and then we get over it and we say, 'I love you, Mom. I love you, Dad,' you know, and then everybody gets over it." She watched him as he just shook his head. Helen studied him curiously. She asked him his name, but he didn't reply. He seemed spacey, as though he was listening to her but not really hearing.

Sixteen-year-old Dwayne told her he was twenty-three and that he'd taken off from home, packed all his stuff and left. She asked him where he was headed, and he admitted he had no idea.

They were interrupted when a van pulled into the store's lot and parked near the market. There was a deli emblem on the vehicle's side. The man driving the van rolled down his window, greeting the guy with a friendly, "Hi. Good morning, Dwayne. What can I help you with?"

"I need some flashlight batteries, Bill," Dwayne replied. "I need eight of them."

"All right," Bill said as he opened the market's door and the two walked inside. "I've only got four, Dwayne, two packages."

"Okay. I'll take those." Dwayne said.

He took the two packs and Bill said, "Well, wait a minute and I'll run back and look in the house first." Unable to find more in the storeroom, Bill sold Dwayne the four batteries, along with two packs of cigarettes, which Dwayne signed for on the Wiers' charge account. To Bill, who had known the Wiers for years, nothing about Dwayne's behavior seemed out of the ordinary.

Helen waited by the pickup. Dwayne had offered to give her a ride to her home half mile farther down the road. At first she'd been hesitant, not wanting to get in the truck with a stranger. But once she heard the exchange between Dwayne and the market owner, she dropped her guard and decided to take him up on his offer.

No longer cautious, Helen hopped up onto the open tailgate of Dwayne's Ford, thinking only of relieving her aching feet. When he came out of the market, he stood near her and took up the conversation where they'd left off. He told her he'd been waiting at the market so he could purchase the batteries. It was still early, not quite 7:00 a.m., and the streets were quiet. A police car drove by the market, and they both watched it pass.

Dwayne commented, "They're probably looking for me."

Helen thought nothing of the remark. People said that sort of thing all the time when they saw the police.

Dwayne opened the passenger side door of his truck and said, "Come on. I'll give you a ride home."

Helen asked him where he was going. He repeated what he'd said earlier, that he didn't know, and asked her if she had a place where he could sleep. She told him she had a tiny trailer and her niece and her niece's boyfriend were staying there besides Helen's two young children. It was likely that her boyfriend Michael was there too.

Dwayne remarked, "Whatever." He said he would still give her a ride home. The front seat of the pickup was packed with sound equipment. The disordered piles looked to have been loaded in haste. Dwayne moved some of the mess to clear the seat for Helen.

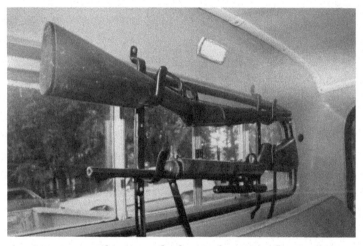

A crime scene photograph shows the two rifles in the gun rack of the suspect vehicle. Helen Haven's was unnerved when her floppy hat caught on "something" behind her in the truck's cab. She had gotten into the vehicle with a stranger, and now she realized he had guns.

Helen climbed into the Ford, the looming dread of even one more step on her blistered feet outweighing her sense of caution. She sat back against the truck's bench seat, and her wide-brimmed hat caught on something behind her in the cab. She turned to put her hat back on and flinched when she saw two rifles in the rack mounted in the truck's rear window. She was afraid of guns.

Dwayne interrupted her thoughts by asking for directions to her residence. They pulled into her short driveway and she thanked him for the ride, suggesting that he drive to the end of the road. There was a school down there and, since it was Saturday, no one would be on the property and he could sleep in his pickup undisturbed. By now it was after 7:00 and getting light out.

Michael, Helen's boyfriend, was walking into the house as the two pulled in the driveway. He turned around and approached the truck with a beer in his hand. Helen introduced him to Dwayne. Dwayne asked Michael if he had any more beer. He shook his head and said it was his last.

Irritated, Helen questioned Michael. "You don't have any more beer anywhere? After all, he gave me a ride home." She looked at Dwayne and asked him again how old he was.

"Twenty-three," he repeated and added that he had Thai stick (a particularly strong form of cannabis) with him. Michael's eyes widened with interest, and he turned toward Dwayne, deciding to invite him in and suggesting that they smoke Dwayne's marijuana. The three sat at the kitchen table, where Michael and Dwayne lit up for a morning high.

Without warning, Dwayne said something about shooting his dad.

Helen asked whether it was Dwayne's real father or his stepfather.

"Real dad," Dwayne replied.

Helen didn't give the comment much thought. She figured he was just talking, without meaning anything. Michael and Dwayne drank beer and the three continued in unremarkable chatter until Dwayne said something about one of them turning him in.

Helen said she was so tired she wasn't about to walk the half mile back to the store to make a call to the cops to "turn your ass in." Still not believing him, she turned and looked directly at him, and asked, "Where did you shoot him?"

Dwayne said, "At my home." He told her he'd been partying and he and his dad had been fighting all week. He'd done acid and crank and smoked his Thai stick while drinking.

Helen said, "The combination of those substances isn't good, you know."

Dwayne replied that he "couldn't handle it anymore," and it was "just getting real bad." He "needed to leave and find something new."

Oblivious to Dwayne's admission and without explanation, Michael said, "This party's over." Standing up, he opened the front door, intending to head outside.

Dwayne looked at Michael as he stood to leave and said nothing. Helen watched him. She flipped on the light and noticed how large his pupils were. He seemed like he wasn't there.

Disinterested in further discussion, Michael announced, "I'm going to split, man. See you later." He walked out, closing the door behind him.

Helen fidgeted uneasily in her chair. Who was this guy whose black eyes were void and whose conversation was so disturbing? She wished Michael hadn't left her alone with Dwayne.

He told her again, "I really did shoot my dad."

Helen didn't want to believe him but decided to keep him talking. She asked him how he'd done it. He said he believed his dad was on his side, in his bed, and he shot him in the neck. The last thing he remembered was his dad grabbing his neck and starting to turn. Then he loaded his stuff in the truck and left. Anxious to validate his claim, Dwayne showed her the spent cartridge he had in his pocket.

Helen, still in disbelief, told him she hoped it wasn't true. But if it was true, he'd screwed up his life and the lives of many other people. They continued in conversation as she walked with him out to his truck. She talked about her relationship with Michael and what a jerk he was. Dwayne wanted to stay in touch and asked Helen to call him later that morning. He said he would be at Hank Allen's place, and he gave her the phone number. She wished him good luck and, with a sense of relief, watched as he gunned the engine and the two-tone pickup turned back in the direction of the Applegate Valley.

The time was 8:00 a.m. as Dwayne drove 80 mph back to the trailer on Murphy Creek Road. He wandered inside and was greeted by Scooter who, after taking a look at Dwayne, suggested he just sleep it off. Fifteen minutes later, Dwayne was passed out on Scooter's couch.

***

Since her daughter, Jennifer, had dance lessons in town at 9:00 a.m., Mrs. Locke decided to drop Donette off at the Wier home on their way to Grants Pass. Certain that Don was home, seeing his work truck was parked in the driveway, Mrs. Locke let Donette out of the car at 8:30 a.m. The garage door was open, so Donette walked into the garage and entered the house through the side door. All was quiet except for the excited whimpering from Snooks, who greeted the girl soon after she stepped in.

Jennifer's mom assumed Don was home when she saw his work truck in the driveway Saturday morning and thought nothing of dropping Donette off at the house.

The side door from the garage opened into a narrow, dimly lit hallway with doors on either side to the bedrooms. As Donette walked into the hall, the first door on her right was Dwayne's room. The door was ajar, and she peeked in to see if he was home although she didn't expect to see him since his truck wasn't parked outside. *He must be staying at a friend's,* she thought. His room was empty, the bed unmade as usual. She continued down the hall and looked into her room, which was off to the right. Everything seemed as she'd left it. When she glanced into her parents' room, off the hall to the left, she could see her dad was still asleep because the bed was under a window that let in filtered outdoor light. Surprised by seeing her dad sleeping, she thought, *He never stays in bed this late—never ever.* Don was an early riser, always up before seven. *He must've had an extra late-night or a really hard night.* Snooks circled Donette's feet, anxious to have attention.

Donette ruffled the dog's coat and talked to the pooch. Then she walked toward the front door, put her overnight bag down, and hung her jacket on the coat rack near the door. Deciding to wake her dad, Donette walked into her parents' room.

"I walked into the bedroom and I started to get up on the bed and I said, 'Dad...' And then I saw the blood. So, then I walked around the other side of the bed that he was actually laying on. And I remember his arm being out of the covers. He never slept with a shirt on. I remember feeling his arm. It was cold. I knew he was dead. I remember thinking, *What do you need to do? You need to call 911, but then what?* So, I thought, *Just call Mom and she'll tell you what you need to do.* I remember coming back into the kitchen to get her phone book, to get Grandma's number and then going back into the bedroom and calling from the bedroom. I was dazed and don't know why [I went back to the bedroom] but whatever the reason, I didn't want to leave him in there alone. So, I went back in there. We had an old rotary phone where the dial spun around when we dialed each number. I remember it was avocado green. I called and my grandma answered. I didn't want to say anything to her so I said, 'Hi Grandma. It's Donette. Is Mom there?' "

The long and busy week had caused Cherie to sleep in later than she'd intended. As she slipped out of bed, her thoughts were on the reunion celebration scheduled later that day. Carrol called to Cherie to let her know Donette was on the phone. Somewhat miffed by the call, Cherie asked her daughter why she was calling again. After all, Cherie thought to herself, didn't Donette realize how expensive these long-distance calls were, especially since there had been many during the week? But a split-second later, she felt intensely anxious; a foreboding had crept over her. She heard quivering in her daughter's voice.

Cherie coaxed her, "What's wrong? What's going on?"

Donette said, "Dad's dead. There's blood all over the bed, and he won't wake up."

Cherie was silent for a moment before gasping out the words, "Oh my God, Donette! Don't say that!"

Donette repeated the dreaded words. "He's dead, Mom. There's blood all over the bed and he won't wake up."

Her daughter's words were filled with such a crushing horror that Cherie refused to believe them.

She blurted out, "Oh my God!" Her voice was charged with agitation and fear.

Donette heard her grandmother's panicked voice in the background reacting to Cherie's words. "What? What's going on?"

Then, once again, it was her mother's voice, distant, terrified. "Donette told me Don's dead!" For several moments, Donette picked up muffled bits of conversation between her mom and grandmother. Suddenly, Cherie placed the phone back up to her ear, gripped by the realization that her young daughter was on the other end of the call and needing to feel reassurance from her mother.

"Listen to me carefully," Cherie told her, struggling to steady her voice. "I want you to call Jon and Sam and tell them exactly what you told me. Let them know I said you should go to their house. I'll call 911 to get help out there, but I want you to stay with the Alhroths." Cherie asked if Dwayne was home, and Donette said that he and his music stuff were gone. She'd noticed there was no equipment in his room when she peeked in as she walked down the hall, not realizing the gear had been locked in the trailer outside.

As soon as Donette hung up from the call with Cherie, she dialed the neighbors' house and repeated to Jon what she'd said to her mom. She asked, "Can you come over?"

Without hesitation, Jon told her, "I'll be right there."

Donette walked to the front door, unlocked and opened it. She stood in the doorway, feeling like it was forever before she saw Jon coming down the driveway. She watched as Dave Raska, Jon's brother-in-law, pulled into the Ahlroths' driveway and exited his car. Jon waved for Dave to join him and they headed to the Wier home. When the two men entered the house, Dave went directly into the master bedroom to check on Don's condition and Jon calmly encouraged Donette to sit down while he called the ambulance.

When Dave came out of the bedroom, he nodded to Jon, indicating Don was gone. Jon talked to the Josephine County 911 operator while Dave reassured Donette that they were doing everything possible to get help. Having completed the emergency call, Jon noticed that Donette was still in her pajamas from her sleepover and encouraged her to get dressed. He thought it best that the girl go over to his house before the emergency personnel arrived, telling her that she could watch TV and that he and Dave would wait at the Wier home for help to arrive.

Donette walked the short distance up the driveway to the neighbors' house. Sam, Jon's wife, was at work at the local hospital. Donette entered the house. CSPAN was playing on the television set. Donette described her circumstances:

"I didn't know where the remote was or how to change the channel. I remember just sitting there staring at the screen and thinking. Then I heard the ambulance, and the fire trucks pulled in. I remember deciding I'm going to go back over there and see what's going on. I remember walking back over and seeing a fireman. I couldn't tell if he was going in the house or coming out.

"Then our friends Linda and Larry pulled in and Linda saw me and yelled, 'Donette!' and she came running over to me. She said, 'Come on. Let's go back to Jon and Sam's house.'

"A deputy from the sheriff's office came over to Jon and Sam's to talk to me. At the conclusion of the interview he commented, 'You're very calm. You're calmer than I would expect.' I was just straightforward. I answered his questions. Matter-of-factly kind of thing."

When asked about Dwayne, Donette replied, "I never felt fearful of Dwayne. Even when I found my dad it never crossed my mind that Dwayne could be responsible." When she didn't see Dwayne on Saturday morning of October 18, she just thought he was at a friend's house. "I knew my dad was murdered because there was blood everywhere. I knew someone had killed him. But no one came to mind.

"I remember Sam coming home from work shortly after that. And she was the one that told me. 'I need you to listen to me.' Sam sat down in front of me and said, 'I want to let you know that your dad has passed away and that he's dead.'

"That's when I started crying. Because I think, up until that time, I was in shock, in robot mode almost, just going, when your adrenaline kicks in. And I started crying and then asking, 'When is my mom going to be here?' "

As soon as Cherie hung up the phone, driven by a surge of adrenaline and overcome by shock, she grabbed a Bible her brother-in-law Bruce had in his hands. She ran outside to nowhere in particular and collapsed on the grass sobbing, pleading with God to give her a scripture, give her something from the Bible to help her to make sense of what had happened. She knew Don was probably dead.

Her mind searched for explanations. Perhaps Don had been hurt at work, or maybe something had hit him. He could have had a cerebral hemorrhage from a head injury. She called the house to see what was going on.

Jon answered.

"Jon," Cherie gasped, "is he alive? Did you call the ambulance?"

Jon assured her he'd called the ambulance. As for Don's condition, he mumbled, "I don't know. It doesn't look good." He suggested that when the sheriff's deputies arrived, she could talk with them.

Concerned about her daughter, Cherie asked him to take care of Donette and keep her at his house. Jon promised he would. The two discussed Cherie's travel plans to get her home, and she said that she and Carrol would take the earliest possible flight into Medford. Jon assured her that he, Sam, and Donette would pick them up at the airport.

At 8:50 a.m., the Josephine County Sheriff's Office received a call from Community One ambulance that they were in route to an address on N. Applegate Road and that the sheriff's office should send a unit. Almost simultaneously, the sheriff's department received a phone call from Michael Sharp. He reported that his girlfriend Helen had accepted a ride from a guy who had claimed to have shot and killed his father earlier that morning. The stranger had told Helen that he was going to a friend's home at an address on Murphy Creek Road.

When Cherie reached Deputy Barbero at the scene, she flooded him with questions. Panicked and fearful, she "demanded to know the condition of her husband." Barbero wrote in his report, "and I advised her that he was deceased. She also demanded to know the method of his death and I advised her that I believed he'd been shot. Mrs. Wier became very hysterical over the phone, but I managed to obtain some details from her." When the sheriff initially showed up on the scene, Ron Dague and Jon met him at the house. The two men advised the deputy they suspected that Dwayne was responsible for Don's murder. With that conversation in mind, the deputy questioned Cherie about Dwayne, then added to his report, "The Wiers have had problems with their son, Dwayne Wier, but that she [Cherie] was unaware of any in the past few days. She further related that there have been past problems with her son being involved with drugs and alcohol and some recent minor problems." After getting information from Cherie describing vehicles that belonged at the residence, Barbero asked her about her travel plans home. "She advised me that she had a scheduled flight out of San Diego airport at 3:00 p.m. today." Then, due to Cherie's emotional state, he wrote, "Mrs. Wier was too hysterical to continue a further conversation and I advised her that she would be contacted later in the day with additional information."

Cherie's brothers, Gary and Denny, had driven to San Diego for the reunion and both had been at Carrol's house when Donette called. By 10:00 a.m., slightly more than an hour after Donette's call, Denny and Gary left San Diego, stopping only to pack personal items, and made the twelve-and-a-half-hour drive to Southern Oregon, arriving before Cherie and Carrol secured emergency plane tickets to fly home. The Alhroths readily opened their home to the family since the Wier property, now a crime scene, had been taped off by law enforcement.

***

Dwayne woke about 10:00 and noticed his pickup wasn't where he'd parked it. Scooter admitted that he'd used it to go to the store.

"Ok, that's cool," Dwayne told him.

Scooter asked if Dwayne had any cigarettes, and Dwayne told him there was a pack on the dash of his pickup. Scooter left the trailer to get a smoke. He sat in the truck, pulled out a cigarette and lit it up, then decided to return to the trailer. As Scooter entered the residence, he saw Pat Harrison, Scooter's roommate and a mutual friend of Dwayne's, pull into the driveway. Pat came into the home briefly, then he, too, decided to go back to his car and get a cigarette.

Aided by Michael Sharp's tip, Josephine County Sheriff's officers Lieutenant Warren and Deputy Barbero arrived at the Murphy Creek address. The two officers parked their vehicles out of sight of the residence and approached the trailer on foot. Deputy Claar, already on the scene, had sighted the two-toned Ford pickup at the location and called for backup. The three officers immediately observed a male subject exiting the residence and detected the distinct odor of burning marijuana wafting through the open door. The male subject coming out of the trailer was later identified as Pat Harrison and was taken into protective custody and removed behind the police vehicles for safety. Harrison advised the deputies that three other people were still inside the residence. One of them was Dwayne Wier.

Unaware of the law enforcement presence outside, Dwayne walked out of the trailer toward his pickup. Deputy Claar could tell that Wier didn't appear to see him with his gun drawn, as Wier casually vacated the Murphy Creek home. When Deputy Claar yelled, "Sheriff's department, freeze!" Wier turned toward Claar, looked at him, but continued toward his pickup, ignoring the command. When Deputy Barbero heard Claar shout the order to freeze, Barbero moved to assist Claar. Barbero had a clear view of the front of the trailer and watched Dwayne as he kept walking toward the driver door of the suspect vehicle. Barbero and Claar had seen the two rifles hanging from a gun mount secured on the inside of the cab's rear window.

Claar again shouted, "Freeze!" having already made the decision to fire if Wier continued to move toward the truck and touch the door's handle. Both deputies had their service revolvers drawn and pointed at Dwayne, ordering him to stop. Dwayne continued to snub their warnings and moved closer to the truck while looking directly at Deputy Barbero with what the deputy called a "cold and indifferent stare." Just as Dwayne reached for the driver's door of the pickup, Claar pulled the trigger on his weapon. Abruptly, Wier altered the direction of his hand from reaching for the truck's handle to putting both hands up in the air above his head. Deputy Claar was able to catch the hammer of his gun with his thumb, preventing the weapon from firing. Only a fraction of a second prevented Claar from discharging his weapon in what would likely have been a fatal shot. Finally complying with the order, Dwayne placed himself in a prone position on the ground before the two deputies.

Barbero asked Dwayne his name, to which he replied, "Dwayne Wier." The deputy emptied Dwayne's front pants pocket of a watch and a can of smokeless tobacco. He handcuffed Dwayne, placing him under arrest and into the back seat of Lieutenant Warren's patrol car, where Warren advised Dwayne of his constitutional rights. Dwayne signed a permission slip for the deputies to search his pickup. Shortly thereafter, Lt. Warren transported Dwayne to the Josephine County Sheriff's Office in Grants Pass.

CHAPTER 9 – THE DAYS
FOLLOWING THE CRIME

The earliest emergency flight the airline could provide Cherie and Carrol would land in Oregon after 11 p.m. More than anything, Cherie wanted to see Donette and feel her arms around her daughter. Knowing Donette was at the Ahlroths' home, Cherie feared the girl would overhear well-meaning family and friends discussing what had happened to Don. While still in San Diego, she called friends Ron and Sheri Dague to ask if Donette could spend a few nights with them. The couple lived nearby and had kids Donette's age whom she knew from school. If Donette would be comfortable anywhere at this time, Cherie thought it would be with the Dagues. Ready to help, Sheri picked Donette up from the Ahlroths' home that afternoon. Though upset that their late arrival would prevent her from seeing Donette, Cherie consoled herself knowing her daughter would be settled at the Dagues' for the night and she would see her the first thing the next morning.

Cherie and Carrol exchanged few words on the plane ride from San Diego; instead, they clung to each other in despair. Once they landed and the women entered the terminal, they were surrounded by a group of friends who offered hugs and condolences. Cherie spent the hour-long drive to the Ahlroths' home questioning Jon about what had happened, and he did his best to provide answers. The conversation stopped as they reached the bend in the road near the Wier property and the car's passengers turned to look at the caution tape traversing the driveway. Resembling some macabre spider's web, the yellow tape cordoned off what had been their home.

The following morning, Cherie drove to Ron and Sheri's to see Donette and make arrangements to come by the Dagues' every evening to pray with Donette and tuck her in bed. Donette tried to talk to Cherie about what had happened. Disturbed about the blood she'd seen, she worried that her dad had been in pain. Cherie knew Donette needed assurance from her, needed hope that the events of the last two days would somehow turn out to make sense. She didn't know how to respond; she needed comfort for herself. What words were there for either of them? Cherie hugged her daughter and told her that when her daddy was shot, he'd been sleeping. He hadn't been aware of what was happening and had awakened in the arms of Jesus. Cherie's faith in God was the consolation she had to hold onto; it was all she could give to her daughter as she held her close.

***

After Lt. Warren arrested Dwayne at the Murphy Creek residence, he transported the prisoner to Josephine Memorial Hospital. There Dwayne was given drug tests and a physical. Two hours later, he was moved to the sheriff's department for further investigative interviews and an evaluation by a psychiatrist. Since there were no facilities in Josephine County equipped to house violent juvenile offenders, at 3:00 p.m. on the 18th, Dwayne was taken to the Jackson County Juvenile Detention Facility (JDH) in Medford. According to the report of the transporting deputy, Dwayne spent the majority of the forty-five-minute trip in silence, looking out the window. As they neared Medford, he began to ask the deputy questions, wanting to know how long he would be in JDH and how long he would be in prison. The deputy replied that he didn't know.

***

Barbero was the last officer to leave the Wier residence. Prior to his departure, he removed the bedding in the master bedroom. He secured the crime scene at 5:50, locking all doors. The keys to the home were left at the Ahlroths' house. Since law enforcement had completed their investigation at the property the yellow tape came down, and the family was given access to the residence. Denny and Gary were the first to go into the house and did their best to get the place in order. The brothers, along with Ron and Sheri Dague, disposed of the master bedroom mattress and scrubbed the rug. Despite the efforts of the thorough cleaning crew, a stubborn stain remained on the master bedroom's carpet, an ugly reminder of the crime that had taken place. Cherie and Carrol moved in by early evening, but Donette would stay at the Dagues' for the remainder of the week.

The day after the tragedy was Sunday. On a typical weekend, Don, Cherie, and Donette attended the morning service at Calvary Chapel in Grants Pass, but today was anything but ordinary, and Pastor Ron Hayworth found himself delivering the shocking news of the atrocity to the congregation. Since the church was a small one, most attendees knew one another and Cherie had felt comfortable phoning Ron to tell him Don had been killed. Pastor Ron shared what little he knew about the terrible incident with those who came to church that Sunday morning and encouraged church members to offer prayerful and practical support to Cherie and Donette.

Marilyn and Melody were two of the members who attended church that Sunday. Neither knew Cherie, but after hearing her story the friends decided to call her. Marilyn phoned Cherie and made arrangements for them to visit later that morning. Cherie welcomed Marilyn and Melody into her home, grateful for the company of Christians. Distraught in her circumstances, she desperately needed the calming presence and spiritual encouragement of like-minded women.

"We're going to be here with you from now on," Marilyn told Cherie, who held onto her words. "We'll come over and visit you and we'll spend time with you." Marilyn was true to her promise and the women formed a lasting friendship. God hadn't forsaken Cherie. It was a joyless time, but He had sent two special people into her life to bring her camaraderie.

After her newfound friends left, Cherie and Carrol drove into Grants Pass for their appointment with the funeral home director. A myriad of decisions needed to be made and

Cherie, unable to remember what day it was, relied heavily on Carrol to get through the three-hour meeting. Cherie's thoughts drifted elsewhere, anywhere but where she was. She looked blankly at the counselor when he asked if she wanted to schedule time for a viewing. He explained that grief counselors recommend the practice as it helps loved ones say goodbye to the deceased. After conferring with Carrol, Cherie agreed to schedule the visitation, choosing a time in the morning before the memorial service.

The two grieving women left the funeral home worn out, longing to go back to the house and sleep, to close their eyes and awaken to a world where Don's murder was nothing more than a dreadful nightmare. But as exhausted as Cherie felt, she was intent on meeting with Dwayne and didn't want to wait any longer to see him face-to-face. She dropped Carrol at the house and picked up Denny. The two drove the thirty miles through the Applegate Valley to Medford. Even though she was determined to get answers from Dwayne, Cherie had no capacity for anger; that would come later. She wanted to understand why her son would murder his dad. *Why* would Dwayne have shot Don? Drug and alcohol use, as well as stealing, were at the center of the increased conflicts at home. There had never been any concern about Dwayne acting out in physical violence toward anyone. When she'd been told that Dwayne had been arrested for murder, the reality that he was responsible wouldn't sink in. Answers were all she wanted now. Cherie considered her future, navigating a life without her beloved Don and comforting Donette who missed her daddy. The prospect weighed heavily on her, but the thought that Dwayne, whom she loved despite their troubles, was responsible for all of it was more than she could bear.

Cherie found Dwayne sitting with his head down at a table in the visitation room. He said little. Undeterred by his demeanor, Cherie pressured him with questions. "Why did you shoot your dad? Why, Dwayne? Why?"

He muttered, "It was the drugs, Mom. It was the drugs." Dwayne cried, but his tears struck Cherie as disingenuous.

The thirty minutes Cherie sat with Dwayne provided no insight as to what had happened or why. She'd hoped to see indications of remorse, but there were none. Sitting at the table across from Dwayne, she stared, bewildered, at the teenager. Snippets of images from their past crossed her mind: The day she and Don came home from the adoption office proudly carrying Dwayne. Camping trips and Boy Scouts during his childhood. The early teen years when Dwayne was initially excited about music and learning to drive. She could only shake her head. How in the world had they ended up here?

Her first visit with Dwayne left Cherie with more questions and no answers, though she wondered what answers she'd expected to hear and what comfort his answers could bring her. Before she left, she requested that the detention officers watch Dwayne for any signs of remorse.

Driving home to Murphy, Cherie ruminated over her visit with Dwayne. He'd always loved his dad. Since Don worked long hours, disciplining the kids had fallen on her shoulders. She'd believed that Dwayne cared more for Don than he did for her. She still had no resolution to her despair, and no answer as to why Dwayne had taken Don's life.

Finally home after the exhausting day, Cherie stood in her bedroom with the closet door open. The funeral home director had given her instructions to provide an outfit for Don. In the kitchen, Carrol fixed dinner, and Cherie's brothers had gone into Grants Pass to run errands. Transfixed, she stared at the clothes hanging in tidy rows. Ever since the phone call from Donette, she'd been carried to and fro by her emotions with Don, her love, gone. The thought of him absent from her life overwhelmed her with sadness, and she couldn't see how she would ever accept the reality of his death. Still in shock, she stumbled through the necessary tasks that loomed in front of her, steeling herself to do what needed to be done, fearing to let down her guard, feeling fragile. She carefully chose what she knew Don liked to wear, what he was comfortable in. She set aside his brown wool shirt and a pair of tan Levi's dress pants. On impulse, she removed the shirt from its hanger and buried her face in the wooly fabric, trying to breathe in Don's smell. Crushed by loss, she clutched the shirt, searching for any fragment of Don that he'd left behind.

Monday morning, on the second floor of the Josephine County Courthouse, Carrol, Cherie, and her two brothers were packed together in the courtroom for Dwayne's first appearance. There were few empty seats due to the presence of curiosity seekers and reporters, as well as Cherie's supporters, who gathered to witness the detention hearing of the sixteen-year-old accused of murder. Cherie sat stupefied, listening to Deputy Barbero, one of several to testify, when he took the stand and described that during the arrest, Wier "seemed extremely cold and indifferent to his own life." Barbero recounted that Wier had refused orders to stop (as Dwayne approached his truck) although he was "being held at gunpoint." Barbero also told the court that Wier admitted to shooting his father and indicated that he'd planned the crime "in detail." The assigned probation officer, Maureen Crumine, filed charges based on the information provided by the law enforcement agencies. Judge Gerald Neufeld ruled there was enough evidence for the court to assert authority over Dwayne. Due to the seriousness of the charges, Neufeld pronounced that Dwayne was to remain in custody.

The hearing concluded, and Dwayne met with his court-appointed attorneys to discuss details of his case and another specific issue that was on Dwayne's mind. He wanted to attend Don's memorial. He knew that a service was scheduled for Wednesday, and he petitioned his attorneys to secure permission for him to be present.

Following his conference with his lawyers, the Josephine County Sheriff's Department transported him back to the Juvenile Detention Facility.

Terry Soeteber, Josephine County Juvenile Department Director, informed the media that the next step in the case would be an investigation to determine whether Wier should be tried as a juvenile or remanded to adult court. Soeteber said he didn't know how long the investigation would take. Headlines in the Grants Pass paper that afternoon read, "Son Held in Dad's Murder." The article would be the first of many that updated locals on the shocking crime and the events that followed. The friendly town, shaken by violence to one of their own by one of their own, devoured every detail, wondering how such a tragedy could happen in their peaceful community.

News of the crime was picked up by the Associated Press and distributed beyond the local level. On the evening of October 20, Cherie received a phone call from her niece who lived near Boston. The niece expressed concern about Cherie and Donette. Cherie questioned her, wondering how she knew about the shooting, and was told by her niece that she'd heard a report about the tragedy on the evening national news. Stunned to know the story had received national attention, Cherie was barely able to reply. The whole country now knew what had happened to her family.

On Tuesday, October 21, Dwayne called his attorney, again requesting permission to attend his father's funeral scheduled for the following day. At first Dwayne was told that "they were working on it," but later that afternoon the court officially denied approval.

In the meantime, the detention staff monitored Dwayne's behavior. During his first four days in custody, he was described as "generally cooperative, staying to himself and showing little or no emotion." When Cherie next saw him, the experience was much the same as her first visit. Dwayne offered little communication and gave no indication of remorse.

Cherie and her family spent most of Tuesday coordinating details of the viewing, memorial service, and graveside ceremony with Pastor Ron and the counselor from Hull and Hull Funeral Home. The Calvary Chapel family had arranged a full dinner following the memorial. The day promised to be long and emotionally exhausting, but Cherie and Carrol were attentive to every aspect, wanting to make the gathering an appropriate honor to Don and to show appreciation to those who came to give him tribute.

Relieved to know her daughter wasn't in the middle of conversations about funeral plans and visits with Dwayne, Cherie was thankful for the Dagues' hospitality. Tuesday night, Cherie knew she needed to talk with Donette about what she could expect to happen at the services the next day. Haunted by the knowledge that Donette had found her daddy dead and in a pool of blood, Cherie wished she could erase the image from her daughter's mind. The counselor from the funeral home had said that viewing the body of the deceased is often helpful in the grieving process. Cherie explained the open casket to Donette and told her there was a time scheduled at the funeral home when family members could visit separately from others. She persuaded Donette to accompany her, believing that if Donette saw Don in a more peaceful and staged setting, she might forget the bloody scene she'd witnessed. Donette didn't want to go but complied because she could tell it was important to her mom. In reality, Donette's memory of finding her dad wasn't a gruesome one. There was blood on the bed, but very little on Don. Donette described her dad as looking like he was asleep. But the staged viewing at the funeral home didn't give the impression of a person sleeping. Instead, Don's ashen skin tones and obvious makeup only served to create an artificial and morbid look. As Donette peered closely at her dad's face, she saw the residue of blood on his neck that someone had neglected to remove completely, attempting instead to cover up the red blotches with makeup. Donette recoiled from the repulsive sight, forever harboring the ghastly image in her mind, and Cherie felt her heart sink as she realized that, although she'd thought Donette should see her dad at the funeral home, it probably would have been better if she hadn't.

Later that same day, Cherie stood with family members greeting a long line of people waiting to share stories about Don and express condolences. Pastor Ron spoke of the grief accompanying Don's sudden death. He encouraged those present to remember the promise in God's Word that assures the believer. "We do not sorrow as those without hope. People are not in their pain and sorrow alone," he reminded them. "God's presence is in the midst to carry us through and we can have faith that we will be reunited with other believers in heaven one day."

A selection of Don's favorite worship music played, familiar guitar songs they'd routinely sung during Sunday services. Several people spoke publicly, expressing their admiration for him. Hugs and tears, funny stories, and condolences were passed around between people whose lives had been touched by Don.

A graveside ceremony followed at Granite Hill Cemetery and concluded with dinner at the church. One stranger who approached Cherie owned a grocery store thirty-five miles north of Grants Pass. The man generously told Cherie about his encounter with Don.

"Don happened to come into my store one day to get food to snack on while driving home. I was fixing this sign on top of the building. Don jumped right in and helped me. He climbed up the ladder and went clear to the top." The man smiled at the recollection. "I was afraid to go up that high but Don climbed right up there! After he helped me, Don stopped every so often to get to know me." He looked at Cherie and added sincerely, "He was a wonderful man. Always there to help somebody any time."

Despite the sadness of the day's services, the family was cheered by hearing guests share personal stories about Don.

The day after the memorial, family members, with the exception of Carrol, prepared to drive back to California. Planning to rise early for the long drive home, everyone had retired except Cherie and her sister Vonnie. Cherie described the experience that followed. "My sister and I stayed up late talking. After she went to bed, I was restless and had trouble sleeping, but suddenly I had a strong sense of God's presence in my room. The impression was so powerful that I could almost hear His breathing, and His presence was so convincing that even though I couldn't see Him, He felt more real to me than the furniture and walls that I could see around me.

"The next morning, when I woke up, I had this feeling of goodness that came over me. Again, I felt His presence and the assurance that God was going to allow everything to be better, even though death had visited our home. I needed to know He was there with me and I felt that comfort.

"That day, my family left to go back home and I was going to be by myself except for Carrol, and of course Donette. We fixed breakfast for all of us. We said our goodbyes and everyone left. My neighbor Jon came over and said he'd be there if I needed anything. I told Donette not to hesitate to ask me for anything she needed. We prayed together and for several months I slept with her in her room at night. When she went back to school she was doing okay. The teachers said they'd let me know if they noticed anything about her behavior that appeared out of the ordinary."

God had revealed His transcendent presence and comfort to Cherie in her time of loss to remind her that He was near even when she didn't sense Him. The days and months ahead would be difficult beyond imagination and as she began to live out her loss, the sense of grief would bring great sadness, but her spirit knew that no matter the depth of grief or fear ahead, she wasn't alone.

CHAPTER 10 – THE CRYING ROCK

On October 23, five days after the murder, Dwayne compiled a list of topics to discuss with his attorneys:

1. Home arrest – <u>discuss</u> and <u>convince</u> <u>November 3 release</u>.
2. Glasses – need them
3. School work from J.C.C.S.
4. Find out where my truck is; when and if my mom can get it. Cost?
5. Discuss hiring of two or four more attorneys to convince home arrest under <u>very restricted</u> basis.
6. <u>DO NOT</u> remand me to adult court and <u>do not</u> charge me for an offense more serious than it is.
7. It should work out because I have the <u>most</u> powerful judge and lawyer behind me – <u>Jesus Christ!!!</u>
8. Rehabilitation program for drugs and alcohol <u>and/or</u> family counseling. At <u>my</u> cost!

Three days later, while housed at JDH, Dwayne scratched out a letter to his mother and sister. It was the first correspondence of over 350 letters Dwayne would send to Cherie during his incarceration. He wrote:

"I know you're having a hard time right now and so is everyone else, including me. You should not be afraid of me for any reason. I promise you, just because it happened once does not mean it will happen again." He tried to persuade

Cherie to tell his lawyers, and any court official, that she and Donette weren't opposed to having him come home under house arrest. He emphasized that if they let anyone know they didn't want him home, he would be kept locked away. He pleaded, saying he would live in alternative secure housing (such as a teen home for runaways) if they refused to have him at home. *"This is not what I want and I'm sure it isn't what you or anyone else in the family wants."* He continued, *"I did not want this to happen any more than you did, but it happened and now we have to learn how to accept it."* He tried to support his request. *"Jail will not do a damn thing for me!!! It will only make me more unhappy and more stressful!!! I don't want to lose you and Donette!!! I have lost enough already!!! I am responsible for you and Donette now! Please come and talk to me! My brain is going to peg its needle at the insanity mark if I'm here much longer! Help me PLEASE! Then, when I'm released, I'll help you. I love you both."*

The remand hearing to determine whether Dwayne would be tried in juvenile or adult court would take place in mid-December. In the meantime, streams of investigative interviews continued. Donette again described discovering her dad's body after coming home from the sleepover. Detectives commented about Donette's maturity for her age, her clear recollection of events, and the calmness of her answers to questions. They were impressed with her frankness and felt uneasy about the ten-year-old's unusual composure, even commenting on it in their reports. Cherie spoke with detectives who asked about Don's and her parenting philosophy and Dwayne's behaviors since childhood. Investigators wanted to know particulars about Dwayne's drug use, his parents' attempts to discipline him, and their efforts to find good counseling. Answering the questions with candor, Cherie held nothing back, privately hoping that as she divulged details about Dwayne's history, someone could tell her why he'd killed Don.

Carrol stayed through October and most of November, keeping Cherie moving. On days when the weather was pleasant, the women went outside to work in the yard, taking breaks to walk down by the river. Having Carrol around prevented Cherie from slipping into depression, and cheering Cherie helped Carrol deal with her own grief. When the time came for Carrol to go back to San Diego, adjusting was hard on them both.

After Carrol had gone and Cherie and Donette were alone, Cherie spoke with her daughter about their future living arrangements. She asked Donette if she wanted to move out of the house. To Cherie's surprise, Donette didn't hesitate in answering that she wanted to stay. After all, Donette replied, this was their home. In addition to the trauma that had come about there, living on the large property meant there were practical issues to address. Cherie questioned how she could maintain the place without Don, and on a personal level she had doubts.

In mid-November, Cherie received two letters from Dwayne, one written to her and the other addressed to Donette.

To Cherie, Dwayne relayed information from his attorneys, letting her know that if he were incarcerated at MacLaren he would *"be one of the top 20! If you don't understand Top 20's, it means that I would be in with the 20 most violent and dangerous people there? Please pray that I don't go."*

To Donette, he expressed concern about his case and asked her to pray for him. He talked about her school and remarked that the detectives had commented to him about how intelligent they thought she was. Then he wrote about the death of their dad. *"Look, I know this whole thing is very discouraging for you and Mom, and it is also very discouraging for all of us. But don't hate me for what I've done, okay? I'm very sorry this all happened. Dad is with God now and I know he is happy. I think we will have to learn to accept this and simply believe that he is not gone forever. We will see him again in heaven and we will be a family again.* " He finished by touching on the fact he would *"be gone for a while"* and in the meantime *"please do not sell the truck or my equipment* [music]."

Over the eight months of Dwayne's imprisonment in JDH, Cherie visited him every six weeks and saw him when he appeared in court in Grants Pass. Dwayne had been given permission to call home, but Cherie temporarily put an end to this privilege after noticing that Donette was upset by the calls. When Cherie met with Dwayne, she primarily shared Bible verses with him. Dwayne never told her why he'd killed Don, nor did he appear sorry. On one occasion, having her own need for answers, Donette accompanied Cherie to visit Dwayne. When the three of them met in the visitation room, Donette asked Dwayne why he'd shot their dad. He didn't reply with a straight answer but rambled in a nonsensical way, avoiding her question. After that fruitless visit, Donette saw no reason to visit Dwayne again, only seeing him once more when she testified at his remand hearing.

Amid the emotionally draining visits with Dwayne, her worries for Donette, and her own adjustments to a life without Don, Cherie relied heavily on the stabilizing influence of her faith to give her perspective. Church family was everything to Cherie. She latched onto each message that was taught Sunday mornings and Wednesday nights, looking for hope that transcended the struggles of her daily reality. Her faith and the encouragement from her church friends were the threads that kept her going. Whenever the church doors were open, she and Donette were there. "Pastor Ron was wonderful. He came over after it happened and prayed with me and we'd talk about everything. He talked to both Donette and me. He had me coming in once a week and would give me scriptures to read and pray with me. He gave me good counsel. I knew I had to keep close to the Lord, that the Lord was my source and protection, that He'd get me through it when nobody else could.

"We were studying the book of Job at church when Don died, and I remember sitting in church thinking I was Job. There were so many tears I shed during that time."

There is no other book in the Bible filled with as much loss and grief as the book of Job. Job suffered greatly despite his faithful walk as a follower of God. His loss wasn't the result of personal wrongdoing, but the consequence of living in a fallen world. Job was grief-stricken and wondered where the God he believed in was in all of his sadness. Cherie sat in every service, listening intently to the story of Job, clinging to any morsel of lesson to be learned from how Job was able to trust God through sorrow.

Marilyn met Cherie the day after Don's murder. The two remained close friends for over thirty years.

"I remember Marilyn was always there. She sat with me during those times, patting me on the leg and saying, 'It's okay, it's okay.'

"A lot of people called me at night, helping me to be at peace. I never got mad at God because I knew it wasn't God that caused it [the murder], it was Dwayne."

By accident, Cherie devised another surprising form of therapy. She'd always been sociable and after the murder, she found herself frequently talking to strangers when she went to town. When someone Cherie didn't know approached her, having recognized her from articles in the paper, and would say, "You look really familiar to me. What's your name?" Cherie would answer, and the person would respond awkwardly with words similar to, "Oh yeah, you're the woman whose son killed her husband, right?"

Cherie would say yes, and then the two would strike up a lengthy conversation. For Cherie, there was relief in getting out all her emotions and thoughts through conversation rather than burying her feelings inside. Not everyone wants to talk of their personal circumstances. In fact, most people would rather not talk, especially to strangers. But Cherie quickly realized that the more she talked about her situation the better she felt. As she verbalized her cares to others, she diminished the weight of the emotions tormenting her.

Alone at home, however, Cherie didn't do well; she continued to be overwhelmed by grief. She longed for Don. When waves of sorrow engulfed her, she found herself sitting on the kitchen floor, pleading with God and craving answers.

Her broken heart implored, "I know You are here. But it's hard. I just can't believe that this happened. I just can't believe it."

Despite repeated attempts to spend her days doing laundry and necessary domestic chores, Cherie recognized her emotional weakness when home alone. More often than not, she spent days in town doing anything to preoccupy her mind. Her unplanned social outings continued to reap positive results. She took to shopping at the Goodwill, often going with Marilyn or Melody, but occasionally venturing out alone.

Maybe friendliness is easier to find in a small community, and people shopping at the Goodwill enjoy browsing and lingering and chatting with other customers. Maybe the pretty, forty-six-year-old widow looked like a nice lady to talk to. Or it could have been that God brought people her way. Whatever initiated the encounters, Cherie shared her story with people who were curious. They would tell her she was a strong person. *Am I?* she wondered. She didn't feel any stronger, but the interaction and conversations helped relieve her sense of isolation.

While her mother dealt with her grief by staying away from home, Donette settled back into school. Cherie wanted her daughter to have counseling. Convinced Donette would benefit from talking to an expert and someone not in law enforcement, Cherie suggested the idea to her. Donette resisted, saying she didn't need to talk to anyone. Cherie knew having to repeat the story again wouldn't appeal to Donette, but she worried about the mental fallout if Donette didn't eventually talk to a professional. Cherie understood how upset Donette must be emotionally, though Donette didn't often show her sadness. How could an eleven-year-old child make sense of such circumstances? She wouldn't force Donette into counseling and took comfort in the favorable reports from the school and Donette's repeated assurance that if she needed anyone to talk to, she had friends who would listen.

While Donette confided in her young friends, Cherie was learning that some individuals she considered friends would disappoint her. She never knew what caused the change. These former friends no longer sought Cherie out or called her as they had before. One woman told Cherie that her doctor said she shouldn't talk to Cherie anymore because talking to her would "give her [the friend] a nervous breakdown." Trying to understand the insensitivity of these people, Cherie thought, *Maybe they can't deal with the awfulness.* It was disconcerting that folks turned away. She knew some people refused to face what had happened to Don. Was the tragedy a reminder of their own mortality?

Did people wonder if similar events could play out in their own families? She would never know what was behind the changes. Maybe turning away was all they could do.

Disappointed by people who walked out of her life, Cherie grew closer to her true friends and found pleasure in her encounters with people she met in town. In the evenings, by the time she came home from her window-shopping outings, finished dinner with Donette, and tidied up the kitchen, the sun had gone down and it was dark. The enveloping shadows were accompanied by quiet and emptiness. No longer distracted with tasks or serendipitous conversations with strangers, Cherie tried to brace herself against the loneliness that came with the dark. Despite her resolve, she couldn't control the sorrow. Nightly, she crawled under her covers longing for untroubled sleep that wouldn't come. Donette would hear her mom's restlessness and come near Cherie's bed and whisper, "It's going to be okay, Mom. It's going to be okay," and Cherie would feel all the worse for burdening her daughter.

"More than once, Donette would come home from school and I'd be sitting in the middle of the floor, still in my pajamas, sobbing uncontrollably, not being able to deal with things, wondering how I was going to make it without Don."

Cherie knew that for Donette's sake she needed to find a way out of her depression. Being responsible for her daughter gave Cherie a reason to live beyond herself. Cherie's resolve to be strong for Donette drove her down to the rock by the river, the one where Don had caught his first steelhead. Naming it her crying rock seemed right, because it was there she prayed and cried out to God. Especially if Donette was home and Cherie couldn't contain her sadness, she would make the trek to the river's edge where she could let her emotions out. She didn't want her daughter to see her again in tears. The crying rock represented happy memories, but now it provided a refuge.

One morning, Cherie dropped Donette off at school and decided to stop back by the house before driving to Medford to see Dwayne. She recalled how the week right after Don's death, her family members had gently pulled her aside to talk with her about Dwayne. Everyone was concerned about her emotional frailty and protective of her well-being. All her relatives and longtime friends were united in their advice to her. They told her she had no obligation to maintain a relationship with Dwayne. In fact, they discouraged her from doing so or from feeling guilty about moving on without him. He'd severed his ties with the family by his actions and now he was paying for it. She and Don had done their best to help him, family told her. She needed to let Dwayne go, for her own sake, and for Donette's. Now, she thought of this advice as she walked down to the water. Flocks of ducks and geese bobbed in the river's currents, basking in the tranquility of the day. Before she knew it, Cherie found she'd wandered near the rock, and though she wasn't agile like Don and unable to perch on the boulder's top, she found comfort in the solidness of the rock's surface and leaned against it. She cradled her face in her hands and began to weep.

Cherie found a place of solace, healing, and prayer near what she referred to as her "Crying Rock." The rock still lies near the Wier home in Southern Oregon.

The crying both exhausted Cherie and refreshed her. She wiped the tears from her face, realizing she'd completely lost track of the time. Her mind turned to Dwayne's adoption. Thinking back, she recalled how excited she and Don had been to finally have a child of their own and the soberness of the courtroom when they'd sworn to raise this little one to the best of their ability until he was eighteen years old. She thought about Dwayne now, seventeen years old and in JDH, and the horrible thing he'd done.

Sitting on a low protrusion of the rock in the warm sun under the perfectly blue sky, Cherie realized that the vow she and Don had made in that small LA courtroom was a promise to God and a promise to Dwayne, no matter what. *An oath,* she thought, *is just words until there's a moment in time when one is called upon to live it out.* Cherie recognized that in spite of her feelings or the depth of her grief and anger, she had a responsibility to raise Dwayne until he turned eighteen. Dwayne's decision to murder Don had made him the property of the State of Oregon's prison system. Nevertheless, in whatever way she could support Dwayne, it was her duty to do so. She knew she would need to set boundaries with him, and that she had no obligation to accept his life choices or yield to his manipulations. She wasn't sure exactly how she was to live out this promise to Dwayne, but she knew she loved her son and would be there for him in some way. Her family members had encouraged her to disown him, even pointing to his adoption as a reason to walk away. After all, they said, he was adopted anyway and not really her son. It was true he was adopted, but she and Don had never thought of him that way. Dwayne had been their son from the moment the social worker placed him in her arms. The fact that he was adopted changed nothing. Dwayne had fatally hurt Cherie and Donette by taking Don's life, relatives said. She had no obligation to forgive him, they told her.

Cherie knew this advice from family and friends was well-meant. She recognized her inability to sort through her own emotions, knowing she feared the violence Dwayne was capable of, and she blamed him for taking her husband and Donette's father and ruining her life. She couldn't make sense of the conflicting thoughts in her mind, but she knew she'd chosen to keep the promise she and Don had made the day of Dwayne's adoption, and she would have to trust God to teach her how to live that out day by day.

CHAPTER 11 – TRIED AS AN ADULT OR JUVENILE?

On Tuesday, December 16, Dwayne's remand hearing began. Cherie had been told that there would be three days of testimony from law enforcement officers, detectives, and forensic specialists detailing every gruesome aspect of the crime. She would testify and so would Donette. The hearing would determine whether Dwayne should be tried as an adult or under the jurisdiction of the juvenile court. The judge would consider whether Dwayne was mature enough to understand his conduct, his amenability to treatment in the juvenile system, the protection required by the community, and the aggressive, violent, premeditated, or willful manner in which the offense was alleged to have been committed. If convicted in juvenile court, Dwayne could expect to be incarcerated in a youth facility until he turned twenty-one and then transferred to adult prison until the age of twenty-five, at which time he would be released. Being remanded to adult court would net him a minimum of thirteen years' confinement. After initially being housed in the MacLaren Youth Facility until age twenty-one, he would be transferred to an adult prison for the remainder of his sentence. The remand hearing was a mini trial of sorts. Following the testimonies and presentation of evidence, Circuit Court Judge Gerald Neufeld would determine whether or not Dwayne would be tried as an adult.

On day one Dr. Michael Sasser, a Medford psychiatrist who had interviewed Dwayne the day of the shooting, was called to the stand. Sasser reported that Wier had a dislike for his father that had grown over the past two years and that he [Dwayne] wanted to do away with him. Dwayne told Sasser that his father treated him like a ten-year-old and had falsely accused him of wrongdoing such as stealing jewelry from his mother and taking cash from other family members. Dwayne said his parents were pushing him into a career in computers or similar fields that they thought were practical. He wanted, and aspired to be, a professional rock musician but felt as if he'd been pushed in the wrong direction and that his life had been intruded upon by others. Dwayne told Sasser that he "has never really felt like part of the family and has no sense of attachment emotionally to either of my parents or my sister."

Wier admitted to Sasser that "tension had been building between him and his father and he [Dwayne] expected an eventual confrontation and was preparing for it by lifting weights to improve his physical strength. Sasser relayed that Dwayne explained in detail the steps he took the night of the shooting, including how Dwayne acquired access to the weapons, which weapon he chose and why. He described his "hiding it and preparations for after I had done the crime," what he planned to take and where he devised to go. Sasser described Dwayne's demeanor during the interview as "showing absolutely no emotional distress." Sasser saw "no sense of remorse, despondency, or regret over the death of his father." Dwayne referred to his behavior with the word "kill," indicating "at least apparent knowledge of the finality of the act." Sasser also acknowledged that there was "no immediate conflict or altercation with his father and that there was no sense of duress which precipitated his action."

Psychological tests administered by Sasser indicated that Wier had "poor impulse control, little empathy for others, and social apathy."

"Wier," said Sasser, "presents in a rather self-righteous, self-serving, emotionally indifferent manner." By Dwayne's report, he was taking drugs on the night of the offense; however, "his rather clear description of the events, the purposeful nature of his behaviors, and the fact that they were planned and not a result of some type of uncontrolled impulse, suggests that he was well in control of what he was doing, despite any substances he may have used." Sasser diagnosed Wier as "having an anti-social personality disorder. The likelihood of curing anti-social disorders is almost nil," he said, "unless the individual demonstrates some ability to feel guilt or remorse." In his opinion, Wier "was a danger to society and would continue being dangerous." He noted that "there was no evidence of mental disease or defect." In Sasser's opinion, "Wier would have no basis for an insanity plea."

Lt. Jim Warren of the Josephine County Sheriff's Department testified next, explaining he had talked with Dwayne immediately after the shooting and on several other occasions. When Warren asked Dwayne why he killed his father, Wier responded, "because he was an asshole." All that he was feeling was "kill." Warren reported that although he observed that Dwayne appeared "somewhat under the influence" at the time of the initial interview, "he was not impaired. Wier could hold an intelligent conversation and carry on a straight line of thought." The lieutenant also testified that Wier voluntarily handed over a shell casing that was in his pocket, saying it had come from the bullet that killed his father.

Following Lt. Warren, family acquaintance Larry Dirksen was called and asked whether he'd ever witnessed Dwayne acting out in physical violence toward his father. Dirksen replied that he hadn't and added that Dwayne had told him he used drugs because "he liked the high, could play music better, and drugs made him feel like one of the group."

Cherie listened to the testimonies. With each witness came new revelations of Dwayne's behaviors and mental aberrations. Her heart broke into a thousand pieces as she listened to others talk about the boy she and Don had been excited to adopt, the one she loved and had helped with his homework and taken fishing. How had life gone from finding marijuana in Dwayne's drums to sitting in a courtroom discussing details of Don's murder? She knew she would have to tell the court about Dwayne, his unusual childhood behaviors, and their attempts to get help. *I guess someone will listen to us now*, she thought. *Why couldn't we get help before?*

On Tuesday, after Cherie dressed herself, she turned her attention to her daughter. Today, the second day of the remand hearing, the court would call Donette to the stand to ask her about finding her dad's body. Donette was in her room and had gotten out a favored outfit she often changed into after school. Cherie noticed the casual pants and t-shirt on Donette's bed and, after asking her if those clothes were what Donette had picked out to wear to court, she told Donette she needed to wear something nicer—a dress, or skirt and blouse. Cherie went to the closet, offering suggestions, but Donette protested, insisting she be allowed to wear the clothes she'd already picked out. Mother and daughter argued. Cherie took a green skirt from Donette's closet and calmly told Donette she expected her to put it on. Angry but compliant, Donette dressed in the skirt. The tension in the room was high, each of them on edge anticipating the day ahead. Cherie struggled to redirect the mood as they headed to the car, while Donette's thoughts were on how much she hated the green skirt. It was wool and the fabric made her itch.

Donette was eleven; her birthday had been three days after the crime. Sitting on the wooden bench next to Cherie, she looked around the imposing courtroom, unruffled at the prospect of answering questions she'd been asked at least a dozen times. After Donette was sworn in, the district attorney began his questioning, patiently directing the girl to recount the details of that Saturday morning two months earlier. Initially, her testimony proceeded as expected and she methodically explained coming home from the sleepover. Shortly into her narrative, and despite her efforts to fix her eyes on the district attorney in front of her, Donette looked into Dwayne's face. He was sitting at the defendant's table positioned at an angle behind the attorney, his dark eyes fixed intently on her. The sight of him, and connecting him with the events of that Saturday, were too much for her. Her voice began to quiver and then crack. Tears welled up in her eyes as the reality of her loss and the reason for it swept over her. Unable to hold back her reaction, unrestrained tears ran down her face, and she began to sob. The DA, sympathetic to the young witness, gave her a few moments to recover her self-control, then gently repeated his previous question. But Donette couldn't regain her composure. Being required to answer questions with Dwayne sitting at the defendant's table was too much for her. Cherie rose from her seat demanding that the interview be stopped, insisting that the court had Donette's full statement on paper. Officials on both sides concurred, as did the judge, who excused Donette from the stand. That day was the last time Donette would ever see her brother. For a long time, Cherie would remember the image of her daughter's face and the tears on her cheeks as she sat on the stand.

The hearing continued with the district attorney playing a taped interview with Dwayne taken by Lieutenant Warren the day following his arrest. In this statement, Wier had changed his story about the killing, claiming, "I don't know why I shot Dad; I was just stoned. If I had been straight, it wouldn't have happened." Wier said he couldn't remember the amount of drugs and alcohol he'd consumed and declared he got along well with his dad and actually preferred him to his mom. On the day of his arrest, Dwayne had said he shot his father because he was abusive and picked fights with Dwayne and recalled, in explicit detail, how much Valium and alcohol he'd consumed.

Detective Pugsley, who was in the room when Warren interviewed Wier at the hospital, said Wier told them he went into his father's room to get the key to his pickup before the shooting.

"I wouldn't have shot my dad if I hadn't had a way to get away," Wier had told Pugsley.

The court turned its attention to the evidence of Don's payroll check in the amount of $2,100 that was found on the Wier property by an investigator. When asked about the check, Dwayne alleged that his father had signed it over to him, claiming it was reimbursement to Dwayne for work on his truck. A writing expert from the Oregon State Police testified that Don's signature on the back of the check was actually forged by Dwayne. It was presumed that Dwayne had planned to use the stolen check to fund his getaway, but had dropped it as he fled the residence. Other testimony included reports from the probation and juvenile officers regarding the different options for incarceration if Dwayne were adjudicated in juvenile court versus remanded to the adult system.

Cherie took the stand on day three of the remand hearing. She told the judge about Dwayne's childhood, explaining how she'd felt something was wrong with him from a very young age. She described her desperation in trying unsuccessfully to find competent counseling for Dwayne and their family, starting when he was in the fifth grade, then off and on during the next six years. She told how she and Don found Dwayne with marijuana when he was thirteen, and how they frantically tried to stop the behaviors that followed: the stealing, running away, and use of harder drugs. They'd been hopeful when Dwayne agreed to sign up for Program 180, a substance abuse rehabilitation center, but that effort also failed. Dr. John Brandenburg, the director at Program 180, would later testify regarding his contact with Dwayne and state that Dwayne had a severe amphetamine addiction when he was admitted to the rehab program.

After Cherie finished her testimony, Dr. Hugh Gardner took the stand. He presented a second psychiatric evaluation that had been conducted on October 30 at the request of Dwayne's attorneys.

Dr. Gardner's six-page typed assessment concurred with that of Dr. Sasser with additional observations as follows:

1. Dwayne reports he has used crank, marijuana, alcohol and recently Valium. He supported this habit in part by dealing, selling the amphetamine derivative, crank, for $80 a gram. He is somewhat misinformed about Valium; he feels he has taken a 15 mg size though it doesn't come in that size. When asked to describe the tablets he states they were white and scored, which is the 2 mg size. He states he drinks about a case of beer a week ordinarily, and it is his want on the weekends, apparently, to do what he calls "party." Which would seem to be taking a half case of his parents' beer, going into a room and getting drunk and vomiting, and also at the same time using marijuana and apparently whatever other drug he can get his hands on. It is curious this episode of drinking in the bathroom and vomiting, he states he does quite frequently. He states his parents have never heard him, as his bathroom is in the opposite end of the house from theirs, also apparently, they have never smelled the vomitus. Indeed, on the night that his father was shot, he states that he did this again. He took a half case of beer from the kitchen, went into the bathroom between perhaps 1:00 and 2:00

in the morning, drank the half case of beer and he states he vomited twice. This information he hadn't previously given any interviewers, and certainly would all but negate him having any toxic levels of any type of substance. The absorption rate of Valium would have precluded it getting into his blood stream, at least the tablets that he took after he returned home with his father.

2. When I asked him what should be the outcome of the affair, he indicates he probably shouldn't go to MacLaren or to prison, because somebody might beat him up. He should perhaps go to a hospital and have Christian-type counseling. At no time during my interview with him, did he seem to indicate an appreciation of the seriousness of what he had done. At no time, again, was there any indication of remorse, sorrow, emotion, etc. Indeed, he represented the entire problem as being the outcome of his drug use; therefore, he shouldn't be held responsible, and he states that his mother now understood this.

3. When talking about the shooting of his father, he at first states that he didn't know why he did it and says that he didn't remember anything about it. I asked him if that was the whole story, and he asserted that it was. He said then the only thing that he remembered was after the shooting, he looked at his father for about five minutes and wondered why he did it.

4. In his description of events leading up to the shooting he stated that when his dad answered the phone, he went to bed, took a couple of Valium at that point; then he stated he got up and "kissed Dad goodnight and I went to bed." He didn't talk about getting the rifle. He stated that he got up at 1:30

or 2:00, went to the kitchen, got the half case of beer, went to the bathroom, got his joints and pills, and proceeded to party. He states he drank the half case of beer in an hour, which as I have mentioned he frequently does on weekends, and he got sick on this particular occasion twice. Somehow, he realizes that he at some point got the gun and loaded it, and he looked at me with a rather sarcastic sneer, and said, "I obviously took aim and fired." He continued in the same vein, "The boogieman didn't do it, I was the only one there."

5. One notices that in the three different interviews, he consistently uses the term "aimed" in relation to his shooting his father, which would indicate a sense of deliberateness. His memory for the events, in my opinion, is very vivid, and his pretense of being intoxicated is untrue. It is also apparent that prior to his boozing and drinking, he had planned to do what he did, as he had procured the weapon and gotten the keys to the trailer. Also, in talking to me, he indicated that he had taken the father's paycheck from the dashboard of the father's truck, and forged the signature.

6. In conclusion, it is further my opinion that Dwayne Wier possesses the sophistication and maturity to appreciate the gravity of shooting his father. It is apparent that he has rationalized his action at this time in a true antisocial fashion, and feels no personal remorse for his father's death. It is also my opinion his amenability to treatment and rehabilitation is very slight. He represents a grave danger. The shooting of his father was a premeditated offense.

On Thursday, December 18, following the conclusion of the remand hearing, Judge Gerald Neufeld ruled that sixteen-year-old Dwayne Wier would be tried as an adult for the shooting death of his father. Dwayne was arraigned the following Monday, December 21, on the charge of murder, the trial date tentatively set for January 20. Dwayne's attorneys, Ben Freudenberg and Dennis James, told the court at the time of their client's arraignment that they planned to file an appeal challenging Judge Neufeld's ruling.

With the court proceedings on hold until January, Cherie thought spending the holidays with her sister Vonnie would be a helpful distraction. But it's likely that nothing could have alleviated their heartaches. Mother and daughter took a five-and-a-half-hour bus ride to Redmond, Oregon and despite Vonnie's efforts to cheer her sister and niece, Christmas that year was horrible. Donette sat under the Christmas tree, hugged her teddy bear, and sobbed. Cherie, helplessly unable to comfort her grieving daughter, felt the same way. *How*, she desperately wondered, *do I help her when I am hurting as bad as she is?*

By January 5, when Dwayne appeared in Circuit Court to enter a plea of innocent, his attorneys had yet to file an appeal that they'd promised to do in December. Judge Gerald Neufeld postponed the beginning of the trial to March 10, allowing the attorneys additional time to appeal the decision.

Having entered a plea of innocent the previous week, Dwayne sat in JDH waiting for his attorneys to act on the appeal. On January 11, he turned seventeen. A week later, agitated and reactive to communications from his mother, Dwayne penned a bitter letter to her.

"Will you not give me any credit for being intelligent? When I quote scriptures, I quote them word for word. Just because you are unable to understand various scriptures certainly does not have anything to do with my 'lack of

intelligence.' " He continued to chastise her for not giving him credit for a variety of his qualities and then proceeded to explain why his efforts to appeal the judge's ruling were likely to fail. He referred to the latest psychological report. Dwayne felt that Cherie had provided information to the psychiatrist that reflected negatively on his evaluation. *"In relation to my history; and in the nature of your testimony, you were not very explainable. Therefore, I sounded worse than I really was. Understand now? The only people I trust are my attorneys, so don't ask me to tell you anything regarding my case."* He continued, *"Also, if you have nothing which is encouraging to say to me, then don't say anything at all. I have enough mental pains as it is, so don't speak to me about anything which can add to the hurt! I really do not appreciate you telling me how hurt you are and how much you cry! Stop living in fantasy-land and try to put yourself in my position for once."*

Correspondence from Dwayne had become unwelcome to Cherie because most of his letters were filled with angry rants of how Cherie and Don had ruined his childhood and how his current troubles were brought on by the actions of others. Cherie made a habit of leaving mail from Dwayne unopened on the kitchen counter.

On February 5, Dwayne's defense attorneys filed a motion for a change of venue. The defense contended that the remand hearing had brought out most of the facts surrounding the case and that information could have already affected the views of potential jurors. The attorneys argued that $2,700 should be authorized to pay for a community-wide survey to determine how much notoriety the Wier case had received. Deputy District Attorney Paul Frasier objected, arguing that any problems created by pre-trial publicity could be handled during jury questioning before the trial. Judge Neufeld agreed and said the trial would take place as planned in Josephine County.

When Dwayne's attorneys failed to force a change of venue, Dwayne turned his attention to his former girlfriend, hoping for a favorable boost to his personal life. His correspondence efforts to her detailed his everlasting devotion to her and his dreams of a future together.

"... so now I have to decide what to do when I get out of prison (which will be somewhere between 1991 and 1996). Any suggestions?" He spoke of working as a mechanic and providing a decent income to support married life. He complained how former friends didn't visit him, saying, *"Am I not worthy of any friends? Will nobody ever understand the fact that I have a GD drug problem and not a murder problem?! My own damn mother doesn't even visit me anymore, Do I have to hang myself before anyone will realize what I'm going through? It isn't that they don't understand, they simply won't understand! Fuck them!"* He listed names of people who had testified against him at the remand hearing, those who had said negative things about him. He threatened each one, saying that if he were to see any of them again, he would *"be charged with attempted murder (if not murder, again)! Go ahead and make these witnesses names mud before I make them blood!!!"* He warned the girl not to talk with his mother, writing, *"because she is trying to 'get even' and she may tell you something that isn't true. She needs a psychiatrist a hell of a lot more than I do. My attorneys even think she is somewhat out of her mind. (but please don't tell her that because she's got enough mental problems already)!"*

On February 24, just nineteen days after the failed attempt to get a change of venue for Dwayne's trial, attorney Dennis James told Judge Neufeld that he'd had at least five conversations with his client over the last ten days. In a startling change of position, Dwayne declared that he wanted to forego a trial and change his plea to guilty. Mr. James characterized his client thus: "He wants to show that he can be responsible, that he can own up to what he did and can be forthright." The declaration prompted considerable conversation between Neufeld and Wier. The judge meticulously discussed with Dwayne the ramifications of entering a guilty plea. He questioned Dwayne for twenty-five minutes, wanting to be sure he was entering his plea voluntarily and that he understood the rights he was giving up by doing so. Neufeld asked Dwayne to explain why he thought he was guilty of murder and asked him about his state of mind at the time of the crime.

Dwayne responded by describing how he'd planned the murder and detailed each step. When answering regarding his state of mind, Dwayne explained, "A good example is that I was having problems deciding which gun to use. I wanted the most powerful one, and I concluded it was the 30-30."

James told Judge Neufeld that Wier's only requests in entering a guilty plea were that he be given another psychological exam and that he not be incarcerated with juveniles. James advised Judge Neufeld that Dwayne wanted to counter the impressions of doctors Sasser and Gardner, whose evaluations concluded that Dwayne had a psychopathic personality and was a danger to society. Wier claimed "that the particular incident [the murder] was an isolated incident and wouldn't happen again." Neufeld said that where Wier was imprisoned wasn't in his control because of Dwayne's age.

Almost exactly two months later, the latest twist in the Wier case was reported in the local paper. Dwayne had sent a letter to Judge Neufeld two weeks before he'd been scheduled for sentencing on April 6, requesting to withdraw his guilty plea and asking now for a jury trial. Freudenberg and James had represented Wier until March 23, at which time Wier had informed the court he was dissatisfied with them and wanted to withdraw his plea and be assigned different counsel. The decision on Wier's part to fire his lawyers was heavily influenced by the case of another inmate housed in the Josephine County jail. The defendant in that case, Michael Holloman, had been charged with murder on the same day Dwayne had shot his father. Holloman's attorney had convinced a jury to convict the defendant on the lesser charge of first-degree manslaughter, arguing that Holloman suffered from extreme emotional disturbance. When Dwayne learned of the decision in Holloman's case, he was convinced his attorneys had done a poor job representing him and giving him advice. Initially, he'd believed that by pleading guilty, he would receive more lenient treatment than he would if he went to trial and was found guilty. Wier changed his mind about his guilty plea after receiving advice from at least two other inmates in the Josephine County jail. The court granted Dwayne's request to replace his attorneys and appointed Mr. Steven Rich. Rich would now represent Wier in his motion to withdraw his guilty plea.

On April 21, Judge Neufeld listened to six hours of evidence presented by Rich on Wier's behalf. The judge ruled that Wier wouldn't be permitted to withdraw his plea. Neufeld stated that during the February 24 hearing, he'd discussed in detail with Wier the ramifications of changing his plea to guilty. The only request Dwayne made at that time was that he receive an additional psychological test in an attempt to refute previous evaluations concluding that he had an antisocial personality disorder and was a danger to the community.

Dwayne's request for a third psychological evaluation was approved by Judge Neufeld, and licensed clinical psychologist Edwin E. Pearson was retained. Dr. Pearson spent two hours with Wier on March 17. The synopsis of his report was presented to the court: "Wier formulated the plan for shooting his father while waiting in the truck the day prior to the crime," wrote Pearson. Dwayne advised Pearson "that he had the thought that, 'I ought to shoot that asshole.' " At the time of the evaluation "Dwayne seemed to be patently attempting to minimize any responsibility for the shooting." The impression Dwayne "seemed to want to create was that the entire shooting incident was done without any conscious awareness on his part, and in fact he denied personal responsibility for the shooting death; that is, he blamed the death of his father on drugs and alcohol. He believed himself to be a victim of alcohol and drug dependence."

Pearson continued his report by identifying Wier "as having an antisocial personality disorder. He had rehearsed this scenario in his mind, considering a rifle as a possible weapon. He had a history of problems in accepting limits within the family structure and was facing, on the day that the killing occurred, a very distinct possibility of returning to a drug treatment facility, to which he was very much opposed. In this writer's opinion, alcohol and/or drug abuse may have precipitated some disinhibition in terms of the actual shooting event, but certainly substance abuse cannot be considered to be the primary cause in this incident, which is far more realistically rooted in the personality disorder."

Dr. Pearson concluded his report this way: "Dwayne is seen as an individual who is going to be highly resistant to traditional psychotherapeutic intervention. While he may proclaim an interest in his own rehabilitation, he is certainly manipulative and aware enough to recognize that such statements are in his best interest at this time."

Dwayne minimized his responsibility in the shooting by claiming he was under the influence of drugs and alcohol, but the three psychiatric exams concurred that he suffered from an antisocial personality disorder and that although "drugs may have precipitated his disinhibitions, that substance abuse wasn't the primary cause of the murder." The killing, in Pearson's opinion, "was rooted in Wier's personality disorder and his maladjustment to society."

On May 21, 1987, Dwayne appeared for the last time in Josephine County Circuit Court before Judge Gerald

Neufeld. Neufeld sentenced Dwayne Dean Wier to life in prison. He was ordered to be transported to MacLaren Youth Correctional Facility located in Woodburn, Oregon, and housed there until he aged out of the institution at the age of twenty-one. Incarceration after that would be under the purview of an adult-only correctional prison.

CHAPTER 12 – I WANT TO
BE IN ADULT PRISON

On the very day of his sentencing, Dwayne began to focus his rebellion on the penal system. Despite Judge Neufeld's ruling, he had no intention of being housed at MacLaren. Dwayne's view about the juvenile facility had been influenced during his incarceration, either through conversations he had with inmates or by his personal experience at JDH. Whatever had sparked Dwayne's adverse beliefs about the juvenile prison, his opinion hadn't wavered over the months; instead, he refused to alter his view, insisting to his mother and lawyers that "I will not be in with a bunch of juvenile delinquents." Hell-bent to chart his own course, Dwayne devised a strategy he thought would serve him better than the sentence imposed on him by the court. He didn't have long to wait before acting out his idea, because a week after sentencing he found himself transported to MacLaren.

The operation of the MacLaren Youth Facility is overseen by the Oregon Youth Authority (OYA). Juveniles who have been remanded to adult court land under the authority of Oregon's Department of Corrections (DOC), which manages the adult prison system. Convicted juveniles tried as adults normally would be incarcerated in adult prison. But the DOC, in an effort to place younger prisoners in a more favorable environment, has an understanding with MacLaren to house inmates like Dwayne at least until they turn twenty-one, and sometimes up to age twenty-five, if the prisoner's good behavior warrants. This arrangement is a courtesy to the youthful offender. If a juvenile who has been tried and sentenced as an adult exhibits disruptive or dangerous conduct, he loses the privilege of serving out the first portion of his sentence in the youth correctional facility and is permanently transferred into the adult system.

Dwayne arrived at MacLaren shackled in full body restraints and flanked by two corrections officers. The belly chains around his waist were connected to handcuffs that limited his arm movements and ankle cuffs that restricted his foot motion and caused him to shuffle awkwardly as he walked. While these restraints may have mentally demoralized some prisoners and fostered submission, Dwayne's heavy chains only fueled his attitude of self-importance, and the look in his eyes indicated that he was up to no good.

Soon after the initial intake, and once his body chains were removed, Dwayne watched for an opportunity when the guard was momentarily distracted and violently shoved one inmate into another, causing the second man to land on the floor. Having calculated his actions, Dwayne moved swiftly, taking advantage of the man's prone position, and turned to strike the prisoner he'd first pushed. Within moments, Dwayne made sure the altercation escalated into a full-on brawl involving a group of inmates and forcing the prison's administrators to take radical action with him. Hopefully, from Dwayne's viewpoint, he'd secured his objective and would be expelled from the facility. MacLaren's contract with DOC assumed a zero-tolerance for housing combative troublemakers, and Dwayne's orchestrated fist fight resulted in his hoped-for conclusion. If Dwayne wanted to go to adult prison, MacLaren authorities were quick to move him out of the juvenile facility. The explanation for Dwayne's stubborn refusal to be housed at MacLaren remained a mystery. Despite the counsel of Judge Neufeld and his attorneys, Dwayne's distorted reasoning would land him in living conditions far worse than he could have imagined.

Dwayne's intake processing had been interrupted when he assaulted the two inmates. The initial evaluation procedure, which needed to be completed at MacLaren, was temporarily put on hold when authorities opted to relocate Dwayne immediately to the Oregon State Correctional Institution (OSCI) in Salem. Dwayne would be housed at OSCI for several days, then returned to MacLaren to complete initial intake before being moved back to OSCI for the remainder of his processing.

In the secure transport vehicle riding to OSCI in nearby Salem, Dwayne sat smugly, once again shackled, thinking to himself how his plan was moving along just as he'd hoped. However, while formulating his scheme, he hadn't considered that OSCI housed four times as many prisoners as MacLaren, and that these inmates were older and tougher, generally of higher security risk, convicted of more serious crimes, and often repeat offenders. He was about to step into the adult prison world clueless about what sort of life awaited him.

Dwayne wrote to Cherie eight days after his sentencing, eager to boast of his success in forcing his transfer to OSCI. He told her of his brief stay in Salem before returning to MacLaren for a portion of the intake process. The date was May 29. He explained that he was currently housed at MacLaren for a two-day evaluation but would be returned to OSCI after the assessment. He described his time at OSCI and said he found the conditions were better there than at MacLaren because there was more to do at the adult facility (varieties of classes and programs) and at MacLaren an inmate could only sit on his ass in a single cell and do nothing but write letters. He wrote that he *liked OSCI, so much in fact, that I would prefer to stay at OSCI even if the sentence was three times as long.*

Returning to OSCI, Dwayne continued through orientation and admissions. He received physical and psychiatric evaluations, and was photographed, fingerprinted, and issued a DOC inmate identification card. He was told to shower and provided with clothing and bedding as well as personal hygiene items and packets with handbooks detailing rules of conduct. A counselor was assigned to him who would determine his custody classification. The DOC used a scale that weighed risk factors such as criminal history, seriousness of current crime, and whether there was evidence of recent drug use. Risk factors and classifications helped corrections officers categorize prisoners so they could be assigned to appropriate housing units for security purposes and have access to needed services such as GED classes, church services, or the infirmary. High risk individuals with a history of negative behavior were considered a threat to the safety and security of the institution, staff, and other inmates. Dwayne's murder charge, his recent use of drugs, his display of aggressive behavior at MacLaren, and his high likelihood of continued violence toward fellow inmates earned him a high-risk score. Having received his bedding, Dwayne was assigned a housing unit and cell. Following his brief stay at both institutions, he believed that he could accurately compare the quality of life at MacLaren and OSCI. Despite Dwayne's first impression, he had yet to discover the realities of either place, having only observed both facilities during the structured intake process. He hadn't experienced daily life in the general population, nor had he yet been introduced to the segregated housing cells referred to as "the hole."

Satisfied to be settling in at OSCI, Dwayne wrote to Cherie of meeting with his counselor, who had advised him he would have a parole hearing in September and told him that he should expect to do at least seven years and six months. *"Do you want me to put you on my visitors' list?*

You may want to visit me some day—you won't see me for a real long time. " He wrote, *"I really wish I would have listened to you and dad a long time ago. If I would have only listened, I would not be where I'm at now! I mean, I'm having a difficult time accepting the reality of all that is happening. When people ask me what I'm in here for, I just tell them 'murder' and when they ask me who I killed I say 'never mind.' "* In the postscript he wrote, *"Mom, pray that I'll come out of prison alive."*

Despite the conciliatory tone of Dwayne's letter, less than ninety days into his sentence, Dwayne's defiance of prison rules landed him in the hole. These cells were occasionally used to separate a single prisoner from others for his own protection but, for the most part, the hole was a place of isolation designed to be harsh and punitive. The austere twelve by seven-foot cells were reserved for inmates who committed serious rule violations such as assault, possession of drugs or weapons, or attempted escape. The length of punishment in these cells was dependent on the severity of the offense and could last as long as six months. The privilege of visits or phone calls was prohibited for prisoners in the hole, but they were allowed to receive and send out mail. On August 5, as Dwayne sat out his punishment in isolation, he wrote Cherie a letter describing his version of how he landed there.

"They put me in the hole last Friday for a bunch of bullshit. I'm being charged with conspiracy to escape and conspiracy to introduce a firearm into the institution. It is a 20 year 'beef' (which means if found guilty, I would get an additional 20 years added to my sentence)." He explained he would be taking a polygraph to determine his truthfulness regarding his involvement with the planned escape. He complained that the *"damn cops"* had taken everything away from him and left him with only a bed, a comb, a toothbrush, and half a bar of soap. He alleged the *"pigs"* were keeping his mail from him. He ended the letter

asking his mother to send him money when she sold his music equipment.

A month after Dwayne ended up in the hole, a letter to Cherie reported more disturbing news. Not only was Dwayne still in the hole, but he claimed he'd unsuccessfully attempted suicide twice by hanging, using his bed sheets. He explained that his last try had landed him in the safety management unit where he *"had been strapped down to a metal bed in a seclusion room for four days then unstrapped and kept under observation for two more days."* He wrote, *"Today the psychiatrist, the nurse, and the unit sergeant sent me back to OSCI and said that they couldn't care less if I commit suicide because they said I'm no good for anyone and I'm no good for society. I told them I wanted to change, but they don't believe me."* Dwayne pleaded for Cherie not to disown him and said he thought he was *"turning into a paranoid schizophrenic."* He thanked her for her prayers on his behalf and said, *"I think I'm feeling remorse finally. I've been thinking a lot about what I did last October as well as how I've hurt you and Dad by doing all the rotten things I've done. I wish Dad was here so I could apologize for all the hurt I've caused him. To me you and Dad are my real parents. You were both too good to be stepparents! I'll never be able to accept what I did Mom; but will you forgive me?"*

Even though Dwayne had expressed feelings of remorse and wanting to live a better life, thirty days later, he reported he'd flipped out for a third time and was sent back to the psychiatric unit at the Oregon State Petitionary (OSP), a maximum-security prison. He said he'd cut up his left wrist and forearm in different places. Without explanation he switched topics, thanking Cherie for a recent letter she'd sent him that had included photos and then he asked her how his pet cat was doing. Regarding a recent discipline, Dwayne wrote, *"I was on water restrictions for a week because I flooded my cell 2 weeks ago."* His appearance before the parole board had added twenty years to his sentence, which meant a tentative release date for December 11, 2006. *"My counselor is going to try and get me transferred to OSP permanently. I'll be better off over there because they have more school opportunities and jobs that pay up to $6 a day. They are all single cells, better food, and I have friends there. The psychiatric unit over there is better and more comfortable to me than general population over here at OSCI."* Referring to a comment in a recent letter he'd received from Cherie, he wrote, *"Yes, I know God is not through with me yet. He has a perfect plan for the life of everyone, but only time will reveal what it is."* He requested she send him money when he was transferred to OSP, saying that he had to pay restitution for the two sheets he tore up, which he used to try to hang himself. In what Cherie considered a sarcastic tone, Dwayne ended his letter with his view of a recent psychiatrist assessment of him. *"Don't worry about what the psychiatrist said. He said the same thing that Dr. Sasser, Dr. Gardner, and Dr. Pearson said, that I'm 'very dangerous, anti-social, and manipulative.'"*

By now, Dwayne was disillusioned about life in adult prison. His letter the following month was full of angry justifications of his own behavior blaming the prison guards, claiming they'd provoked him by their actions. *"This time I was charged with 'being accused of possession of a dangerous weapon'! They are trying to tell me they found a 'shank' (improvised prison knife) in my mattress! Which also is just another of OSCI's absurd, damnable lies that staff members seem to be in the habit of telling."* In the letter's final paragraph, Dwayne wrote, *"Mom, I do not think you are ready to hear the true reasons why I killed Dad! I think you should read a little more about my personality first. I've read a book called Abnormal Psychology and Modern Life. You would be surprised at what I learned."*

Dwayne had begun to play on Cherie's need to know the true reasons why he'd murdered Don by taunting her and then refusing to divulge insights. When another envelope appeared in her mailbox, she didn't open it immediately, deciding instead to put it aside on the kitchen counter. When she did read the letter, Dwayne's explanation for killing Don was slightly different from the reasonings he'd used before. *"As for killing Dad, I thought about doing it when I was 14. It started when Dad took me out of 'Black Diamond' (that band I was in). I wanted to kill him then and that's when I started planning to get myself out of his control any way I possibly could (such as running away). I tried every way possible, but, since nothing worked (you kept making me come back) I used the last resort which was to kill him. So, I did. There was no way I could have controlled my drug habit while I was on the streets. I remember smoking the first joint when I was 12 years old, and ever since then, I always wanted more and more."*

Dwayne described the confusion he'd experienced during his teen years, telling Cherie how Don had purchased beer for him and even let him drink and drive twice, while on other occasions his dad would preach to him about not drinking. He felt his dad was two-faced about such things. Were these statements true, Cherie wondered, or was Dwayne simply making up reasons to justify his murder of Don? *"Well, there it is, the whole truth about why I did it—how I did it is unimportant, although I didn't do it as planned. If I did it as planned, I wouldn't be in prison; but it's too late worrying about it now."*

Cherie had wearied of the reoccurring content of Dwayne's letters detailing his latest rule violations and the disciplinary action that followed. Unsurprisingly, when she received his next correspondence, he launched into a full report of the incident that had first landed him in segregation, writing that he'd had a hearing regarding the charges and now felt free to tell all.

"I did plan an escape," he told her, describing an elaborate (perhaps imaginary?) scheme involving the use of UZIs, fake IDs, and transportation out of the country. He claimed, *"I was to be a 'hit man.' I snitched on some guys but that didn't help me any; it put my life on the line. And this is the last time I will tell the truth to a cop."* Life in adult prison wasn't quite what he'd imagined and Dwayne didn't hold back saying so. *"OSCI is the worst place to be, not the best, and if my counselor won't transfer me then I'll kill him!"*

Ironically, given Dwayne's constant complaints about his life in OSCI, two months later on Christmas Eve, his short note to his mother pointed out her unwillingness to adjust to her circumstances. *"Merry Christmas! Don't let yourself be upset all the time. It isn't good for you. Be happy and thankful for what you do have and stop trying to live in the past. You can't do that."*

Dwayne's comments did include a slice of truth. Cherie was living in the past and was upset most of the time. She continued to be obsessed with understanding why Dwayne murdered Don. There were hints here and there between the lines of his letters. If only she could piece them together to make sense, maybe she wouldn't feel tormented by what happened. Considering every option, Cherie wondered if Dwayne's behavior could be driven by a physiological derangement. After all, his childhood had been riddled with mysterious illnesses, and much of his development had been noticeably different from that of other children. She agonized constantly about how the baby she and Don had raised could have turned into a killer, even if he'd been using drugs. Reflecting on their parenting style, she believed that she and Don had been fair with Dwayne, clear about expectations, and consistent with consequences. Maybe they should have been tougher on him, or easier? How could they have understood him when he kept to himself? Were there traits in Dwayne that she should have noticed but hadn't? She'd known they were failing at parenting as the two of them watched their son slip deeper into substance abuse.

Now, Cherie read books about mental health and searched out specialists who studied behaviors as they related to biological factors. There were indicators that pointed to physical abnormalities in Dwayne's brain that had never been explored. She hoped to discover a way she could have her son tested for a chemical imbalance and made contact with the American Institute for Biosocial Research in Tacoma, Washington. In 1988, she contacted staff with the Research Institute and made extensive inquiries, but found the expense of testing was cost prohibitive and it would be impossible to arrange testing for Dwayne due to his incarceration.

Cherie had no funds for extras. Barely able to generate enough income to get by, she found herself irritated to have to repeatedly refuse Dwayne's pleas for money. Without Don's income, the family struggled. From Cherie's point of view, Dwayne had committed a heinous crime and was incarcerated as punishment and to protect society. She had no desire to make life easier on him.

In the spring of 1988, Katheryn, a friend of Cherie's whose daughter lived in Tigard, a forty-minute drive up I-5 from OSCI, suggested that the two of them take a road trip north. Katheryn would visit her daughter, and Cherie could see Dwayne. The letters from Dwayne, which were always accompanied by requests for money and enumerated in detail behaviors that had landed him in the hole, didn't draw Cherie to want to see him. Dwayne's incarceration thus far seemed to have fueled his rebellious conduct and fostered his attitude that nothing was ever his fault. With great reluctance, Cherie agreed to make the trip. The months following the murder had worn her out physically and emotionally. Sadness and loneliness were her constant companions. She didn't expect anything good from the visit and was only going because she'd promised she would. Dreading the encounter, she braced herself for the unknown as she entered the prison

The room was crowded. Inmates sat in assigned places while visitors surveyed the room looking for their loved ones. Cherie scanned the area, her palms sweating as she searched for Dwayne. She finally spotted him in a back corner and made her way through the congested and noisy throng. When she reached him, she sat in a chair across the table from him. Guards monitored every detail of activity, shouting at inmates and visitors alike if rules weren't strictly followed. Dwayne slouched in his chair, head down. Cherie's heart pounded.

She stared at the top of his head while he said nothing. "Dwayne, do you think you could look at me when I'm talking with you?"

"Mom, I can't," he mumbled.

When she insisted, he stammered, "Because... because these guys in here are going to get me if I look at them."

"I'm not asking you to look at them. I want you to look at me," she said.

Despite her repeated request, Dwayne kept his head down. Cherie looked at him, wondering if his subdued behavior indicated he'd been assaulted over the previous months. Clearly, his youthfulness put him at risk. He looked slight compared to the other inmates, almost effeminate, she thought, then quickly dismissed the idea. His impaired hearing didn't help them converse in this raucous environment. Sullen and barely reacting to her questions, Dwayne offered no explanation about "these guys get[ting] him" and she didn't ask further.

Cherie did her best to engage her son, to connect with this young man she'd raised and loved and who now was a stranger to her. Inwardly she was angry with him, but she tried to stifle the feeling, afraid of it. She blamed Dwayne for the loss of Don and the emptiness she felt in her life without him. She talked aimlessly for an hour. She asked how he was doing, but how could he be doing? He looked afraid, though he didn't have visible marks or bruises. His posture reminded her of a stray dog one might see cowering in a corner at the pound. Dwayne didn't talk to her about anything, keeping his head down, his responses barely audible. There was no conversation about the crime. Cherie knew she needed to forgive him and not let her repressed anger take root in her soul. She looked at him with pity while inwardly seething with rage. She sensed a twinge of compassion as she studied Dwayne's prison uniform, noticing it was so tight that she questioned why the staff would have issued clothes that didn't fit him. The encounter was bizarre and confirmed Cherie's doubts that she would come away with new understanding about why Don was killed. She wished she hadn't made the trip.

When Cherie exited the prison, her spirits were even lower than they'd been before she went inside. She climbed wearily into the driver's seat, her facial expression incredulous. "Dwayne was dressed like a girl," she told Katheryn. "His clothing was almost skintight, his shirt tucked in his pants," she reported. Visibly distraught, she couldn't process the visit and wondered if Dwayne had surrendered himself sexually to another inmate rather than be forcibly assaulted. Her mind clouded, refusing to believe unthinkable thoughts. *I can't face Dwayne and my conflicting feelings of anger and a desire to forgive*, she thought to herself. *I can't think about the years we tried to help him and nothing worked.*

The visit set her back emotionally to where she'd been right after the murder, engulfing her in a bleak funk in which she questioned what forces had driven Dwayne to drugs and then murder. She wondered again whether she and Don had missed something as parents that could have changed the course of events. Seeing Dwayne confirmed the secret fears she had about his life behind bars, fears of sexual assault and homosexuality, and she wondered if she was wasting her time staying in contact with him when he seemed bent on a life of rebellion. Peculiar impressions, grim dark images, filled her mind; flashbacks to scenes from the court room, Donette weeping on the stand, Dwayne in the tight prison uniform, her life without Don. She dropped Katheryn off at her house and couldn't wait to get to her own home.

Finally pulling into her familiar garage, Cherie turned off the engine and sat in the darkened car, relieved to be home. Worn out from the day's events, she thanked God for the safe trip and the blessing of the Applegate property that she loved so much. Her thoughts turned to happier family times, and she recalled her promise to raise Dwayne until he turned eighteen. Dwayne had turned eighteen on his last birthday, six months before. She understood that technically, she'd fulfilled her commitment at Dwayne's adoption hearing but inwardly, she felt she hadn't really finished raising Dwayne. She sensed that there was a greater purpose driving her to keep communication open with him. She decided to continue living out her dedication to him no matter her feelings, and she believed that God would take her persistence and somehow use it for His purposes in her life and in Dwayne's. Exhausted, she got out of the car. Her heart was lighter, renewed by hope and resolve. She needed to continue to be faithful to what she knew was right and trust that good would follow. Though she remained steadfast in her commitment to Dwayne, the visit had been traumatizing for her.

She didn't see Dwayne again for twelve years.

CHAPTER 13 – LETTERS
FROM HIS CELL

Even though a dozen years would pass before Cherie visited Dwayne again, the two communicated by letter or an occasional phone call. Correspondence from Dwayne was hit and miss and filled with erratic content. Cherie never knew what to expect from him, and she opened each envelope with trepidation. Scrawled, nasty accusations often filled the pages, while at other times Dwayne seemed congenial and introspective. His focused rebellion toward the penal system had only worsened, as exemplified by the numerous letters he wrote expressing hostility toward inmates and blasting corrections officers for his latest unfair treatment. More often than not, the unwelcome white envelopes would pile up, unopened, on Cherie's kitchen counter.

She'd renewed her commitment to be supportive of Dwayne, meaning that when they corresponded, she took in his chaotic rambling but kept her letters short and avoided commenting about the complaints he enumerated. She consistently encouraged him in the Christian faith by quoting biblical verses and urging him to study the Bible so that he could see life from a completely different point of view. Cherie knew that only divine intervention could bring about change in either of them, realizing that it would take a miracle for her to ever be able to truly forgive him for what he'd done and for Dwayne to feel genuine remorse and take responsibility for his crime. Deep down, Cherie knew that the God she believed in, whose promises filled the Bible, was a God of the miraculous. She was sure that nothing was impossible, but she couldn't imagine how that truth could play out in her situation.

Knowing she couldn't control the direction of Dwayne's life, she decided the time had come to chart her own course. Her friend Marilyn suggested to Cherie that she take a class at the local community college. The course was called Moving On and was tailored for women who found themselves at a time in life when their circumstances had changed and they needed direction and support. The idea appealed to Cherie and she enrolled.

Still struggling with grief when home alone, Cherie found it impossible to focus on her class assignments. She asked Michael Wood, the owner of a small restaurant in Murphy called the Yacht Club, if she could do her homework there. Michael was glad to be of help and invited her to come to the restaurant whenever she wanted. Cherie took advantage of the opportunity and could regularly be found doing her assignments in the back corner booth of the restaurant.

During the next nine months, between caring for her Applegate property and attending her class, Cherie continued to pray for her son and his circumstances and write to him when time permitted.

A letter from Dwayne written on January 12, two days after his nineteenth birthday, stated that he'd begun the new year in the hole for disruptive behavior, disobedience of an order, destruction of property, and attempted assault. The charges would keep him in segregation until June. Dwayne wrote about unrelated subjects, first expressing curiosity about his biological parents and asking Cherie if she would help him locate them, and then jumping to news on his case, reporting that he'd filed with the court claiming his conviction was unconstitutional. He wrote, *"I'm not sick minded or anything. All I was doing is handling a problem which I didn't know how to deal with any other way."* He wrapped up the letter by promising to send photos in the summer. He explained that inmates could purchase tickets that would allow them to have photos taken by an inmate photographer during visiting hours. At the end of visiting, an officer would hand the visitor an envelope with the printed pictures in it.

The snapshots arrived in mid-May along with a smaller envelope addressed to Donette. Donette accepted that her mom had chosen to stay in contact with Dwayne, but she was now thirteen and had no interest in hearing from Dwayne or about him. In the aftermath of her dad's murder, she'd watched her mother struggle through months of grief and depression, and every day she missed her dad. As far as Donette was concerned, Dwayne deserved to be right where he was. When Cherie handed her daughter the envelope with her name on it, Donette opened it with ambivalence, not having the slightest curiosity about what Dwayne would want to say to her.

"I'm only trying to be the 'older brother' I should have been several years ago. If you remember correctly, I was a real asshole to you, Mom and Dad—I've regretted it for the last 3 years, but that won't change anything. I'm now doing what I feel is best." He talked of weight training and getting in trouble. He said he no longer lived in "fantasy land," but then again, nothing about him was the same. He wrote of a waning interest in heavy metal music, saying he now preferred pop and rock. He'd cut back on cigarettes, he said, and messing around with the *"'girls' in here (which of course are actually homosexuals)."* He wrote, *"I've become so accustomed to living in here, I'd have a hell of a time trying to adjust to the free world.... I still have to survive in here. It's a real bitch to have to watch your back all the time—you never know who will get stupid. But you get used to it after a while... I'll be out of prison, maybe not for 10 or 15 years but eventually I will though. Also, I know you have got good reason to be leery of me, but,*

listen to me. What I did in 1986 was wrong and there is really no justifiable reason or excuse for it. I really can't honestly answer what was going on in my brain at that time but I obviously wasn't in full control of myself. I'm able to understand that, now that I've been drug free for nearly 3 years. What I want to say is this... I remember all that BS the state said about me, some of it was true, most of it was not. All that crap about me going to come after you and Mom, that's a damn lie."

Donette only shrugged. All she cared about was that Dwayne was still in prison. She didn't give a thought as to whether any of the content in his letter was true. Besides, she'd started high school the previous fall and her mind was occupied with her social connections and classes. Dwayne's reflections didn't interest her. As she glanced again at the letter, something caught her eye. Surprised, she looked at his signature, particularly the way Dwayne wrote his D when signing his name. She thoughtfully examined the cursive. She'd never picked up that Dwayne wrote his capital D the same way she did when she signed her name. With this new realization, she purposed to change her handwriting so it wouldn't look anything like Dwayne's. She tossed the letter on the kitchen table and walked to her room, anxious to figure out a way to modify her handwriting.

Cherie needed an escape from Dwayne's letters that left her, and now Donette, upset by their disturbing content. The invasive poison oak, star thistle, and blackberries were fighting to retain their claim to the land, and Cherie's efforts to plant anything were met with resistance. The upper part of the property was virtually a rock garden; rock after rock just below the top surface of the soil required the use of a crowbar or pick to remove them. The physical exertion kept Cherie's mind distracted from her worries, and the complete exhaustion from the labor helped her to fall asleep at night.

A month later, when Cherie received a letter from Dwayne, she could tell he was irritated about not having heard back from Donette. Compounding his disappointment was the fact that Cherie hadn't written him for six months. He began the note reporting that he was still confined in the hole but expected to be out in eighteen days, and then he mentioned his sister.

"Like I told her (Donette), I'm not going to be locked up forever, so she can't just pretend I don't exist. Well, she can, but she's still going to have to face me some day. A lot of people will. People may think I'm never going to change, but that's their trip. All I'm saying is none of you really know me—you think you do, but really you don't and you would all understand that if you'd take the time to get to know me.... Well, enough about that. I'll let you decide for yourself. If it's meant to be, it'll be. If it isn't, it won't. Simple."

The summer of 1989 passed without an exchange of letters between Dwayne and Cherie. The break came at a time when Cherie found herself caring for her ailing stepfather. Lois had passed away in 1985 before Don's murder. Since then, Arnie was a regular visitor at the Wiers' place. Cherie had increasingly noticed that Arnie's memory loss seemed to disrupt his daily life and a trip to the doctor resulted in a diagnosis of Alzheimer's disease. Cherie moved Arnie temporarily in with her, hoping she could find foster care that provided assistance for Alzheimer's patients. Housing Arnie at her Applegate home proved unsafe when one afternoon the confused man wandered down to the river and Donette couldn't coax him back to the house. Donette finally persuaded Arnie to leave the water's edge, but both Cherie and Donette were fearful of what could have happened that day and relieved when Cherie made arrangements for safe foster care.

Arnie had settled into the assisted living home in Grants Pass when Cherie again heard from Dwayne. It was September 15 and he was furious. He launched an attack on all Cherie held dear, particularly targeting her views on morality and her efforts to be a good mom. Dwayne chided Cherie for not replying to his letters and determined to hurt her because he perceived she'd purposefully neglected him. *"Well, it seems as if my last 3 letters were just wasted ink. But I'll try one last time."* The rest of the first page reported that he was out of the hole and talked of how his petition to be transferred to a prison out of state had been denied. He then disclosed a homosexual relationship he had taken up with *"a woman who is trapped in a man's body."* He explained the initial connection he and the other inmate had was because they were both former crank addicts and because they were able to help and encourage each other to overcome the addiction. He wrote of their love and loyalty to one another. The remaining six pages proclaimed his decision to disavow any moral standards espoused by Cherie and Don. Defending his choice to enter into the homosexual relationship, he wrote, *"Maybe that's wrong, but so are a lot of things. Right or wrong, it is reality. I'm really sick and tired of people wanting me to live by their standards. I done that with you and Dad for years and, you know what? Fuck you and your standards and morals! If it wasn't for your fucked-up standards, I'd not have killed Dad."*

Dwayne continued his onslaught of shifting the blame for his actions onto his parents. Cherie had questioned the validity of Dwayne's excuse that he "had no other way to deal" with his frustrations about his dad. When she mentioned Dwayne running away, as usual, he managed to deflect the fault back on his parents. *"You said, 'well, why didn't you just run away?' Mom, I ran away a number of times. So, I ask you this, why the hell didn't you and Dad just let me go? I was 16. I could have been emancipated. I'd have made it okay on my own. I may have even made it somewhere in music. Who really knows? You just wanted me to be something I wasn't and still am not and **never will be**! I'm me and that's all I will ever be."*

Dwayne's verbal assault intensified as he used Donette as a means to get under her skin. *"I just hope you don't fuck up her life like you and dad fucked up my life. Yes, **I** pulled the trigger on that gun; yes, **I wanted** to kill him; that's why I shot him in the head with a 30-30 just in case, by some remote possibility, he lived through it. I didn't use such an extremely powerful rifle to make sure he'd be dead because I was scared of him; I wasn't. You really want to know how much I hated him? If I had a full-size picture of Dad, I'd either throw darts at it or tear it into 6x6 inch squares and use it to wipe my ass! Sure Dad was really cool to me at times. He tried to be a partner to me and a friend at times too but when he was around you, he was always contradictory to how he was when him and I were alone...*

*"You asked me where you went wrong. Well, I'll tell you! The first thing that you did wrong was <u>you</u> adopted me: secondly you must have thought you owned me (like a piece of property) because you sure tried hard to run my life for me; thirdly, you were too damn stupid to realize that a man can only be pushed so far for so long before he will take some kind of action to cease whatever the problem may be; fourthly, you should have thought about why I'd ran away so many times and took that as a hint that I wanted to go on my way. But what did you do? You called the fucking police on me and reported me for runaway and theft... I'm not your little baby anymore! What is it? Do you feel I owe you for something? I'll tell you what—I don't owe you a god damn thing! If anything, **you owe me!** Your morals are really fucked up!.*

"Do I seem different? Well, I've changed a lot. I'm no longer going to bite my tongue for anyone! I'm going to stand my ground and speak my feelings freely and fuck anyone who don't like it. Anyway, good luck with your future and tell Donette I love her and wish her the best."

Reeling from the sting of Dwayne's charges, Cherie's stomach tightened and a familiar nauseating sensation swept over her. Knowing Dwayne chose to turn his back on the moral standards she and Don had taught him was one thing, but reading his verbal assaults made her sick to her stomach. As if Dwayne's accusations weren't enough, another letter was included in the envelope, one written by Dwayne's boyfriend David. David wrote of his selfless devotion to Dwayne, telling Cherie how he was giving Dwayne the love Dwayne never got from her and Don.

David started his letter by criticizing Cherie for bringing up the crime in her letters to Dwayne. *"And I think you're fucked up for always rubbing the fact he took your husband. Well you and he took a lot from Dwayne! God the more I think about you, you are more fucked up than what Dwayne says! I don't care what Dwayne did! What you and his dad didn't seem to understand is you were not loving him like you should have! I understand Dwayne! My mom and dad did what you did but I run away and did drugs and gave sex for money. And all of this shit about mental health is nothing. I went to all of that stuff and it don't help! He doesn't need all the testing you say he needs; he just needs me to love him."*

After reading both letters, Cherie collapsed at the kitchen table, unable to sort through her emotional storm. She'd pledged to support Dwayne, but how much more could she take? Maybe the naysayers had been right. After all, Dwayne was now an adult, and she'd fulfilled her vow. Cherie stared at the two letters on the table in front of her, fearing that she would never be able to forgive Dwayne. Two years in prison had only increased his defiance. Cherie knew that as long as Dwayne continued to shirk personal responsibility and blame others, forgiveness would be impossible.

Cherie softened somewhat when Dwayne's letter four months later was contrite. He started and ended with apologies for the last letter and the explanation that behind the nasty and sharp words were, *"my feelings of rejection and hurt because you hadn't responded to my letters. I realize that's really not enough, but it's a start to the future. If I didn't care, I'd not be writing. I want to rebuild a bridge that was burned and destroyed a long time ago. Please give me a chance. I'd appreciate it if you'd write me back and tell me your feelings for me."*

Although Dwayne's correspondence to Cherie reflected a conciliatory attitude toward her, less than a month later his behavior in prison landed him in the hole. Once again, a shank had reportedly been found in Dwayne's cell. In predicable fashion he claimed to have no knowledge of where the weapon had come from, and he told Cherie he was to take a polygraph to validate his innocence. To Cherie the report was more of the same, but she brightened as she read the next few sentences. Dwayne told her that he'd been doing some spiritual reflection and had spoken to a chaplain at the prison. He wrote that he'd *"given my life to the Lord to do with what He wishes. I mean this. It's taken a lot of pain to make me wake up and realize what I was doing to myself and my family."* Dwayne described the difficulties of maintaining a Christian life in prison and the trouble he had trying to change his ingrained behaviors. Yet he said he was resolved to do what was right.

When Dwayne wrote of trying to change his behavior, Cherie wondered if transformation was possible for someone like him. At least three psychiatrists had agreed that he suffered from poor impulse control, was self-serving, rebellious, and emotionally indifferent, all characteristics of an anti-social personality disorder. Dwayne was a danger to society, they said, and would continue to be. From the perspective of the mental health professionals, conversion for someone like Dwayne appeared hopeless.

Still Dwayne continued to show Cherie that there was potential for change in him. In a Mother's Day card three months later, he reported that though she hadn't responded to his letters, he remained committed to writing to her. He sounded upbeat despite having been found guilty of the weapons charge and remained in the hole. He apologized again for the content of the September 15 letter, then wrote, *"I'm ready to grow up. I just wish I would have about 4 years ago. I also wish I'd have stayed at MacLaren. I could've had an opportunity to be paroled right now, this year. I've been real dumb and I kick myself in the rear every time I think about it."* He was expecting some money from the state regarding an appeal he'd won and intended to send some of the money to Cherie and Donette for Christmas later in the year. *"Before I forget, if you still have my hearing aids, will you send them to me? I really need them. I do miss a lot of important things that are worth hearing. People think I'm stupid sometimes and can't comprehend anything, but it's because I don't hear half of what's being said. Sometimes officers tell me something and they think I'm ignoring them, but I just don't hear. It's a real disadvantage."*

Cherie sent Dwayne his hearing aids and settled into her new job waitressing at the Yacht Club. When Michael had encouraged Cherie to come by his restaurant to do homework for her class several years earlier, he knew she needed a job. With Don gone, Cherie couldn't wait to start generating income. The social security benefits for widows and children were welcomed revenue, but they fell short of meeting Cherie and Donette's basic needs. During the weeks Cherie had occupied the corner booth of the Yacht Club, she'd been surprised by how many people she knew who frequented the place. She'd made many friends over the years and everyone knew what had happened to Don when she began working there, and these friends were liberal when it came to leaving her tips.

Noticing Cherie's efficiency and friendliness with the customers, Michael promoted her to manager. The position suited her and she found pleasure in waiting on familiar neighbors and friends. Nights at home continued to be hard on her, but the work at the Yacht Club built her self-confidence and gave her a reason to look forward to every new day.

When Cherie retrieved the letter in her mailbox after an especially long shift at work in late May, Dwayne wrote that he had yet to receive a letter from her and was still in the hole, expecting to be there a few more months. He was seeing two counselors, both of whom were women, one for drug and alcohol therapy and the other for anger management. He told Cherie he was being candid with the women and taking the opportunity of counseling seriously because he wanted to change his life. His recent HIV test was negative and he said he was done with homosexuality. He discussed ideas about realistic career opportunities he thought might be available to him when he was finally released, saying he was tired of prison life and thought he might want to visit places like the Juvenile Detention Center in Jackson County and give advice to the teens that could help them stay out of prison. He wrote:

"This is really not where it's at. Mom, I've not told you a lot of what I've experienced in this place, but it's worse than I'd ever imagined. You may or may not doubt that I'm sincere about the changes I'm making with myself, but I know I'm sincere, God knows I'm sincere, and I believe my counselor knows I'm sincere as well. It's really frustrating because I know how much I've hurt you in the past and I'm sure you're not ready to say 'okay, everything's fine and dandy now' and I doubt you ever will be. At least I don't expect you to. I just want to renew my relationship with you and Donette. I assure you, I'll hurt you no more. Pray and ask God to guide you. If it's his will I know we'll be back on 'fair' terms."

Assurances from Dwayne promising a change of heart failed to eliminate the private fears Cherie had harbored about him since the murder. The shock that Dwayne was capable of violence had never left her. With news of each parole board hearing Cherie grew panicky, wondering when Dwayne would be released, and she decided to seek the services of an attorney. Cherie asked the lawyer to draft a letter to the parole board insisting on a guarantee that the board notify her prior to any short- or long-term release of Dwayne, so she might take necessary steps to secure her safety and that of her daughter. Copies of the letter were to be sent to the OSCI records department and to Carol Zenon, the superintendent of OSCI. Cherie strongly stipulated that her letter remain confidential and that Dwayne not have a copy of the document or know that such a letter existed. Past experience and hostile conversations with him had added to her fears, and she continued to believe Dwayne was a danger to Donette and her. On June 4, 1990, Cherie's attorney composed and mailed out the requested document.

Cherie expected the confidential letter to provide extra protection for Donette and her and give them both an added sense of security. The last thing she wanted for Donette was for her to encounter Dwayne unexpectedly in town or, worse yet, to see him walking up the drive. Cherie tried to take each letter from him as it came, never letting her guard down in case Dwayne let loose with further verbal abuse.

Fortunately, the note she received in September was upbeat, with positive feedback regarding his ongoing counseling and news of a Christian book he'd read that encouraged him. His closing lines read, *"I've learned a lot since I've been here. Perhaps 10 years late, but I'm learning, so all hope is not lost."* He included a bookmark imprinted with the Serenity Prayer and a copy of a Letter to the Editor in the local *Grants Pass Courier* he'd submitted.

The article was titled, "Convicted Killer's Plea: Stay Away From Drugs." In the letter, Dwayne summarized his crime and his incarceration in the Oregon prison system. He warned young people not to give in to the various temptations that they encounter, to never think that they have all of the answers, to listen to their parents and not others, and to get help immediately if they feel themselves slipping into trouble. He wrote, beware of the teenagers' worst enemy, the one that causes endless problems: drugs. Previously, Dwayne had mentioned to Cherie of his desire to use his life story as a warning to teens. His letter to the editor seemed to be his first attempt to speak out.

Drugs, however, weren't Dwayne's topic of conversation in the letter that arrived in March. When Cherie opened the decorated envelope, she discovered two filled notebook pages and a card decorated with a smiling bunny. The handwritten words read, *"I want my mommy!!!"* Inside the card Dwayne had written, *"I love you!!! Mom, I hope you like this. I wanted to do something that would make you happy."*

The two notebook pages reported that he'd been feeling pretty miserable lately, but he didn't elaborate. Proud of himself, he gave her details about the grades he was getting in his classes: A in English Composition, C in Intro to Psychology, B in Entrepreneurship. He told her he was signing up for the next semester and listed the classes. He asked for money for soap, writing that *"my face and skin keep drying up and cracking and itching then breaking out because of the lye soap they give us and the hard water. I usually use shampoo on my whole body but I have none. Summertime is coming up and I'd like to go outside. I'm white as a ghost from being in the hole so long so I'll burn very easily and would like to get sunscreen."* Additionally, he requested money to buy deodorant and apologized for asking. He enquired about Donette and mentioned that he'd turned twenty-one on his last birthday, writing he felt like an old fart!

With the positive reports from Dwayne, Cherie's hopes rekindled. Perhaps Dwayne's resolve to do what was right was a sincere commitment on his part. If his letters and his newspaper editorial were any indication, he was showing an interest in the welfare of others. His November letter included a typed page written as an appeal to those caught in drug use. He hoped somehow his words would warn and prevent others from the series of events that had led to his life in prison. He explained that he'd been working with his counselor, Sally Schick, whom Dwayne wrote had *"helped me a great deal. I feel I owe her a lot for helping me to help myself change into a better person. I've learned to accept reality and take responsibility for everything I do and say. I have a heart that can love, care about people, feel hurt, etc.—something I've never really had before I came to prison and even for a long time while I've been here. All I really knew at one point was anger. The change which I feel is a complete turnaround for the best."*

Dwayne wrote about his classes, then became more personal. *"Mom, I really hurt bad over what I've done to us, the family we once were. I cry a lot and feel a longing to change what I've done in the past. I know that those words will never be enough. I want you to know that I love you and Donette and I will do whatever necessary to help you make it through the pain that I know we all feel so deeply."* He appealed to her to visit him, but said he would understand if she chose not to. He wrote that he knew he *"didn't deserve the time of day from you and I'm very thankful you're even giving me the chances you have and I'm thankful for the patience you've shown me too. I know, without a doubt, that you love me and care about me."*

Dwayne had asked Cherie for prayer. Underestimating his mother's Christian devotion, he didn't realize that she prayed for him daily, asking God to help him recognize truth and live well while learning the value of helping others. Although the psychiatrists had warned that change for someone like Dwayne was virtually impossible, Cherie had ignored the bleak prognosis and fervently prayed for change.

In April of 1992, Dwayne sent Cherie two torn-out pages from an in-house pamphlet titled, *Just Another Spiritual Book.* The circular was a publication where inmates could submit questions to be answered by a prison counselor and then the booklet with the questions and answers was distributed to the general population. Dwayne had put forth a question to the counselor and had enclosed a copy of his query and the answer on the torn-out pages he sent to Cherie. Dwayne explained the reason he'd sent a copy to her was because he wanted her to know the truth about how he felt in the days prior to the murder. He said he wanted to be honest with her and himself. In his question to the counselor, Dwayne admitted to doing a terrible thing. He briefly summarized his crime and drug addiction. He told the counselor that he realized he'd caused an enormous rift in his adopted family and that he also was curious about his biological family. Dwayne was looking for advice from the counselor on how to resolve his family relations in some way at this point in his life.

In his query to the counselor, Dwayne described his circumstances this way: "*You see, my dad was an ex-con. He was also two-faced. For 3 years, he'd condoned and participated with me in many illegal activities. Yet, when Mom would find out or Dad got in a weird mood, he'd physically assault me for doing exactly what he was condoning and doing along with me. This became very confusing for me. I eventually felt very stressed and wanted out of the 'trap' I was in with my dad. I tried running away. I tried reasoning with my parents to let me go on my own. This did not work, and problems got worse, so I killed him. At the time, I seen no other way out. Now I regret my decision. Please give me some advice.*" He signed the letter, asking Cherie to send him money for necessities.

If Dwayne had intended his excerpt from the booklet to be a statement of contrition, he'd fallen short. Cherie viewed Dwayne's explanation as another example of him justifying his actions by placing the blame elsewhere. In this case, he blamed Don. Cherie briefly considered whether this was Dwayne's way to make known hidden disturbing behavior on Don's part? His awful claims about Don deeply bothered Cherie. Still, she didn't believe them credible.

When Cherie opened an envelope from Dwayne two weeks later, the most recent troubling update became her newest source of worry. The information that Dwayne conveyed was all too familiar to her. His health had declined, requiring reoccurring medical trips. Mysterious, seemingly unrelated symptoms that had plagued Dwayne since childhood had resurfaced in various forms. He was seeing an endocrinologist and a nephrologist. The nephrologist believed Dwayne had a rare hereditary kidney disease that manifested in his ear and eye problems. Dwayne wrote, *"I've been tested for numerous things and what they found is an abnormally large amount of protein and blood in my urine. Also, my ankles are swollen. They've been like this for a long time now and that's what I'd gone to the doctor for to begin with, to see why my ankles were swollen. After several months of testing, I'm told I have this problem that is not treatable and may have to have a kidney transplant sooner or later. I go in for a kidney biopsy in three or four weeks. This will determine whether or not it's treatable or hereditary and untreatable."* He listed the names and numbers of his medical providers and invited Cherie to call them if she had questions or wanted more information. As usual, he signed off his letters by mentioning Donette and hoping things were going well at home.

Three months passed before Dwayne had answers. On November 27, he was diagnosed with Alport syndrome, a rare genetic condition characterized by kidney disease, hearing loss, and eye abnormalities. Symptoms of the disease typically appear in male patients during childhood and can progressively escalate in severity. Most affected individuals will experience end-stage renal disease and deafness by age forty. Dwyane was frightened by the diagnosis and, in a letter to Cherie that same day, he expressed worry about his prognosis. *"I've been quite concerned with my health ever since I found out I have this disease. It's pretty scary. You know how I've always been about blood and guts and all that, and to think of dialysis or major surgery to stay alive gives me a very eerie feeling."*

Having shared all of the information the doctor had told him about Alport syndrome, Dwayne asked about Donette and then apologized as he requested money for toiletries and a pair of shoes. Low tops were issued by the prison, and his excessively swollen ankles sagged over the edge of the shoes, causing discomfort. With the cutbacks at the facility, toothpaste had been replaced with baking soda. He said he understood if she lacked the resources to help.

A month later, Cherie found a bulging manilla envelope in her mailbox crammed with documents related to Dwayne's recent academic performance. Folded copies of his certificates of completion showed proficiency in residential blueprint reading, introduction to electricity, and wiring. He'd also fulfilled the requirements of an alcohol/drug workshop and breaking barriers class. Cherie looked through the certificates while thinking how she'd always known Dwayne was capable of doing well if he tried and how glad she was to see him applying himself. She was proud of him and was quick to respond with a letter congratulating him on his success.

In the meantime, between the certificates and doctor visits, an undercurrent of disagreement involving money had been brewing between Cherie and Dwayne. When Cherie's grandfather passed away, he left money in an account for Dwayne. On May 17, 1993, Dwayne's letter expressed frustration regarding his inability to get into the account that held the money. The funds were to be kept for him with Cherie acting as trustee. Initially Dwayne had asked, rather apologetically, for access to some of the money, giving Cherie reasons why he needed it. But over the months, when Cherie didn't acquiesce, he became more insistent, demanding availability to what he thought was rightfully his. The letter was no nonsense. Rather proficient with legal matters by now, Dwayne included a couple of official forms with instructions about what Cherie needed to do to permit him into the account. If she refused, he said he would force her to comply, which he said he would rather not do.

While Dwayne and Cherie bickered over the inheritance money, Dwayne had been moved out of OSCI as a preemptive protective measure. Dwayne and cellmate Scott had been transferred to OSP and placed in Administrative Segregation because the men had been named as vital witnesses in a serial murder case in Multnomah County. Dwayne wrote, *"We are testifying against a guy named Scott William Cox. Cox was here at OSCI last summer and if I remember correctly, I think I was in Josephine County jail with him in 1987. My friend and I testified against him last Wednesday in Multnomah County court and we'll most likely be called upon to testify again around September when Cox goes to trial. The guy told me a lot when he was here. He is a real sick individual. Cox was a truck driver whose hobby it was to pick up prostitutes, raping them and then stabbing them. And he beat them up badly too! The guy is a maniac!"*

Dwayne had been sickened by Cox's boasting about his crimes to him, and he and his cellmate had notified corrections authorities of the prisoner's gruesome exploits. Because of his willingness to turn state's evidence, Dwayne and his cellmate were at risk of retaliation by friends of Cox. Dwayne wrote he was, *"running around here in fear. It scares the hell out of me and my friend. What's more is the guy would ultimately come do his time here where Scott and me are at. Mighty sweet of them."* Anytime an inmate turns state's evidence he is automatically in danger of retaliation, especially with a prisoner like Scott Cox involved. Payback was likely to be deadly.

The difference between OSCI and OSP was obvious to Dwayne right away. OSCI was built in 1959 and housed a maximum of 880 medium security inmates, whereas OSP was constructed 100 years earlier and held 2,242 maximum security prisoners. Oregon's death row inmates were incarcerated in OSP. Dwayne described the prison as *"a pretty scary place and I'm sort of glad I'm in PC. It comes complete with cockroaches and flies crawling around in every cell. All they give you here is baking soda to brush your teeth and you must buy your own toothbrush, lye soap, a good for one shave Bic razor, a few sheets of newsprint to use as writing paper... you must buy your own pen or pencil, toilet paper, a plastic spoon and fork, 2 plastic cups, and clothes that don't fit."* He added on the positive side the food was much better than he had at OSCI and the correctional officers, so far, seemed more respectful to the inmates and honest.

Not only were some of the conditions at OSP more to Dwayne's liking, but other fascinations had surfaced and grabbed his attention. During Dwayne's six years of incarceration, the topics brought up in his letters to Cherie had been all over the place. Even so, when correspondence arrived on June 17, Cherie wasn't prepared for the report sent to her by an anonymous acquaintance of Dwayne's. More than with any letter she'd received thus far, she found herself ill equipped to handle the news.

"I am the best friend of your son/daughter. I'm not sure whether you refer to Dwayne as a son or daughter, so please forgive me if one of those terms offends you. For ease of writing I'll stick to my normal reference to "him." I call her 'D' (Dwayne's nickname)." The friend explained that he'd gotten Cherie's address from Dwayne as an emergency contact. He wanted to let her know that D was going through some very difficult times right now, and had been for a while. He wrote that D was having problems with *"her sexual identity. This is a subject you'd be better able to*

help her with than I would. When D got off the phone with you yesterday, she walked over to me and started crying, I guess she didn't want to tell you about it. I imagine this is just as hard for you as it is for D. In spite of D's physical appearance, D is a woman." The writer appealed to Cherie to *"listen to D and be there for her and let her know you care. Since I've known D, she's been crying and hurting inside over the pain she caused all your family, friends, and you. It is one thing to be truly sorry for something that has such a tragic ring to it, but it is a totally different thing to be eaten up by it, slowly and surely, never for 1 minute able to forget what was done. That is what's been happening to D... She has a few things she'd like to tell you, but she's afraid to hurt you or lose you... You're the only one who can drag all the negativity in her to the surface so it can be dealt with.. .and the mother knows best. Thank you for your time, A Friend."*

Cherie was shaken by the revelation provided by the anonymous writer. She'd worried that prison would introduce Dwayne to homosexuality, but she'd never considered he would question his gender. This letter forced Cherie to ponder what other torments might be haunting her son. She didn't have long to wait, because a lengthy letter from Dwayne arrived four days later.

The letter was written on six pages of newsprint (front and back) and filled with Dwayne's attempt to understand and explain his gender confusion. He wrote, *"All of my life, I've felt female on the inside. I wanted to look like one, act like one, dress like one, etc. But I couldn't and I could certainly not be a man either. It's just not me."* He talked about the differences between homosexuality and transgender. He explained his desire to behave as a female and his interest in makeup and fiddling with his hair. He wrote of his intention to *"try to get these ignorant shrinks here to put me on Estradiol* [an estrogen hormone] *so I would feel more like myself"* eventually. He said he was hoping in due course to have the sex organ reassignment surgery done. He reported that he'd mailed off papers to the court to legally change his name to Denis Lynn Smith, saying that he couldn't care less if anyone approved. He told Cherie he was also referred to as "D."

In an attempt to convince Cherie of his long-time struggle with his gender, Dwayne reminded her of an incident that happened at home when he was twelve. The Kirby vacuum cleaner salesman was talking to her at the house when Dwayne walked through the room. The man remarked, *"What a pretty daughter you have."* Dwayne remembered thinking at the time, *"That to me was one hell of a compliment. I loved it and I've cherished it, as it is one of only a few 'true' compliments I've gotten. That's why I remember it."*

He told her that he'd hinted to his dad that he was different, feminine, female, but never came right out and told him. He wrote about his early girlfriends and how he never felt right. He felt *"rejected as a woman and, because of my femininity, rejected as a man as well! Do you see why I was so messed up now? I never wanted to tell you any of this. I've been enough of a problem to you, Dad, Donette and everyone else. I've been afraid you'd disown me completely if I told you. I was sure Dad would have. The only thing I didn't like about Dad was he treated me like a boy, a guy, like a male. I despised him for that. But I was too afraid of how he'd respond if I tried to tell him I'm a female."* Dwayne asked Cherie if she was beginning to understand him and told her this was not *"something I've all of a sudden become. It's all been carried within me, thought out thoroughly, and finally accepted and understood. It's hard for me! Do you think I'm 'cold' because I was antisocial or whatever? It is because of who I was inside, what I looked like outside and the constant conflict it creates! I sit here crying my eyes out as I write about it because it is not easy. I don't need or want a shrink for anything, except to prescribe Estradiol.*

The only thing that's ever been wrong with me is I have the <u>*WRONG BODY! Sincerely, your daughter, NOT son*</u>"

CHAPTER 14 – I WILL
CARRY IT TO MY GRAVE

Cherie studied the last page of the letter, struck by Dwayne's claim that he was a woman. She shuddered as she reread his belief that what had been diagnosed by psychiatrists as an antisocial personality disorder was actually Dwayne's introverted response as he tried to cover up "who he [really] was inside." She dreaded opening the accompanying second letter and found her fears confirmed as she read more details about his hidden feelings.

Dwayne wrote by admitting that *"maybe I should have told you about these feelings I've had a long time ago. I don't know. I was afraid to tell anyone. It's only been for about the last couple or so years that I've let myself come out little by little."* He told her he'd developed a greater understanding of what it was to be a transsexual by reading several books on the subject and the information in them had reinforced his certainty that he was transsexual. He wrote about an inmate he'd met who was also transsexual and said he felt they were like-minded in many ways. *"The only therapeutic remedy is sex reassignment surgery. And, the reality of it is that I'm never going to be totally happy or able to live a worthwhile life unless I have the body to match my personality. The two, as it is at present, just don't mix."* He was hoping that *"after seeing the prison psychiatrist I may get put on hormones. That would be a relief to me. Love, D"*

Cherie shook her head, thinking back over the past eight years. *How much worse can all of this get?* she wondered. *Dwayne has never felt comfortable in his own body?* She'd noticed peculiarities in his behavior, but she hadn't once considered that confusion over his sexuality was at the root. This revelation of Dwayne's secret struggle caused Cherie to wonder whether she and Don could have done more to be attentive parents. Both of them had been busy with the property and later, the construction of the house. Don had worked long hours. In the midst of caring for the family, had they been too busy to notice other problems Dwayne may have been facing?

During the next month, Cherie found herself brooding over Dwayne's claim that he was transsexual, and she was mentally exhausted from trying to make sense of the disclosure. When she received his next letter, she was relieved to see he focused on the long-disputed funds held in the Jackson County Federal Bank. He was grateful Cherie had released the funds and happy to report that he'd received a check for the balance. Cherie had seen little reason to continue to deny Dwayne access to the account, knowing the money was legally his. She was surprised when less than a month later she received a check from Dwayne for $200. Included was a note specifying that the money was what he'd promised to send to her to purchase Christmas gifts for her and Donette. Other than the $200 Dwayne sent for the presents, Cherie never had any idea how Dwayne spent his money from the inheritance.

The quarrel about the bequeathed money now settled, Dwayne turned his attention fully to his upcoming testimony at the highly publicized Scott Cox trial. He'd written to Cherie about the Multnomah County case, reminding her that it was because of this trial that he and his cellmate Scott had been moved to OSP. Cox was accused of the rape and murder of two black women and was about to plead guilty to a lesser degree of murder. Dwayne, outraged by the news that Cox's murder charge had been reduced, complained to Cherie, *"Some justice system!"* On September 15, 1993, Scott William Cox was convicted on two separate counts of homicide in Portland, Oregon. He was the prime suspect in at least twenty additional unsolved murder cases.

While Cherie worried about Dwayne living among sadistic criminals, she still wasn't prepared for him to be released. Whenever she was notified of an upcoming parole board review, she wondered what would happen if Dwayne was released into the community or, worse yet, if he were to escape. Safety concerns for herself and Donette had prompted Cherie to contact her attorney, Ronald B. Versteeg, the previous October. At that time, Mr. Versteeg had drafted a letter to the parole board and OSCI on her behalf. It was now January, and Dwayne was housed at OSP. Cherie requested that Mr. Versteeg confirm that the original letter, sent to OSCI, had been copied for the authorities at OSP and that they would send confirmation verifying receipt of the letter. In the original document, the attorney had stressed the importance of Cherie being notified of any planned release of Dwayne, and had asked that the letters requesting Cherie's desire for notification would be handled with the strictest confidentiality.

Mrs. Wier, the attorney wrote, feared reprisals from Dwayne if he knew of the letters. Mr. Versteeg requested that the OSP offices and the parole board send confirmation to his office verifying receipt of the October letter, as well as the January letter. *"It is of extreme importance to Mrs. Wier that Dwayne does not have access to this* [January] *letter"* and that *"NO COPY of this correspondence be placed in Dwayne's file."* Trusting that her lawyer had ensured that she would be notified if Dwayne were to be released and that her wishes would be kept confidential, Cherie did her best to set aside her fears.

In early October, three months after Dwayne's parole board review, Cherie opened a letter she found so noteworthy that she jotted the words "very important" on the envelope. Dwayne began by explaining the events of Don's murder in 1986, citing details he hadn't previously disclosed.

"I'm really not sure how to explain 10-18-86. I do know that it was not Dad, nor you; it was me. I know when the idea first popped into my head—when Dad and I were on some logging road helping that guy at Jantzer logging who everyone called 'Beaner.' It was right after Dad picked me up from school. I'd stayed in the truck the whole time and had been doing drugs all day (as usual). I was 'high' and thought I probably could've passed a 'drunk test.' I was in something of a daze. After that idea came into my head, when I seen Dad's gun in the front seat of the truck, I could not get the thought out of my mind. I kept feeling compelled to act on my thought and kept trying to block it out of my mind altogether and I couldn't. It was as if I'd become obsessed with it and had to act on it. I'd almost acted out twice before I actually did. Once while he was on the phone to you, and once right after that, but I could not do it. One part of me was telling me, 'no, don't do it,' and a greater, more overwhelming part of me was urging me to do it. I tried to go to bed, but I couldn't sleep. So, I went into the bathroom and took some more drugs, thinking that if I got stoned enough, I'd forget whatever it was that was bothering me so much and just fall asleep or pass out. It didn't work that way—instead, it only got worse.

"Mom, I know what the forensic guys said about the blood and urine tests, and I realize a lot of people didn't believe me when I said I'd taken some of the drugs I did, but I KNOW what I took. I'd taken 8 Valium over the course of that entire day (10-17-86 and the early hours of 10-18-86) three of which were right before the fact. Also, I'd smoked around a gram of pot before the fact. Dad had just bought a ½ case of Hamm's beer too. He'd drank 2 and there were 3 left when I was done drinking. I'd taken enough stuff to

make a horse pass out. There was an outside force putting pressure on me to carry out my thoughts.

"During the drive home, after Dad, Beaner and myself ate dinner at a restaurant somewhere, I could almost sense that Dad knew what was going to happen before it did. I wanted to talk to him about it, and tell him what was going on in my mind, and I just couldn't get the words to come out. I remember asking him if I could have my guitars back the next day and I can remember almost begging, pleading, nearly ready to cry. I've never forgotten what he said, 'Well, I don't know, maybe. We'll see if tomorrow gets here.' Those were his exact words. I think I was looking hard for a reason to let tomorrow come and fight back against whatever it was in my head that was telling me, or rather, insisting, that I take his life.

"I still don't know how I'd even managed to use that gun and not miss. I'd NEVER been able to hit a target with that gun before. I was a lousy shot. I could hit a target maybe 2 or 3 times out of 20, and only the outer edges at that. Also, I have no idea how or why I knew where to find the keys to the truck and to the trailer. I don't know how I was able to drive on North Applegate Road in the middle of the night going as fast as 95 mph and no slower than 70 until I got toward the stop sign where N. Applegate meets Williams Hwy. I'd hit the same speeds from Scooter's house to E and I Market as well and that lady I seen walking down the road while I was at the E and I Market I was trying to 'pick up' on. All of this is a mystery to me.

"I didn't WANT to take Dad's life. I want to go back in time so that I can do everything over and different from around August of 1986 and up. I think about Dad all the time and I wish there were some way I could communicate with him. If there is, I haven't quite found it yet. But I can hear his voice inside from time to time, giving me advice. And I listen. I know you and Dad both deserved a much better-behaved son than I ever was, and I'm very sorry I

was the way I was. I miss you both. A lot of what Dad taught me, or had tried to teach me, I'm only just now learning. Things like how to be a good guy—how to be a real man— being mature, being responsible, being honest to others and above all, to myself. As far as my sexuality is concerned, I really don't know how to answer your questions. From time to time I'll feel a homosexual urge or feminine urge or vice versa. As time has passed though, these feelings have become less intense."

The reason Cherie marked the letter "very important" is unclear. Perhaps she found it significant that Dwayne commented on characteristics in his dad's personality that he now found valuable or maybe she was relieved that Dwayne's feelings about his sexuality were no longer in the forefront of his thoughts. Dwayne had expressed regret in his lengthy letter, Cherie thought, but he still fell short of showing genuine remorse, and she didn't find Dwayne's explanation of the events the night of the murder particularly illuminating. In fact, she didn't perceive that Dwayne was accepting responsibility for his crime any differently than he had during his testimony in court seven years before when he'd blamed "the drugs." In this letter Dwayne had added a twist. He contended that he'd been influenced by "an outside power" that "was putting pressure on" him to kill his father. Cherie was puzzled and irritated by the claim. What was Dwayne alleging in this new assertion? Were evil spirits to be blamed?

When Cherie received a letter on December 12 from Clay Johnson, Deputy District Attorney for Josephine County, a possible motivation for Dwayne's emphasis on his drug use as an excuse for the murder became obvious. Ever since Dwayne's crime, Cherie had become well acquainted with staff in the DA's office. Recently, Clay Johnson had been her primary contact, and he'd called her to tell her to expect an important letter from his office. Mr. Johnson had asked Cherie to read through the information in the letter and then call him for an appointment to discuss the contents. The letter from Mr. Johnson said that Dwayne had submitted a commutation application and was appealing to Governor Barbara Roberts to have his sentence commuted. The enclosed copy of the application, dated November 22, 1994, was a five-page form summarizing Dwayne's crime and stating why his sentence should be commuted. Dwayne's answers to some of the questions revealed his plan to blame his actions on his drug use.

Q. Briefly and accurately explain the events surrounding your offense.

A. *I shot and killed my father while he was sleeping, with a deer rifle. I had a serious drug problem and was under the influence at the time. I was physically beaten by my father as punishment for my drug problem and became deathly afraid of him as a result. In my chemically clouded rationalization, I did not know of any other solution to end his physical punishments.*

Q. Describe your family situation and responsibilities.

A. *My mother and I are on speaking terms, although we've agreed that it's best that we each go separate ways. I am single.*

Q. The reason(s) for my application are as follows: Explain why you believe the governor should use her power to grant you clemency.

A. *I have learned how to work out my problems maturely. I know I'll never commit a crime again because I've corrected the aspects of my past self-destructive, antisocial behavior which ultimately ended in tragedy. The skills, treatment, and ambition to succeed, which I've acquired during my incarceration ensures my ability to be and remain a law-abiding, productive member of the community. I humbly ask to be released on parole in 2 years. This would satisfy the statutory minimum sentence as well as the newer sentencing guidelines of 120-121 months.*

With the possibility of release on the table, Cherie's fear of Dwayne occupied her thoughts. Donette was eighteen and aware of Dwayne's application for commutation. Both women were on edge until official notification came from Governor Roberts' office denying Dwayne's request and they could, temporarily, breathe a sigh of relief.

It was the week before Christmas when Dwayne was notified that his application for commutation had been denied. Nevertheless, he sent to Cherie what had become a regular holiday gesture, a pen and colored pencil Christmas card. Dwayne had drawn an image with candles and a red bow and had written inside, *"Mom I wish you a Merry Christmas and a happier New Year. Thank you so much for being my mother. In spite of everything bad in the past, you and Dad were the best parents anyone could have ever wished for and I'm thankful for that."*

Each year Cherie wrote far fewer letters to Dwayne than he wrote to her. It's apparent that the two communicated by phone, as Dwayne occasionally referenced a phone call in the letters, but there is no record of how frequently they talked or which of them initiated the calls. The first letter Cherie received from Dwayne after the 1994 Christmas card was four years later, on February 28, 1998. His note was short, condescending, and sarcastic. Presumably, he was irritated that Cherie had made little (or no) effort to stay in touch with him.

He wrote, *"I apologize for having delayed writing to you for so long. I know damn well that you care, otherwise you'd not have been so persistent in getting in contact with me. I sure hope I am not that big of a disappointment to you. It's really difficult in this place. You don't have even a clue as to what I go through in here. Yet I do the best I am capable of doing."* He said he was seeing two different therapists regularly and was taking Prozac for obsessive/compulsive disorder as well as for depression and anxiety. Dwayne told her that he was having another parole board review hearing in about a month. He'd been told that *"there are three people, who wish to remain confidential, and who do not want me paroled. It was suggested to me by one of the staff here that you and Donette were two of these three. Is this true? If so, why? Do you honestly think I'm some sort of monster who should rot in here? I did this crime when I was 16 years old! And here I am, damn near 30! What's more is I am quite capable of living a <u>clean</u> life on the streets."*

Dwayne reiterated how life for him was *"no country club,"* then reported that his television wasn't working and he had no money to replace it. *"I'd ask you for financial help but I know you and Donette won't do shit for me. It may seem trivial to you, but to me it's all I've got! There's nothing left for me in this hellhole. No matter how hard I try, they don't seem to want to give me a chance to live normally! So tell me what am I supposed to do? Pray? Yeah, right!... Anyway, I guess I'll write back if you respond."*

Shortly after receipt of the letter, Cherie sat down and scratched out a response. Twelve years after the crime, she found herself disturbed by reoccurring grief, and the ability to forgive Dwayne continued to elude her. She didn't appreciate the tone or implications of his last letter and she didn't hold back her thoughts.

She wrote, *"I have never stopped being a mother, but I still have lots of pain over what you did to Dad and it will never leave me. I will carry it to my grave. Life has not been fair to me or Donette but we have tried to learn to cope and it takes all the strength we have. But we're doing it and you need to do the same."* She showed no sympathy for difficulties he experienced in prison and wrote, *"Prison is supposed to be hard on you; it's punishment for what you did."* Mildly pleased he was in therapy, she thought it was good he was taking advantage of resources that would *"help you to cope and learn to deal with everything that you're having trouble with. Stick with it all, and learn as* much as you can to <u>help yourself.</u>" She wrote, "*Life itself is tough; even out here. I'm having a hard time making a living myself. I didn't ever plan on having to work. I was a housewife and mother. I worked at home. But that was all taken away from me and I was forced to get a job.*" She reminded him that on her birthday she would turn fifty-eight. She'd only been able to find work as a waitress. And while customers were generous with tips, she still made only $10 an hour. "*No one wants to marry a woman that has a son in prison for murder because they don't want to deal with the problems that come with that, let alone the problems of dealing with... when they get out. I'm really on my own. But I'm tough and I'll make it or die trying.*"

She switched the topic to his upcoming parole hearing and the subject of the three anonymous people who didn't want Dwayne paroled. She lied to him, anxious to convince Dwayne she had nothing to do with interfering in his parole review. "*I do not know anything about your file or the three people who wish to remain confidential and do not want you paroled. It is not me, and certainly not Donette. <u>Who was the staff there</u> that suggested this to you? I would like to know why he's saying this, also do you honestly think I have any say in whether you are paroled or not?*"

Cherie blasted Dwayne for his comments that prison was no country club, telling him she didn't feel sorry for him. "*Dwayne, I didn't have anything to do with you going to prison and as far as I know no one else did either. You created all this for yourself. Please stop blaming me or anyone else for what's happening to you. Dad was only 48 years old. He lost 40 or 50 years of good living because of <u>you</u> no one else.... No, I don't think you are a monster at all, but I don't think you have a clue either about life and living and what kind of life I've had because of you or you wouldn't have wrote a letter like this to me. You think you're the only one that has suffered all these years. Well you're wrong. A lot of people have and especially me and*

Donette. It's been real hard, but by the grace of God and His never ending mercy, I'm doing the best I can, and I don't complain. Without the Lord in my life I would not have made it. He gives me the strength and determination to keep going.

"Prison isn't supposed to be a <u>country club</u>; it's supposed to be hard and tough and you're not supposed to like it. You are in because of the wrong you did. <u>Punishment.</u> I didn't appreciate the anger and the swearing you directed at Donette and I and this kind of letter you wrote to me. You should be thankful to me that I even write you at all. I've been the best mother to you and you certainly don't deserve it nor do you appreciate all I've done for you. How dare you write a nasty letter like that to me. I am hurt and angry— hurt because you haven't got a clue, you don't understand at all. If you did you wouldn't write that Donette and I won't do SHIT for you. Just think back Dwayne. Of all I've done for you. How dare you. It hurts and it also angers me. I'm going to do one more thing for you but that's going to be the end of my doing for you."

Cherie reminded Dwayne of the $200 he'd sent to her for Christmas gifts. She was returning the money to him. She told him not to ask for money in the future. She was out of work and there was nothing extra for him. *"You have an attitude and it really shows. Yes, you need to pray and get your life right with the Lord. That will help a lot. And quit feeling sorry for yourself and start thinking about others and how you can help them. Take your eyes off of yourself. Reach out to others and learn to be kind and kind-hearted. Do good deeds. Help your fellow man. You'll see that will change you and you will not be so depressed. Light up your own life.*

"I can't get into your mind or know what you are thinking. But by the letter you wrote me, it shows no compassion or real understanding for what Donette and I have had to go through in the loss of Dad, only feeling *sorry for yourself and wanting us to do more for you, and being angry because we haven't. You have to realize that your pain and unhappiness is because of you and what you did, not us! Our pain and unhappiness is also because of what you did. And yes pray! Pray continually seeking God for His forgiveness. Try to make up for all the wrong you've done, be a better person. I wish what you did had never happened. Oh, how I wish it never happened. But it did and we're all paying for it literally. We have to live with the pain. You took a life. You have to give your own even though you were '16.' You knew it was wrong and you made the choice and now you're reaping the consequences. That's life. We all have to pay for the wrong we do at some point in our life. God is a just God. He is fair with us. But life isn't always fair. Love, Mom"*

Cherie had been furious with OSP personnel since receiving Dwayne's letter in which he claimed that "one of the [OSP] staff" told him that Cherie and Donette were trying to prevent his parole. This news alarmed and angered her. Who would have said such a thing? Cherie already feared the release of her son. If Dwayne knew she'd tried to keep him behind bars, and he was released, he would come after her and Donette for sure.

Notification of Dwayne's upcoming review by the parole board arrived in early April. The hearing was scheduled for July 28, and she was invited to attend the meeting in person or "appear" by phone. Thinking back to her correspondence with Dwayne about the anonymous person(s) trying to influence the board's decisions, Cherie sat down and wrote a brief note to the board. *"To the Board Members, first of all I would like to request that this letter and its contents be kept strictly confidential. As I do not wish to be present or on the phone, would you please send me an audio tape of the proceedings? Thank you. I do not want Dwayne Wier to know I am writing this letter. I still fear him. And according to the content in the letters he writes me, he should not be released. Thank you, Cherie Wier."* Hoping to make more of an impact, Cherie enclosed a copy of Dwayne's letter from February 28 in which he accused her of trying to interfere.

In the preceding months, Mr. Versteeg had sent what was labelled as confidential correspondence to the parole board as well as copies to the offices of the director of the prison and their records division. The privacy of these letters had been breached to the extent that Dwayne had somehow learned of their existence. The chief reason for the attorney's letters was to ensure his client's, and his client's daughter's, safety. Instead, the disclosure of the private communication had only increased the tension between Cherie and Dwayne and put Cherie and Donette at greater risk. Her fear of Dwayne heightened, Cherie composed a letter to Mr. Mitch Morrow, the current OSP deputy director, explaining how errors on the part of his prison staff had fueled the mistrust between her and her son and severely added to her and Donette's fear of reprisal. How was it, she asked, that Dwayne had been given any information regarding her and her daughter's involvement in information sent to the parole board? She told her story, desperate to have Mr. Morrow understand and appreciate her fears:

"I am his mother. I have tried to keep a rapport with Dwayne during his stay in prison, to encourage him and keep him going in the right direction, trying to cause him not to lose hope and that has been hard for me. Also, in the case that he was ever to be released, I didn't want him to have anything against his sister or I. So, I have tried to guide him and not get angry. But now I'm angry, and this is why. I've been afraid to write this letter because Dwayne is someone I don't know any more. When he shot and killed his dad while he was sleeping, I said I don't know him. I couldn't believe he could do such a thing, but he did. That's been 11 ½ years now and the pain and hurts are still there... My anger is not only directed at Dwayne but at someone on your staff. Someone has done a great injustice to my daughter Donette and I. To tell Dwayne that we are two of three people that are preventing him from being paroled? This person that said this is putting our lives in danger and that scares me and makes me fighting mad. I have worked very hard to keep a good rapport with my son.

"I have heard too many horror stories about prisoners getting out of prison and committing similar crimes. I don't want my daughter or I to be a victim again! I love my son but I fear him if he were to be out of prison because of the crime he committed. I would never be able to trust him again. But I want him to continue to have hope, hope that he may be out someday. Please find the staff member that is saying these things before he endangers others' lives, but be discreet. I don't want Dwayne knowing about this letter, its contents or that I sent you his letter. Please keep it confidential. Please respond soon, and do something about this. Thank you, Mrs. Cherie Wier"

She included a copy of the letter from Dwayne dated February 28, 1998, in which he'd described being told by corrections staff that it was likely that Cherie and Donette were affecting the parole board rulings.

Not long after Cherie mailed her letters to the Oregon State Prison and parole authorities and her letter to Mitch Morrow, she received correspondence from Dwayne that focused on his current health news and personal musings. He'd been transferred to OSCI after he'd been badly assaulted at OSP. Although he would have preferred to stay in OSP, he said he was going to try to make the best of his present situation. He told her the latest news about his kidneys wasn't good; according to the specialist, they were operating at ten percent capacity. This meant that dialysis would likely need to be started within the year. He admitted, *"That's really scary to me, especially as much as I can't stand needles."*

His writing turned reflective as he considered his life situation, saying he was more fortunate than many because, *"I have someone who cares. I'm glad you wrote me that letter* [referring to her lengthy, biting correspondence in early 1998] *because it has really made me think about a lot of things which I've neglected in the past. For this I am truly sorry. I never realized this before, but I feel like a real selfish jerk now that I see things from a different point of view. I'm sorry for directing my anger toward you and Donette. The reason I express anger is so I won't feel the pain. I try to camouflage my pain with anger because I'm afraid to feel hurt and ashamed to be hurt by my own cause. Does this make any sense at all?"* In the postscript he commented, *"Thank you for the money. I feel bad that I even mentioned it, although I do appreciate it very much."*

Cherie winced every time Dwayne asked for money. She was frugal by nature, but since Don's death, she'd had to be extra vigilant to limit unnecessary spending. Working at the Yacht Club for the past ten years had been a godsend. The patrons of the restaurant had tipped Cherie so generously that she'd been able to take Donette to Hawaii on her twenty-first birthday two years earlier. The Yacht Club had provided steady work and charitable tips but even so, Cherie's paycheck was below minimum wage.

During her years waiting tables, Cherie and Michael became close friends. Not only had she worked for him at the restaurant, but Michael was a building contractor by profession and had enlisted Cherie's help by paying her for labor on several construction projects. He recognized Cherie's work ethic, and he knew she could use the money. Besides, he frequently needed additional labor on his jobs, even hiring Donette to paint or stain woodwork. Michael exchanged the time Cherie put in on a project for a percentage of the profits he received after selling the renovated homes. The extra income allowed Cherie to have a sustainable living and kept her from losing her own property.

Whether Cherie was serving at the Yacht Club or running errands for Michael, she was tired when she got home and occasionally overlooked letters from Dwayne. When she opened Dwayne's card dated June 15, she read that his disease had caught up with him and that he'd been on dialysis for the past two months. He'd been referred for a kidney transplant. He wrote, *"It has certainly changed my outlook on everything!"* He'd been transferred back to OSP and said, *"I am trying very hard to turn my life around for the better. I have been making a serious effort to be a Christian."* He asked her to pray for him and reported another parole hearing coming up the following month. He ended his letter by saying that he'd selected this particular card because *"I mean what this card says. If I'm not mistaken, I have not said these things yet and it's been 12 years. I wish the best for both of you."* The inscription on the card read, *"We all make mistakes at one time or another. Some are small while others are large but, with forgiveness and understanding, they all become the lessons of life. I'm sorry—I hope that you will forgive me."*

When Dwayne appeared before the Board of Parole and Post-Prison Supervision in July of 1998, the board reviewed a document submitted by OSP. The correctional institution had given Dwayne a positive recommendation regarding his behavior during the period from December 1994 to December 1997. OSP suggested the board take into account inmate Wier's positive behavior when making a determination whether to consider a reduction in his sentence. Despite the favorable endorsement, as Dwayne reported the outcome to his mother, the board's action wasn't all that great for him. The board had the authority to release Dwayne or add to his sentence. They chose to reduce it by six months, which still meant many years before he would be free. Disappointed, Dwayne was resigned to the board's ruling. *"It's God's timing and no-other. That was the first time I've ever really had to explain what happened that night and it was quite haunting, to say the least. I cannot imagine my mind being so twisted and oblivious to reality, and yet it was."*

Dwayne's news reporting disappointment with his parole review was followed by the report of another setback when he admitted he'd been put in the hole again. This time he was disciplined for sending a card of encouragement to a nurse who had trouble accessing his vein at the dialysis center, adding that inmates were prohibited from sending personal notes to prison staff. Wanting Cherie to understand dialysis, he wrote explaining the process as he saw it. *"It's called hematolysis. It consists of 2 huge (15 gauge) needles being put in your arm acting as an inlet and outlet. It takes the blood from the body, runs it through a series of filters, causes changes in blood chemistry and then puts it back into the body. It's a treatment that I must go downtown for 3 times a week each for 4-hour sessions. It's a permanent thing. The only way I will ever be 'normal' again is if I have a kidney transplant. I have been referred for a transplant, but unless I actually have a donor, my chances are not all that great—especially being a prisoner. Eventually, when my kidneys shut down completely, I will no longer be able to urinate and will have to rely on the dialysis machine to draw out the excess water. As it is now, my kidneys function minimally. In other words, I am only able to pass freely a fraction of the amount of liquid I take in. It has really been a strengthening experience, ironic as it may be. Without dialysis, I would die within a very short time. I just put it in my mind that it'd take a whole lot more than that to bring me down. Thanks to the grace of the Lord, it has not broken me down yet."* Dwayne's surgeon told him bluntly that if he didn't have dialysis he would die. He admitted that as the doctor told him about how the vascular access operation would work, he'd started to cry, but then it was like he heard or FELT a voice inside telling him, "You are stronger than this."

The sensation of an inner voice rooting him on led Dwayne to thoughts of how his dad had responded to injuries sustained in his work so many years ago. He remembered his dad's hurt back, the time when a sliver of metal had lodged in his dad's eye, and the serious ankle sprain his dad had sustained when he jumped out the back of his work truck, landing on the uneven surface of a poorly maintained logging road. *"Dad was stoic when it came to such things,"* Dwayne wrote, remembering. Then he reminisced about when Don had cut the cast off his own leg and how he'd helped Don remove his stitches. His dad had been resolute and never let illness or injury keep him down. *"I find myself trying to be a man whom he'd have been proud to call his son."* Dwayne wrote on about memories and regrets, missing family. *"A lot of experiences I wish I'd never had, yet, these 'mistakes' and experiences have molded me into becoming what I am today and I am not displeased with the result. My regret is having to learn it all the hard way—the 'school of hard knocks' you used to say. And I never would listen. Even now—I still seem to always learn the hard way."* He said he believed his intentions were good and his heart was in the right place, though he continued to struggle with his choices. *"I've stepped onto the right path."*

Dwayne's search for meaning led him to investigate a wide range of spiritual paths as varied as Christianity, Buddhism, and witchcraft. He told Cherie he'd benefitted from reading publications written by Billy Graham, which he described as helpful. Delving into martial arts philosophy had taught him *"about discipline, responsibility, and assertiveness. I am no longer a passive, easily influenced, little boy. I'm a grown man and am finally capable of being me. I'm not afraid or intimidated anymore."* He wrote that *"homosexuality no longer has a place in my life,"* describing the behavior as *"one, among many, things I could've done without."*

As Dwayne assessed the condition of his life, he acknowledged his desire to make amends with everyone, admitting that, for the most part, the family wouldn't want much to do with him. He claimed that he wasn't a maniac but suspected that, if he were the one on the outside looking in, he would wonder too.

Ten days later, Cherie received another letter from Dwayne filled with soul-searching admissions. *"Been doing a lot of digging into the past... I was such an idiot back then."* He wrote of how he missed his mom and dad, and *"even Donette. I constantly am longing for that day when I'll wake up from this nightmare. In my dreams, it is as everything is okay; just like it was so many years ago. Yet I wake up to find that we are still caught in the reality of this nightmare. It just seems that it's rather backwards. I always thought nightmares were awakened **from,** not woken **to**.*

"There is certainly nothing which I can ever do to turn back time—though, God, I wish there were—-and we can only go forward from wherever we are. Sometimes I wonder if we will get a second chance. But, in a metaphorical sense, it is like a chess game. Which, actually, is rather similar to life. In the beginning, you have a whole board full of players and literally thousands upon thousands of different ways to go, all of which reap different pros and cons. The more mistakes you've made, the fewer players you have. Thus, the more limited are your options. Get in check enough times and one day you find yourself in checkmate... thus, another life wasted.

"Certainly, I wish I'd had the knowledge I have now back then! But none of us ever do. And to know it all from the beginning would make life rather pointless, yes? No goals, just boring routine. I can't help but wonder how things would've been if I had not have given in to the evilness of that day years ago. Without a doubt, our lives would have been so much better. The drugs were my biggest problem. I wanted to be on top of the world, wanted all my goals to just happen and skip everything in the middle. With the dope, I actually believed I could do this. There was a short time there when I could've pulled out of it... remember when I wanted to go into the Navy? I'd taken the ASVAB test at school and then had gone to see a Navy recruiting officer? The officer had called me back and wanted to meet with me

and you and Dad were against it. This was my way out of the downhill slope and when that door was shut on me, I went back to doing the thing I knew best—drugs and music. I'd always wanted to go into a military school, remember? It really would have been best. I'd had it in my mind that that was the only way I'd truly amount to anything. Deep down, I knew I wouldn't have gone very far in music. Music and the military were the two most consistent career goals I had. And the most realistic was the military.

"If you remember, that began in early childhood. Uncle Denny used to send me all sorts of stuff about aircraft because I wanted to be a pilot. But I was smart enough to know that my hearing, vision, and asthma probably would have prevented that. But an aircraft electrician I could have done. Remember my fascination with uniforms? From a very young age, I always wanted to be in a uniform. Be it Cub Scouts, a Captain Spock Star Trek wanna be, or a rock star. It was a statement to myself, more than anything, that I am Dwayne Dean Wier and I am about something! I'm somebody! When I lost this form of fulfillment, I turned to drugs and this brought back my sense of self-worth. Even now, I find myself focusing on a small array of things—and striving to excel in one or two as my 'uniform' of self-esteem.

"It's been all sorts of things over the years—most consistently martial arts and martial arts philosophy. The study of this has perhaps helped me mature more so than any other means. It's changed my whole attitude for the better. I think even Dad would be proud. It's taught me what I needed to know 15 years ago! Self-discipline, above all. The ability to commit oneself to the process of going from point A to point B. A clock will not succeed a single minute until it has exhausted all 60 seconds of the previous. Just like everything in life. You and Dad always told me that nothing is just handed over on a silver platter. And if it's *worth achieving, it's worth working for. I never listened and should have!*

"The Lord must have a more important task in mind for me to accomplish. I'm unsure of what it is, but I'll know when I face it. Anyway, I only wanted to share some of my thoughts and perhaps give you a clearer understanding of myself. I don't think I've really done that yet. Take care. I will be writing again soon."

Two days after Christmas a letter arrived; this one Dwayne had written with urgency, seeming to sense pressure to make his life matter and overshadowed by vast regrets. His tone reflected his fear that he was on borrowed time. *"How do I make things right? I'll never figure it out it seems. I do not even know how to make things right with myself! Let alone, you or anyone else. An utter embarrassment it is to even face the Lord in prayer. For it is he alone who created all of mankind, he alone who gives us the capacity to be who we are and the choice to become who we become."*

He wrote that God had given him talents that he'd wasted. *"I really need to get my life on track and figure out where I wish to go on the remainder of this short journey of life. I've yet to get a clear idea. All I do know, and all too well, is I've so far accomplished nothing; threw away thus far over 12 years of my life, along with endless opportunities to live as a proper Christian gentleman, and robbed yet another man perhaps 30 or more years of his life (which he probably didn't feel was fulfilled either) took away a sweet little girl's father (and quite likely traumatized her enormously being as how she discovered him) taking away from her the opportunity to have a father, taking away the husband of 24 happy years from a woman who undoubtedly was the best mother a kid could have hoped to have, bringing her own life to a screeching halt and turning her world upside down, and as in a chain of dominoes, expel myself as a son* to my parents, a brother to my sister, as a member of the family and from my own life.

"Do I have a rational explanation or some kind of half-assed excuse to why I decided to destroy our lives? No, I'm sorry, I do not. Although I so desperately wish I did have some kind of answer. Sure, I have come up with bits and pieces, many probablys and maybes some of which may even make a sliver of sense to one so inclined to seek the understanding of a truly twisted mind. However, nothing is really acceptable. So, with the absence of self-acceptance how can there be self-deliverance? How can there be self-forgiveness? Thus, how could I ever expect another to forgive me when I cannot even forgive myself...

"My life ended over 12 years ago. Since then I've been masquerading on one of life's many roller-coasters, which inevitably became merry-go-rounds every time. Discovering then what deja vu is. And here I am now, all these years later, and not 16 years old anymore, but nearly 30 years old... yet, still after all this time, 16 years old. Where do I begin? I'm trying to pick up wherever it was I left off and resume the stages of growth and maturity. The funny thing is that I'm really not all so sure where exactly it is that I ceased growing up. Perhaps, before even the age of 16, which inclines me to think that sometime during my childhood I took a left turn when I should've taken a right turn. This being the only way to really account for those mistakes I made as a teen. Always, with each wrong turn becoming more and more fatal. I was certainly climbing the ladder to the top which ironically, I'd always wanted to do, yet it just so happened that it was the wrong ladder, leading to all the wrong places. I often wonder how different everything would have been had I had the courage to stay on the right track.

"Courage because that is the strength to do what is right even in the presence of fear... It's about as smart as one who is about to begin a long journey across the land. One has *a vehicle in perfect working order and with plenty of fuel. Yet suddenly, for whatever moronic reason, the individual stops the vehicle in the street, gets out, and begins to walk instead and throws away the map as well. Real smart, huh? This person is me. Now I want to back track my steps and somehow reconvene with whatever it is I left behind or shut off all those years ago. Like I said, I know not where to look because I threw away the map as well. How do I find my way?*

"I'm tired of being a convict. I'm tired of playing the game and living a lie. I want to do what's right. I want to become a gentleman. A real man. A man whom Grandma would be proud of, a son whom a father would proudly declare his own, a son whom a mother would love. A man whom a woman would consider a wonderful husband and an outstanding father. Is this too high of an expectation for such a man as me?" He mentioned his desire to write a book, commenting that it might help him find the answers he was seeking. In closing, he thanked Cherie for always being there.

Cherie was pleased by the letters Dwayne had sent filled with what seemed to be genuine insight into his thoughts. As of late, Dwayne hadn't been hostile in his content; instead, he sounded as though he longed for atonement. He told her he was doing his best to try to make things right, not wanting to wait until it was too late. He asked her who she thought he should write to and mentioned he wanted to write to Pastor Ron Hayworth. *"Well, I hope I'm not overwhelming you with my letters. You know, I am truly sorry for not being a better son. I wish we'd been closer, and the same with Dad and Donette too. I suppose, in some way, I am trying to compensate for lost time, past mistakes, etc. And, although I can never turn back the clock, I believe I must do my best to make amends and set things right."*

By January of 1999, Dwayne was having dialysis three mornings a week and, with little opportunity to do much else, he wrote Cherie long letters that often included paragraphs of introspection. In one of these letters, he wrote of how he'd never fit in [with other kids] due to his hearing impairment and the physical restrictions of his asthma. Then he described his reasons for killing his father in a slightly different way.

*"Please don't misunderstand what I am saying here, Mom. I know you want the answers just as much as I do. That's what I'm searching for. I'm just trying to explain everything honestly. I'm tired of being a shithead and I want to turn my life around, and, to do this I must know **WHY** I've been a shithead. Something you probably don't know is that I was intrigued by evil and satanism. I remember a friend of mine had a Ouija board and we would ask it questions. I thrived on anything that could enhance the level of demon strength I could get. I used to make a show of breaking my albums and tapes to 'profess my reformation into Christianity.' But it was all a lie. I only did it because I was hoping to hear the demons tell me not to. I wanted their power so I could have what I wanted. And, of course, to discourage any suspicions of what I was really doing. It was almost as though I were craving to be destructive.*

"I was always afraid I'd be in a situation where I'd be hurt. I'd been beat on a number of times at school, called names, etc. I was ready for a weapon, so I always had either a knife, throwing star—ALWAYS. Even at school. I'd just do a line or smoke a bowl and I was ready to face anything. I think what happened is I convinced myself I was living in a dangerous world where everyone was a potential threat to me in some way...

"When I told the police that I didn't really have anyone in particular in mind that night... I said, 'just kill;' that was no lie. I'd just had it with everything. It wasn't anything Dad did, but he was there so it was typical of me to put all the blame on him; like a coward. Which is really what I was... I know I'm the one responsible for getting myself

into the mess we are all in; I'm just looking for solutions to make the situation better."

Less than a month later, Dwayne wrote of the solutions he was trying to find. *"The answers will come to me I know. I'm getting a little at a time just by getting this out. I have to tell you because I know you care. The therapists don't really give a shit—they just do what they're trained for. I'll figure it out...*

"While I'm thinking of it—sorry for taking that money out of your purse. Remember the $60? It was drugs, I had to have it, or so I thought. I treated you and Dad very badly. I don't know why...

"Please don't get all bummed out though by all this stuff. We aren't getting any younger, Mom, I want you to know that I am at least trying to turn my life around and have started to. And I will succeed this time—I've run out of options, you know. It's just so hard to do trying to find yourself, after you've been lying to yourself and playing charades your whole life. But I'll get it right, I promise."

The next month, Dwayne persisted in his efforts to understand himself and his desire to patch up, in any way possible, his relationship with family members. In that regard, Dwayne wrote to Cherie wanting her opinion. *"I'm feeling a need to send the whole family a letter just to say I'm sorry. Whether or not they choose to forgive will be their choice, but it'll be a big step towards forgiving myself, which I've not yet done. And there's no better time than the present to act. What is your opinion? Would it be a good idea or not?"* He said he'd started to read a book by Charles Colson titled, *Who Speaks for God?* He remarked that in 1998 Colson had done a fellowship at the prison. Dwayne had signed up for it and been called when the meetings were conducted, but he hadn't gone. He didn't know why; he just didn't go. He told her he was reading various Christian and spiritual magazines and books. He appeared to be searching for truth but didn't know where to look. He hoped he would recognize it when he found it.

Later in the week, Dwayne's letter carried on his reference to truth as he searched for meaning and spiritual understanding. He was struggling with what he called the "inner man" (a phrase used by the Apostle Paul in the Bible referring to the spiritual aspect of a person). Dwayne admitted he struggled knowing what he should do, what he knew was right, versus yielding to personal desires.

He wrote, *"In all honesty, I was never really serious when I've made a commitment 'to the Lord' before. In a sense, I wanted to, but not at the expense of my own desires. So, this being my first sincere commitment, I've got to say it has to be the hardest thing I've ever done in my life. I thought it'd be easy and it's just the opposite! I don't want to fail this time because I don't believe that the Lord is going to give me any more chances to come clean. He's given me too many as it is. This time he literally put me face to face with death and pulled me out of the life I was living; or rather, jerked me right off of my path, and opened my eyes and spoke to me. I heard him for what is probably the first time and listened and heeded his words. I know I'm on the right track. Yours, and others' prayers have not been fruitless. I suppose that the more I follow my drive to follow God, everything else will work itself out. Isn't this right? Anyway, every day is a bit easier, but far from effortless."*

On the bottom of the page were the lyrics to a song he'd written titled, "Father, Father."

Oh Father, Father
Where did I go wrong
what would it be like
if we could be back home
Father can you hear me
I feel so damn bad

for suddenly ending all ties
that we all should've had

Chorus
how do I set things right
how can I turn this around
how can I trade in my soul
to bring you back in our life
I'd give anything to go back in time
and do everything that is right

Through clouds of smoke
and strings of snow
all that'd mattered
was that future music show
I was really a fool
but thought I was cool
you tried to show me
like a son should be schooled

Chorus
It's over now
What can I do
I'm sorry Dad
can't live this down
I'd give anything
to make everything
all right

Dwayne had been moved to Snake River Correctional Institute, located in eastern Oregon, the largest facility in the Oregon Department of Corrections system. The prison was considered a medium security facility and new, having been completed a year earlier and housing 3,000 prisoners.

On March 24, Dwayne reported that the food at Snake River was terrific and the opportunities better as far as what was available. The downside was the inexperience of the medical staff in the dialysis unit. He complained of the repeated efforts of nurses to hit his vein, thus turning him into a human pincushion, causing his arm to swell fifty percent. He said he hadn't expected to be transferred to Snake River as the man (Scott William Cox) he'd testified against was also there. *"I'm not at all concerned about this either. I know there won't be any conflict. They sent him to OSP by mistake a couple years ago and I had the opportunity to talk with him. There's no problem. We aren't friends really, but we get along and all."* He'd recently gotten into trouble because he'd been part of a group smuggling tobacco and had been caught. Although he'd played a minor role in the incident, he'd been heavily disciplined and was trying to make the best of his penalty, commenting that he wouldn't allow himself to be discouraged.

Six weeks later, Dwayne wrote that he was still in Snake River and reported that he'd been reading his Bible and other Christian publications. *"There was a time when I would have been embarrassed or ashamed to admit to being a Christian or reading the Bible. No longer! I'm proud to be a follower of Christ! Thank you for praying for me Mom. You have inspired me in a lot of ways in which only a good mother can do."*

By mid-January of the new millennium, Dwayne was back at Two Rivers but his health was declining. In 1996, he'd been strong, weighing 200 lbs. and lifting weights. Four years later, the dialysis treatment and Alport syndrome were visibly taking a toll. He was down to 153 lbs. and his muscle mass had depleted. He was losing interest in exercise and told Cherie, *"The truth is I've just been lazy. They've been having a lot of problems with my fistula (that is, my access vein in my upper left arm). So far, I've had to have 4 angioplasties and am due to get another one. The problems are due to the carelessness of some of the dialysis staff I had at Snake River. I nearly lost my access as a result, which means I'd have had to have another surgery to have a new access put in my other arm. By all odds, I should've lost it even the surgeon who did the first angioplasty was 'absolutely amazed' that the procedure was successful. I know the prayer I said right before the surgeon began is the only reason it was successful. I hope I'll get a transplant soon so I won't have to go through all this. They haven't even put me on the list yet."*

Dwayne told Cherie that he'd begun a program named Pathfinders, a network dedicated to helping inmates. Thus far, Dwayne believed the program to be of personal benefit. He looked to his mom for discernment as to which religious program at the prison he should attend, telling her he didn't want to make the wrong choices, as he often did.

Dwayne ended the letter by disclosing his current battle. *"I've been struggling recently with the 'fag stuff' and even though it disgusts and embarrasses me, I still think about it and associate with those types of people, I shouldn't yet I do. Pray about this for me."*

CHAPTER 16 – A VISIT
AFTER TWELVE YEARS

When the phone on Cherie's bedside table rang before daybreak, the sound woke her from a deep sleep. The caller identified himself as a chaplain from OSP, then immediately apologized for the time of his call, explaining he had news that couldn't wait. Cherie sat up in bed, struggling to clear her mind. The chaplain told her the prison wouldn't notify her, but he wanted her to know that Dwayne was in a coma and had been rushed to Salem General Hospital. He characterized Dwayne's condition as critical and encouraged her to find a way to get to the hospital as soon as possible. The chaplain knew little else about the circumstances, only that the initial investigation suggested that medications had accidently been switched between Dwayne and another inmate. Cherie hung up the phone, frantic, wondering how she would manage to find transportation.

She phoned her friend Jerry who had been helpful to her since Don's murder and asked him if he would be willing to drive her the three and a half hours north to Salem. Hearing the worry in her voice, Jerry said of course he would, telling her he would be there within the hour.

Arriving in Salem, Cherie and Jerry made their way to Salem General's ICU. Cherie found a supervising nurse who told her that Dwayne was stable but still in a coma. She wouldn't be allowed to visit him in ICU and couldn't see him until he was no longer comatose. There was nothing to do but wait.

Fatigued from the car ride and disappointed that she was denied access to Dwayne's room, Cherie noticed a sign advertising a nearby Ronald McDonald House and approached the woman at the desk. Cherie wanted to be at the hospital if her son woke up, or... for whatever happened. Cherie knew the Ronald McDonald House provided rooms to families of sick children twenty-one years or younger, but Dwayne was thirty. Dwayne's age didn't deter the lady from helping Cherie. She said a room would be available that afternoon. Grateful, Cherie reserved the room, relieved that her housing needs were put to rest.

Before leaving the floor, Cherie checked back with the ICU nurses' station and was surprised to learn that Dwayne had been moved to a private room. He was still comatose, but knowing how far she'd driven, the nurse told Cherie that she could see him.

Twelve years had passed since Cherie had seen Dwayne. Her heart pounded as she stepped into the room. The unexpected presence of two corrections officers just inside the doorway startled her. Dwayne would have guards for the duration of his hospital stay, the men told her. Cherie explained that she'd traveled almost four hours in hopes of seeing her son. They said he was still in a coma and the rules prohibited them from letting her into the room. Dwayne would have to be conscious before she could see him. Disappointed, she left the room, letting them know she would be back in the morning.

Jerry drove Cherie the mile and a half to the Ronald McDonald House, dropping her off and handing her twenty-five dollars "just in case." Cherie thanked him and promised to call him with updates.

When Cherie arrived at the house, she was told that each room had a name. Her room was called Faith. Believing the name was a positive sign, she was reminded to have faith that Dwayne was going to recover. The former tenants of the room were leaving just as Cherie checked in and told her that they'd left food on several shelves in the cupboard. The leftover provisions were an unexpected blessing and, to Cherie, further proof that God was caring for her even in the smallest of details.

Cherie woke early the next morning, eager to get to the hospital. She walked the twelve blocks, stopping to pick up two cups of coffee in the hospital's cafeteria, then headed to Dwayne's room. Saying good morning, she handed each of the guards fresh coffee. Her demeanor disarmed the men to such a degree that they allowed her in the hospital room and in no time, the three were engaged in conversation. Cherie and the COs talked for hours during the next four days. Both of the men had known Dwayne when he'd arrived at the prison thirteen years before. They described him as "a different person" now. Cherie told them she'd noticed a subtle but distinct change in Dwayne's letters, although he was still unpredictable. Dwayne frequently wrote introspectively, she said, and he told of searching for spiritual understanding often commenting about others, not always focusing on himself. One of the guards said he was hoping Dwayne would pull through.

The men reminisced about Dwayne's early years and how he'd repeatedly instigated fights that landed him in solitary confinement. Did Dwayne end up in solitary because he was rebellious (as his psychiatrists had described him), Cherie wondered, choosing to push back against any rules or authority? Or had his aggressive outbursts been because he preferred isolation to living in the general population? Whatever the case, there had been one positive outcome of Dwayne's time in solitary. Years later, Cherie learned that it had been during Dwayne's confinement in the hole that he'd begun to read the Bible, the way a drowning man clings to a life preserver.

On the fifth day of her stay, Cherie entered the room and was stopped by a guard. He whispered that Dwayne had come out of his coma. She surprised herself by suddenly feeling awkward. Anxious about Dwayne's condition and fearful he might die while in the coma, more than anything, she knew she loved her son. The call from the chaplain had panicked her about his unconscious state and she'd rushed to be by his side. He was conscious now and familiar painful emotions began to surface. They'd exchanged at least a hundred letters since she'd seen him in OSCI. Inexplicably, Cherie felt as if Dwayne were a stranger. She knew she hadn't forgiven him and she still feared him. Hesitating, she looked into the room and saw Dwayne sitting on the side of his bed, his back to the door. His hospital gown gaped open, revealing a portion of a tattoo. Dwayne looked as though he was in conversation with the guard standing near his bedside and hadn't heard her come in. The guard looked up and seeing Cherie, he pointed toward the door and said to Dwayne. "Here's your mother."

The thirty-year-old man turned around slowly, weakened by unconsciousness, to face his mother. Tears began to stream down his face. He mumbled, "Mom, Mom, it's been twelve years."

Cherie, overcome at seeing Dwayne awakened from his coma and watching the tears on his face, faltered, looking for words as she crossed the room. Feeling slightly defensive, her voice quivering, she blurted out, "I know, Dwayne. But I couldn't reward bad behavior by traveling to support you when you were getting in trouble all the time."

The truth was that she hadn't been able to force herself to see him. His rambling letters and caustic allegations about Don's and her parenting shortcomings had devastated her. Where were the words to articulate her conflicting feelings? She couldn't reconcile the love she had as a mother for her son with the plethora of negative emotions she felt toward Dwayne that had started with Don's murder and deepened with the horrid letters he'd written to her over the years. How could she explain in a way he would understand?

But through the letters Cherie had begun to see a change in Dwayne. She went to him and hugged him, shedding tears of her own. Clinging to each other for several minutes, mother and son wept, lost in their separate feelings. Slowly, Cherie regained her composure. She apologized that she hadn't visited and sought to explain how, after the first visit, she couldn't make herself come back. Dwayne didn't comment. Instead, he asked Cherie to write more. She agreed to do her best. She'd traveled to Salem, Cherie told him, to make sure he was going to recover and had been at the hospital for the past four days, sitting in his room while he was unconscious.

Startled by the news, he longed for assurance. "Really?" he responded, genuinely surprised and pleased. "I'm glad you were here, that you care."

Cherie looked at him closely, seeing his vulnerability. She touched his arm. "I've always cared. I haven't been to visit because seeing you reminds me your dad is gone because you took his life. Facing that reality, seeing you in prison twelve years ago, and now in this hospital, is hard on me. I can't seem to help but take the grief of your dad's murder back home and then... I cry too much."

Dwayne looked at her sleepily, reacting to his medications. There was unmistakable sadness in his large, dark eyes. She told him how she felt badly for him. "But," she said, "you did something tragically wrong. Between the drugs, and the alcohol, and whatever you took before you shot and killed your father, that's something I haven't been able to get over yet. It's still hard on me. So, seeing you before just brought back everything. I couldn't do it, see you again, I mean. I just couldn't do it." She paused and looked at him intently, adding, "But when the chaplain called me and said you were in a coma, I couldn't stay away. I had to see you. I had to be here."

He remained quiet. He was weak, barely able to sit up on his bed. Cherie and Dwayne silently looked at each other for several moments.

Cherie broke the quiet, deciding to speak to him about spiritual matters, thinking now a good time to respond to questions he'd asked her in a recent letter. She affirmed the reoccurring message in her letters to him: the importance of studying the Bible. Cherie reminded Dwayne of the significance of prayer, encouraging him to trust that God has a purpose and a plan even when we don't see it and challenging him to believe that God can take tragedy and use it for good if we trust Him. Dwayne's depleted physical condition kept him from engaging much with her. Appearing to listen with interest, however, he rallied vaguely, his mother's presence acting as good medicine for his soul.

Cherie and Dwayne talked about what he'd been doing and how he'd managed to take the wrong medication. "Somebody switched it," he told her, though he couldn't grasp how it had happened. There was no further conversation about the crime. Cherie knew talk of Don's death would have stirred up too much for her. Instead, they discussed Dwayne's life.

The timing was right when Jerry showed up. Dwayne was weary, and the nurses had advised Cherie that he'd talked enough for one day. Dwayne and Cherie embraced, both full of sentiments, reluctant to let go of their time together and promising to improve their efforts to stay in touch. Cherie left the room, relieved that she'd made the trip.

When Dwayne wrote on June 12, it was his first correspondence with Cherie since their visit in the hospital. He was exuberant. *"Mom, I'm so happy that you came up to see me. It made me realize that I was so wrong about you. All these years I have felt like you just didn't want anything to do with me and that the only reason you wrote at all is because it was simply the Christian thing to do. Now I know how wrong I was and how very lucky I am to have you as my mom! I know now that you love me and I'm still your son in spite of all that's taken place and that means probably everything to me. I hated to see you go when you had to leave. It was the most comforting experience I've ever known—just you being there, being my mom!*

"I'm so sorry for putting you through so much. And I thank you for never giving up on me. I know I have treated you very, very bad at times. I'm terribly sorry for those things. I really miss and regret having thrown away these last 13 ½ years and the 16 years before that. I hope you can forgive me. I feel I've really been such a monster."

He went on to tell her that when he was released from the hospital, he'd been sent to OSP's infirmary. He expected to be moved again to OSCI when his health permitted. He wrote about the medication "mix up" that had landed him in the coma. He couldn't imagine how a switch could have happened because the distribution of prescriptions was done in a very methodical manner. He wrote details about how he managed his current medications and how impossible it seemed that there could have been deliberate tampering with them by other inmates. He reassured her that despite his drug abuse history, he wouldn't risk his health by taking pills that weren't prescribed to him.

Dwayne sought her prayers about the occurrence of very disturbing dreams that had consumed his sleep and shaken him emotionally. The dreams tormenting him had been full of evil, demonic images. While attending chapel services, he'd told Father Mike about the dreams and the priest promised to pray for him and said he would let the guys in the chapel know that Dwayne needed prayer. Dwayne said he was praying with increasing regularity and felt the occurrences of the nightmares had lifted somewhat.

He spoke of the night he'd been taken to Salem General and his belief that his cellmate Chris had saved his life.

He told Cherie that when he'd first started to react to the medication, he "*couldn't breathe. I remember asking him (Chris) to call the cop down because I was having trouble breathing. When the cop got there, I told him I can't breathe and he wasn't taking me seriously and started saying stuff like I took some speed, etc. when I was really trying to say I can't breathe. I remember Chris carrying me from our cell up to the officer's area.*" If Chris hadn't intervened, Dwayne told her, he probably would have died in his cell. With the delay in getting medical attention due to the CO not taking Dwayne's symptoms seriously, along with the intensity of the reaction he'd had to the meds, Dwayne felt it was a miracle he hadn't died. If there was an investigation into the incident to determine what medications had been switched or by whom, he never let Cherie know.

Grateful to be alive and appreciative of his mother's visit, Dwayne wrote paragraphs recalling details of pleasant childhood memories. He talked about specific places they'd gone as a family, fishing and camping trips, and boating on the river. He treasured every memory and regretted how he'd been as a kid.

Cherie and Dwayne corresponded regularly over the next six months. When Cherie opened a letter from Dwayne in January of 2001, she was upset by a disturbing medical update regarding his Alport syndrome. The progressive, degenerative nature of the disease required careful monitoring and treatment. Despite the best efforts of Dwayne's physicians, the insidious condition would suddenly cause new and horrific symptoms. Cherie never knew when a novel problem would strike and Dwayne would send her information about his latest hospital stay. The return address on this envelope indicated he was back at OSCI.

"*Mom, I apologize for not writing sooner. I was in the hospital from 12/18/00 to 1/5/01, in OSP infirmary 1/5/01 to 1/10/01. I had a bad infection above my new dialysis access in my leg. A fever of 105/106. It spread and ended up in my lungs. I was coughing up blood and black stuff. My face broke out in big, pus-filled sores (Type 2 herpes simplex) as a result of the infection. In a nutshell, I've got 9 lives! A gift from God, of course. They say I almost didn't make it again. I'm okay now. Getting better any way. Been on heavy narcotics for pain because of complications at dialysis (they tried using my old access in my arm and ruptured it). I was getting morphine and Percocet then Roxicet, then hydrocodone, now codeine. I've been sort of spacey, but the pain is quite a lot to bear still. I'm starting to doze off so I'll close."*

Dwayne's two-week stay in the hospital for treatment of the secondary infections had done him in. Recovery was painfully slow. Three months later, Cherie felt the discouragement in in the card that came. He wrote in small, cramped handwriting. *"I'm so tired of living a lie and trying to meet everyone else's expectations of me. Sure it's difficult for people to accept. It's difficult for even me to accept! The fact is, Mom, yes, I have what is called a gender identity disorder (also termed transsexual). For many years the few people I've been close to have known and still do know me as Denise or Dee for short. I tried to legally change it back in 1992 but I had nobody on the outside to post the notice for me. I had all the paperwork done and submitted to the court.... Thank you for opening up this door for me—I've wanted you to know and tried to tell you once before but I knew you had a problem with it so I remained Dwayne to you.... I'll write you a long letter this week though. I'll be happy to explain a lot of things. Love you, D"*

When the promised letter arrived ten days later, Dwayne had written on paper that was pink, thin and crinkly, like tissue paper. Desperate to have his mother understand his struggle, he'd included two pages from an unknown publication that defined transsexualism, in hopes the article could explain what he couldn't. He told her that his feelings were exactly like those described in the article and that he'd always experienced these thoughts. He explained that his confusion with himself was partly why he was a loner. He always felt out of place. He told her again of his enjoyment in wearing makeup and fixing his hair. He said it had nothing to do with sex or his prison environment, (responding to Cherie's implication that living with all males had influenced his behavior as he sought to find intimacy in a sexual encounter). He admitted to preferring clothes that had an effeminate cut to them and then thanked her for wanting to understand, adding that it meant a lot to him.

A conversation about Dwayne's confusion in regard to his sexuality wasn't the discussion Cherie wished to have with her son. She didn't understand the disorder that she'd never noticed in him as a youngster, and she certainly didn't grasp his attraction to feminine qualities. Dwayne was right. The topic was hard for her to hear about, and she would have preferred that he kept that portion of his life to himself. But she did know it was important that Dwayne believe she cared enough about him to want to understand his struggle. So, she did her best to listen to his explanations.

The first letter of the New Year brought more news about Dwayne's sexuality. The details were ambiguous, but he'd gotten in trouble again; this time the charge was sexual misconduct. *"Things are not going well for me at all. I try to do the right thing and all, stay out of trouble and every time it seems that some obstacle is always there to make my life difficult. I got thrown in the hole last night, accused of sexual activity, that supposedly took place while my cellmate was doing whatever he was doing close to my butt and I'm facing the opposite way with my back to him sitting at the table reading a magazine."*

Dwayne complained that all of his books and magazines had been confiscated. The books, he told her, were resource materials for his classes and included a workbook for self-teaching Spanish. To make matters worse he'd recently been told, on a medical front, that he had hepatitis C. *"I'm tired of everything and I simply cannot endure it any longer."* He'd made the decision to refuse further dialysis treatments and let the disease run its course. *"I don't know if I'm right with God—I'd like to believe I am, but I doubt it. All I know is that I want out of this miserable life."* He apologized for the contents of the letter and wrote, *"This is something I feel I must do because there's no other way out of my misery. I have kidney disease, hepatitis C, secondary hyperparathyroidism, myoclonuses. I can't hear worth a damn, can't see very well (20/50 or bouts with double vision). I have felt like crap ever since I started dialysis. I weigh only 133 pounds. My teeth are ruined, the enamel has been wore off the inside due to frequent vomiting. I've given up on the transplant now with the hepatitis C. I'm tired of trying so hard to not get very far. It's too much. It's a lot of things. I'm sorry Mom. I just see no way with which to resolve any of this. I love you Mom and you'll be in my heart always. I send my warmest farewell. Love, Dee"*

Even though Cherie found the contents of Dwayne's letters disturbing, she'd grown accustomed to reading of his emotional highs and lows and knew the prison staff wasn't responsive to hysterical phone calls from panicked mothers; however, as the trend of despair continued in his letters, Cherie began to take Dwayne's references to death more seriously.

He was still depressed a month later when he expressed discouragement with a disease that would never improve, the recent loss of his books, and his bleak perspective of life in general. He set out to put his affairs in order. He wrote to Cherie about sending her the power of attorney over his personal business, particularly relating to medical choices. *"You and only you have legal authority to make any medical decisions in the event I am unable to for whatever reason. If I ever go into a coma again or anything like that, please make your decision after seeking Dr. Richard Stor's advice. Only his. And my only other clause is please don't keep me on a machine if I'm totally dependent upon it to breathe for me, etc. Just make sure they make it painless. I know I won't make it too much longer—I can sense it. I'll write you again tomorrow I promise."* He wrote down the name and phone number of his therapist, Ann Heath. Since Dwayne had begun to organize his personal life in the case of his death, he'd made a practice of keeping Cherie advised of his key caregivers. Cherie noted on the envelope to call the therapist, writing next to the counselor's number that Dwayne was unusually depressed and crying out for help.

The fatalistic tone of Dwayne's letters and the inclusion of the power of attorney forms prompted Cherie to call his therapist. She cried while talking to the counselor, certain her son was suicidal. The desperation of her emotional phone call filtered down to Dwayne and, on February 21, 2002, he wrote to her. *"My counselor called me out yesterday and informed me that you'd called up here to health services and was crying and quite distressed. Mom, I am sorry. I had no intentions of sending your emotions into a chaotic upheaval. I don't want to be a burden or some type of disheartening cross for you to bear. I am more concerned about your well-being than I am of my own battles. Ms. Leigh, my counselor, was asked by medical staff to convince me to 'blanket over' the pain and 'paint a pretty picture of the situation so as to lessen your grief.' I told her, quite frankly, that I will not lie to you. Only because of the unpredictability of the present circumstances I'm facing, I just want you to know exactly what has happened and is going to happen. Particularly considering the bleakness of my health I felt compelled to be straight with you about things."*

Attempting to reassure her, he continued, *"Mom, please don't cry and worry, okay? I know God will help see us all through this. Have faith in the Lord. Have faith in me* because I too have faith in the Lord. Please don't cry over me mom. Easier said than done, I know. But hang in there, please!"

Despite Cherie's call of panic to the therapist and Dwayne's note feigning an emotional stability he didn't really feel, his true mental state hadn't improved. When Cherie opened another letter a week later, she was disheartened to read that Dwayne's depression had expressed itself in non-compliance as he reacted to an incident in his cell and, once again, landed himself in segregation. *"I was taken here yesterday because I supposedly refused to move, which is a damn lie. They wanted to move me from the bottom bunk to the top bunk so they could move this 300 plus pound black guy (whom I've never gotten along with) into my cell. I'm not even going to try to explain it to you you'll call up here and they will say I'm lying or whatever. I'm tired of this shit. I try hard to follow the rules. I have never knowingly or intentionally refused to obey any order given by staff, nor have I ever disrespected staff. I'm just a number to them that guarantees the allotment of a generous sum of money from the government. I'm tired of battling endlessly and getting nowhere. It doesn't matter what's right or wrong, I will always be wrong, alone and without support. I have compelling evidence in my favor—it doesn't matter because the system is corrupted."*

The last letter that Dwayne would write while at OSCI arrived on March 2, 2002. His circumstances, as well as his emotional state, hadn't improved. *"I'm sick, wasting away to just skin and bones. It won't be long before I check out, and I welcome it. It can't happen soon enough. I have no life, nor will I ever amount to much being totally dependent upon a machine for my mere survival. It's all pointless.*

"Eventually I will be transferred to Two Rivers Correctional Institution in Umatilla along with all the other dialysis patients. It isn't going to be a good thing but I cannot stop it. There's nothing you or anyone else can

do—I brought this all upon myself when I took Dad's life. I'm sorry for all I have put you through and hope you'll forgive me. Dee"

CHAPTER 17 – TRANSFERRED TO THE DESOLATE UMATILLA PRISON

On April 1, 2002, Cherie received notice that Dwayne had been moved to Two Rivers Correctional Institution (TRCI) in Umatilla, Oregon. The prison had opened in 1999 and housed 1632 maximum security inmates. To get to Two Rivers from Murphy would mean a trip of eight hours for Cherie, traveling up the I-5 freeway four hours to Portland and then turning east on I-84, which runs along the Columbia River Gorge separating Oregon and Washington. Cherie's friend, Katheryn, who visited the prison with Cherie, described the trip to Two Rivers this way:

> "Driving through Portland it is beautiful, green and foresty. You drive about 30 miles from Portland before passing Multnomah Falls, the fourth highest falls in the US. But as you go along inland, it gets sparser and sparser. Rocky cliffs butt up next to the road's shoulder on one side and the Columbia River follows the highway on the other. Then, without warning, it turns into wasteland, deserty looking. I'm traveling, or if anybody is traveling, excited to see a loved one, the excitement of going. Then all of a sudden, the terrain is just getting more ominous. It's getting more... where am I? Desolate. Then, where is this? This isn't any place I want to be. That was a shock to my system when going. Where is he? Where am I going? When I actually got to the prison itself

(and I have a picture of it) there is no grass; there's no anything. It's just all ground, barren, stark, ugly."

It would be during Dwayne's stay in this bleak wasteland, home of Two Rivers Correctional Institution, where he began to show some consistent positive change.

Two weeks after Dwayne was transferred to TRCI from Salem, he directed his attention to what he considered to be shoddy treatment of patients in the newly constructed dialysis center. Dwayne was incensed. *"The truth is this place violates the very dignity of human beings."* He was angry about what he considered substandard medical care and the recommendations a doctor had given him since his arrival. The clinic's doctor had suggested treatment that opposed all that Dr. Stor, Dwayne's longtime trusted doctor while at OSCI, had decided was best for Dwayne. Dwayne was particularly disturbed about the new doctor, whom he described as *"a little nerdy looking jackass."* To Cherie he wrote, *"This doctor was talking about the grafts (such as is in my leg) and he said they do not last very long and if I'm lucky I might get five years out of it and that I should consider having one put in my arm again. I said, 'no way. I won't do it.' What's more is they are decreasing any maximum potential in the life of the graft by using larger needles. They are using 14-gauge needles, rather than 15 gauge, thus, making a bigger hole. I do not believe I will live long enough to ever see parole or the outside world. I've already been on dialysis four years and I'm on my third access."*

By the time he'd been incarcerated a month at Two Rivers, Dwayne had filed a formal complaint with the Oregon Health Licensing Office (HLO) claiming hemodialysis patients at the facility were subjected to *"incompetent and unsafe practices."* To Director Susan K. Wilson of HLO, Dwayne wrote:

"As a hemodialysis patient myself, and having been educated and trained to safely practice self-administration of my treatments, I have become quite familiar with hemodialysis treatment protocol. Because I have reported this ongoing situation in good faith and have addressed the matter to you only as a last resort, I trust that this issue will be investigated and justice will prevail. Notwithstanding the hemodialysis patients concerned are incarcerated, the fact is that human lives are being placed in jeopardy as a direct consequence of unlawful conduct."

Later that same month, Dwayne forwarded to Cherie four letters he'd received, responding to the complaints he'd filed referencing hemodialysis treatment. Two letters were from the Department of Corrections, one from the HLO, and one from the Department of Human Services. Dwayne's accusations had caught the attention of all three agencies. After a short investigation, the determination was made that the corrections officer in the dialysis clinic shouldn't have been acting in a clinical nature in the infirmary even though he was under the supervision of medical staff while assisting. The administrator of the DOC's health services division admitted that *"the officer should not be participating in your hemodialysis care. I am also informed by health services staff, your grievance to them resulted in an immediate cessation of his actions."* Despite the fact that Dwayne's hand was slapped with the words, *"In the future, I encourage you to utilize the grievance process properly,"* he considered his efforts a victory and was rather proud of himself for bringing the safety practices of the clinic under the scrutiny of the governing agencies.

When Cherie had been notified of Dwayne's transfer to Two Rivers, she thought it was unlikely she would visit him now that he was housed so far away. She'd seen Dwayne in Salem, the year after the murder, when Katheryn had accompanied her. At that time, Katheryn had never imagined that fifteen years later she would be there to visit her husband, who was now also incarcerated. Since Dwayne and Katheryn's husband were both now housed at Two Rivers, Katheryn believed that divine intervention had provided a way for the two women to travel together for visits and proposed the idea to Cherie. Recent communication from Dwayne had been free of hostility and Cherie wasn't entirely opposed to the suggestion.

Katheryn and Cherie were companions on many trips up and down the state of Oregon visiting their loved ones in prison. Through their alliance, they encouraged each other.

As she entertained the notion, Cherie decided to get her name put on Dwayne's visitors list. To be approved she needed to submit an application and agree to a background check. Authorization would be completed within sixty days. Once Cherie was informed that her application had been approved, she half-heartedly consented to go to Two Rivers with Katheryn.

The 1988 visit to OSCI was seared in her psyche; it had been traumatic. "I was fearful of going up there," said Cherie. "But I thought, I've got to do this for him. I think I was fearful of just going to a prison, and it's so far away, and not knowing what he looked like, and what he was like. You can read a letter, but that doesn't tell you what the person is all about. I needed to go to know whether he was sincere about making a commitment to overcome the struggles within his being and that he was doing what he said he was."

As Cherie packed for the trip, she reread the visitors' dress code. She knew the rules mandated that women dress modestly. What hadn't caught her eye was the stipulation that ANY blue clothing for visitors was forbidden. In case of a riot, the guards needed to be able to distinguish the prisoners from the visitors. Wanting to be in compliance, Cherie double checked her bag.

On June1, 2002, Cherie and Katheryn drove the 400 miles to Umatilla, planning to be gone three days. They'd left late Friday, about 10:00 p.m., driving all night, stopping for gas and later at a rest stop to get presentable for the first visiting session Saturday morning. Afterward, they camped at nearby Hat Rock State Park and slept before going to afternoon visiting at the prison. Sunday morning, they would visit Dwayne and Katheryn's husband in the morning and drive back to Southern Oregon that afternoon.

After the nighttime drive to Umatilla, the first glimpse Cherie and Katheryn had of the penitentiary was a slight rise in the distance where an austere building stretched out low and long against the horizon. As they drew closer, Cherie was silent, amazed by the massive size of the structure. Surrounded by acres of sagebrush, the prison looked severe and dismal. When the women took the turnoff to Two Rivers, Cherie couldn't help but notice the vicious razor wire fencing that encircled the perimeter. As they pulled into the lot, Katheryn explained that the parking spaces nearest the prison were reserved for corrections personnel and visitor spaces were farther away from the prison's entrance. Bold lines down the center of the lots designated where friends and relatives were allowed to walk when approaching the building. Once on the grounds of Two Rivers, Katheryn advised Cherie that the visitor's every move is watched, and strict rules dictate all manner of behavior. To Cherie, the towering concertina wire enclosing the compound looked horrific.

Cherie climbed out of the car thinking about the prison's security cameras watching everyone exit their vehicles. Katheryn had warned her about the chaos. Cars rolled in, filling the parking lot, and people milled around, calculating the best approach to the prison's entrance. A crowd had begun to form, a narrow cross section of society, a majority of whom were hard looking and ill-kept. Visitors were prohibited from moving toward the door of the prison until five minutes before the designated time. Veterans of the visitation procedure waited at strategic spots. The weather conditions in this part of Oregon brought in gusty winds that blew off the Columbia River gorge year-round, but whatever the temperature, anxious relatives and friends, girlfriends and spouses with children, waited outside. Smokers took one last drag. Five minutes before the start of visitation, the groups stationed in various spots raced toward the prison's main entrance. About a hundred individuals jockeyed for position, vying to be first at the door, elbowing others to get ahead. Those who ended up near the back of the line became aggressive, thinking nothing of shoving others to improve their advantage. The visitors who didn't make it in the first group were packed in a small waiting area indoors. Three benches along the wall accommodated ten to twelve persons each for those lucky enough to reach them first and bold enough to hold their spots. Otherwise, there was standing room only. Since Cherie and Katheryn were there on a weekend, the room was packed.

Two River's solid concrete structure exacerbated the outdoor weather conditions. Sometimes it was so hot inside the prison that it was hard to breathe or, conversely, the air conditioning could be set to almost freezing, making everyone miserable. In the winter months, when the wind blew, it was drafty. Fortunately today, the temperature was mild. Entering the prison, Cherie stuck close to Katheryn as they stood in line. There were lines where the visitors showed their IDs and lines for metal detector screening. There were lines to remove belts, jackets, and jewelry, and lines to write one's name on a signup sheet with the exact time noted. Another line formed where visitors got keys for lockers to store personal items not allowed inside, and more lines took shape where visitors got their hands stamped. A massive steel door with bars opened into the adjoining area where each person's stamped hand was placed under a fluorescent lamp, verifying the completion of the process in the previous room. In room after room, ten people at a time, escorted by two guards, moved through the passages of concrete, steel, and wire. The air was rank with the unmistakable smell of human bodies packed together in the confining space.

The two women managed to push their way into one group, committing to remain together if possible. Katheryn stayed near Cherie, watching the bewildered look on the face of her friend as they moved through the commotion. The slamming of every steel door echoed, layer after layer of steel, barriers to the outside world. The reverberating hollow booms made Cherie shiver.

When they finally entered the visitation room, Cherie gave the officiating officer her name and told him she was there to see Dwayne Wier. Her heart pounded and she could feel sweat on her palms. She knew it was incumbent upon her to have complete knowledge of all of the rules regarding visitation. She'd been told that anyone violating the regulations would be singled out publicly and loudly humiliated by the guards. With the safety of visitors and inmates paramount in Oregon state prisons, there was no leniency when it came to following rules. The officiating CO noticed Cherie's flustered expression and gave her a subtle smile as he pointed to a table near the side wall where Dwayne was sitting.

Cherie squeezed through the crowd of visitors, making her way to Dwayne, who sat at a small wooden table about the height of a coffee table, designed specifically to prevent visitors and inmates from passing contraband to one another. The room was noisy. Some tables were placed against the back wall where inmates with children could sit in a group together. Several tiny rooms were partitioned by bullet-proof glass where prisoners talked on telephone handsets to loved ones. All of the activity created bedlam and for the first time, Cherie realized that visiting wasn't going to be an opportunity for private conversation as she'd hoped. Knowing they were being watched by cameras and guards, and that every movement was subject to scrutiny, she was on edge, fearful she would do something wrong. But despite the nerve-racking noise and uneasiness, she managed to gather her thoughts, take a deep breath, and look intently across the table. She couldn't believe that she was sitting with her son. She'd imagined how he might have changed in the two years since she'd seen him in the hospital. When she'd visited Dwayne at Salem General she'd focused on how weak and pale he seemed, but now it was Dwayne's countenance that she noticed had changed dramatically.

"And when I went there, it brought tears to my eyes. He was totally different. He was meeker, and he wasn't trying to put on any airs, like Dwayne knew that God was helping him, and He was transforming Dwayne little by little."

Even though Dwayne's hearing impairment made conversation particularly difficult for the two of them, and in spite of the boisterous voices on all sides, conversing with Dwayne wasn't as forced as it had been both times she'd visited him since his incarceration. Cherie talked with him regarding his health and hers, the Applegate property, and spiritual matters.

"Dwayne was quoting scripture and easily found references in the Bible I'd taken off the nearby shelf. It was unbelievable. I really was amazed. And that made me know that the Bible studies that he'd been taking had helped him. I believe he was wanting to hear from God and I think God was speaking to him."

When the time was up, Dwayne and the other inmates remained seated at the tables while Cherie filed out with Katheryn and eight others. The process of moving small groups from one secure area to another was time-consuming. Cherie waited in line and for the first time surveyed the room. She noticed that the inmates seated at the small tables all wore denim jeans marked with large, round orange spots at the knees. The prisoners' shirts and sweatshirts had similar orange circles on the left upper chest as well as in the middle of the back. Confused by the deliberate markings, Cherie asked Katheryn about the circles. Katheryn explained that they were targets on the men's clothing in the event of a riot and the guards had to use deadly force for suppression. If an inmate was hit on a knee, he would go down; a hit to the upper body was intended to kill. Cherie was horrified by the thought. She knew the prison was full of convicted men, all of whom were considered a danger to society, but knowing the purpose of the circles on the prisoners' clothing made her cringe as she thought of the ever-present possibility of violence within these walls. Once all of the visitors had been escorted out, the inmates would be moved back to a holding area, searched, and returned to their cells.

Going to see Dwayne had been a good decision, though Cherie was terribly tired afterwards from the emotional energy she'd spent to get through the process. She and

Katheryn camped at the nearby state park. Enduring the same hectic process twice more over the next twenty-four hours, Cherie and the Katheryn took advantage of both visiting sessions, doing their best to have meaningful conversations in the deafening environment.

After seeing Dwayne at TRCI, Cherie started to write to him more often. Once she'd visited him, it was easier for her to believe the positive changes he spoke of in himself were genuine.

When Dwayne wrote to Cherie in August, he referred to her visit in early June, telling her, *"I look forward to seeing you again. Our last visit meant more to me than mere words could ever describe. I want to make the most of this reunification between us, I don't want either of us to be in a position to harbor any regrets in hindsight. We can't go backwards, so we must go forward. I feel that this is what the Lord has intended."*

Then he surprised Cherie by bringing up a subject he hadn't written about for some months. *"I have kept my identity issues under a tight wrap since I've been here for a number of reasons. Only the therapist knows. I chose not to allow it to become common knowledge so that it doesn't become an interference to any aspect of my life or anyone else's. Besides, it could potentially adversely affect my credibility with the courts and in relation to my legal matters in general, and I simply cannot afford this to occur no matter how remote of a possibility it may be. Going back to the identity issue, I think that it is likely to remain unresolved for reasons I will not be able to overcome."*

Redirecting, Dwayne reported that his name had finally come up on the list of inmates who would be called out for religious services. He'd petitioned to be added to the group shortly after arriving at TRCI in April. It was now August and he was pleased to tell Cherie his request had finally been approved.

A reoccurring theme in Dwayne's letters through the years had been to vent to Cherie his complaints about life in prison and, in response, Cherie had encouraged Dwayne to educate himself on Oregon law. She told him that if he had troubles in prison, he would need to find ways to advocate for himself through the legal system. Dwayne took this advice to heart and, believing he had an aptitude for the work, was using his acquired knowledge to help himself and others. At the end of June, Dwayne sent his mom information regarding court cases he'd filed on behalf of other inmates. The documentation showed responses to his filings. Proud of his work, Dwayne asked for financial help from Cherie so that he could sign up for a correspondence class in legal work. He knew she didn't have extra money to send him, but wanted to let her know that he continued to pursue his learning, telling her that legal work was his calling and it was a way for him to help others. Dwayne had begun to be recognized as a jailhouse lawyer among his peers.

While Dwayne advised inmates on legal matters, Cherie found the system on the outside working in her behalf. Victim Notification About Offenders (VINE) was implemented by the Oregon Department of Corrections in mid-2002. This system provided her with notification anytime Dwayne was transported out of the prison for any reason. Cherie had harbored fears, especially during the early years of Dwayne's incarceration, that he would somehow escape or be released without her knowledge and would unexpectedly approach Donette out in the community. The services that VINE provided gave Donette and Cherie a newfound sense of safety. The notification afforded another benefit for her. Prisons don't report medical transportation of inmates to relatives but as part of the VINE, Cherie was alerted whenever Dwayne was moved and knew when he was transported to the hospital.

Fortunately, Dwayne's medical condition had stabilized in recent weeks and he hadn't required hospitalization. Instead, he'd been able to concentrate on providing legal help to fellow inmates and, he told Cherie, he was itching to be able to attend chapel services. Since he'd had access to religious services at Two Rivers, he wrote to Cherie of a renewed interest in his spiritual life. His childhood roots were nondenominational Christian, but Dwayne began to delve into a variety of faiths, questioning doctrines and examining their differences. He met a Pentecostal chaplain named Bob Lovett, whose support affected him deeply. For the first time in his adult life, Dwayne wrote to Cherie that he felt a personal connection with God. He continued reading his Bible and completed multiple correspondence courses on Christian doctrine. He looked into Mormonism, Jehovah Witness, and Catholicism. Jeanine Lovett, Bob's wife, worked as a corrections officer at Two Rivers. She recalled that Dwayne was in the mix of inmates who attended chapel regularly. Her husband interacted with Dwayne often because Dwayne would approach the chaplain after services to ask him questions. Answering Dwayne as best as he could, Bob took note of Dwayne's insightful inquiries and his professed desire for a deeper understanding of Christian teachings.

During the summer and fall of 2002, the letters Cherie received from Dwayne were stuffed with worksheets that demonstrated Dwayne's ongoing interest in spiritual matters. Besides his written correspondence to her, Dwayne included pages that looked like Bible study notes. He knew that Cherie would be pleased to see what he was doing and that he was honestly putting in effort. Well acquainted with Dwayne's unpredictability, Cherie cautiously waited to see if his interest continued. "And it did," she commented. "One class led to another. Everything started changing with him, he started becoming a better person. He could write a letter to me and I could feel the heart in there." Looking over the content of Dwayne's letters in 2002, she pointed out that, "Some of them were really good. You could tell that the heart was changing… and even though he probably still had somewhat of a personality disorder, the Lord was helping to make that lesser and lesser every time I heard from him."

As Cherie witnessed a subtle difference in Dwayne, she noticed change in herself. "More and more I was able to forgive him. I knew I needed to forgive him to be able to move on." Dwayne had apologized and seemed remorseful, but Cherie responded with wary optimism. Where would they go from here? Could she really trust him?

Dwayne told his mom that he regularly met with Chaplain Bob Lovett at the Pentecostal church services and that Bob's wife Jeanine saw him daily inside the prison's housing unit. Mr. Wier, or Wier, as the officers called him, was an inmate on unit seven. The Oregon Department of Corrections requires head counts every day in all state prisons. During the checks, each inmate must be in his assigned cell while the officers take a count of every man in all units.

One evening, while Officer Lovett passed by Dwayne's cell, she saw he was wearing a skullcap and demanded, "Why are you wearing that skullcap, Wier?" Lovett knew that Dwayne was familiar with the rules prohibiting him from wearing anything that covered his head or face. "You cannot have that on."

"Well, I'm so cold," said Dwayne.

Officer Lovett didn't know that Wier was sick with Alport syndrome, but even if she'd known, his illness wasn't her business; her job was to enforce the rules. Appreciating that the facility was bitterly cold and taking pity on Wier, the CO didn't confiscate the cap. In fact, later during her shift, Lovett sought out the captain to secure permission for Dwayne to be able to wear it. She understood that if someone were ill in the frigid conditions, a skullcap would help keep in body heat. The captain was persuaded by Officer Lovett's petition and made the allowance for Dwayne to wear the skullcap at night. Surprised and appreciative of the gesture, Dwayne wrote to Cherie telling her how Officer Lovett had advocated for him. As Cherie read about the CO in Dwayne's letter, she couldn't have imagined that several years later, that very same Jeanine Lovett would open her home for her and Katheryn to stay while visiting their loved ones at the Umatilla prison.

Although Dwayne had been admonished by Officer Lovett for disobeying the rules, in every other regard his improved behavior had kept him out of the hole. He divided his time between attending religious services, working on his correspondence courses, doing research in the law library and undergoing regular dialysis treatments. He frequently busied himself by writing to Cherie but in October of 2002, Dwayne penned a letter to his sister. He hadn't written Donette in years and he longed for her understanding.

"It is not my intention to unearth the past and bring back the pain of years past. I simply want to avoid leaving matters unattended. With my health the way it is, two near deaths [scares due to episodes regarding his Alport syndrome] *have taught me that anything can happen at any time. The Lord has allowed me to survive against highly stacked odds for a reason. Though I don't know for sure, or understand his reasons, I do know that I must not only repent and seek forgiveness from the Lord, but also from those of whom I have harmed during my life.*

"My point is that I am quite proud of what you have accomplished and of the woman you have become. Daddy would have been proud of you, Donette. The good Lord has blessed you greatly.

"The one question that I do not have an acceptable answer for is, "Why?" All I can do is speculate. I can assure you of this however—I do not now, and I did not

then, hate Daddy. Nor have I ever hated you, Momma or anyone else. My perceptions of things regarding Daddy and I, my judgments, interpretations, my fear, were drug-induced. Not imaginary, but enhanced tremendously and misunderstood. This, in conjunction with my already inferior feelings, is what prompted me to take Daddy's life. He was doing only what he believed was best for my sake and for the family's sake. I did not see it like this though. In my eyes I felt like Daddy was trying to hurt me. In addition to this, I wrongly faulted Daddy for my own insecurities. I blamed him for not making me into a better person—like him—but, of course, I never asked either. I merely expected that he would know this, but naturally he didn't and couldn't have. I'm sure you've been told a great many stories about 'why' over the years. Some may have some relevance; most are probably way off base.

"Sis, I do not expect you to write back or anything. I just wanted you to know that I'm sorry and my heart goes out to you. You are and will always be in my prayers. I have no intention of intruding into your life. I just wanted to say I'm sorry and that it is sincere. I love you, Sis. PS Thank you for taking care of Momma all these years. Best Wishes, Dwayne"

A month later, Dwayne wrote to Cherie about his letter to Donette. *"I remember she was always a little genius or something close to that. She had a very strong sixth sense (or intuitiveness). As an individual she always had a remarkable amount of personal power, far more than most adults."* He expressed the hope he had that Donette would write him back, but understood if she didn't. *"Please pray for me about this; about everything really."*

Dwayne's letters continued to be full of reports about his spiritual growth. He didn't complain about altercations with other inmates or disputes regarding the infirmary or with COs. He wrote, *"I feel like the Lord is really touching my heart. I started a correspondence Bible study. The Lord blesses me daily in many ways. I stopped asking for healing or other favors—instead I pray for others."* Near the end of the letter, Dwayne asked for $260 for a guitar. *"I know this is way too much money for you to afford and I certainly can't ever buy one on my own. But this would mean a lot to me and it would be used to play worship music. Is there any way you could ask anyone you know to pool together enough money to make this happen for me?"*

The following month, Dwayne's letter again spoke of his efforts to grow spiritually. He told Cherie, *"Mom, I'm truly trying to live the life of a good Christian. Walking the walk and talking the talk. It's much more fulfilling than being the real butthead I've been for so many years.*

"A friend of mine passed away last week. He was on dialysis too. I prayed for him several hours before he died. He and I had become fairly close. He was mostly confined to a wheelchair, although he was able to walk short distances with a walker. Everyone on dialysis here seems to be going downhill in their health, me included. The only reason I've made it this far is because the Lord has a plan for me. No other reason is probable or would make any sense." Dwayne wrote again about wanting to pursue work as a paralegal. *"It's challenging, rewarding, and very fulfilling. Plus, I'm helping people and that's a good thing."*

Watching the death of his friend made Dwayne realize that he might have little time left to connect with estranged family, so he decided to write his Uncle Bob, one of Don's brothers. Unlike most of Dwayne's letters that were hand-written, the letter to Uncle Bob was one of the few he typed. (In a subsequent letter, Dwayne did confess that the use of typewriters and computers was restricted to tasks such as preparing legal documents. Office equipment wasn't allowed for personal use.)

"Dear Uncle Bob, Mom told me about your cancer. I'm sorry to hear that. You are in my prayers.

"There are no words nor logic to explain away or to otherwise justify what I did 16 years ago, but I will try to explain what was going on in my mind at that time. In no way was Dad a bad father; if anything, he was too good a father. He always spoiled me, even when I didn't deserve it. The one thing I never learned and could not get him to teach me was how to face my fears and not be a coward every time troubles would come my way. Be it problems with kids at school or whatever the case was, I always ran home to Dad and he would take care of everything for me. When I got into physical confrontations, I would become too petrified to defend myself and would again run home crying to Dad, knowing that he would protect me.

"This was the heart of my problems. Certainly, drugs and alcohol use played a big role in my perception of everything, but that came later on. It was my way of self-medicating. I felt like I could face anything and all my fears were conveniently subsided and I could then carry on. But all that this accomplished was sweeping everything under the rug.

*"I felt very inferior as a child. I was hearing impaired, had asthma... I missed out on a lot of things for those reasons alone. Hearing aids only made sounds distorted, louder; I could **hear** fine—I just couldn't **understand** what I was hearing. Then there was the asthma—the medication helped a little but I was still the only kid in P.E. class who couldn't even do one pull up, let alone perform well in any other kind of physical activity. I was defensive bench warmer in football at Lincoln Savage Middle School...*

"I often felt as though I were some kind of a freak.

*"I tried to compensate for this by assuming an outward appearance of importance. I did this through wearing various types of uniforms, such as Cub Scouts, military surplus, Mr. Spock, etc., etc. in a feeble attempt to seem important, that I was **somebody**. The one thing I did do well was music and nobody seemed to care or accept this. At*

one point, I did become very interested in enlisting in the Navy and did exceptionally well on the ASFAB, but I had no support in this either.

"However, illogical as it is, I blame Dad for not being the mentor that I longed for... for not teaching me how to be man enough to handle myself and make him proud. Instead, I was always a "Mama's boy.. Back then, I was ashamed of this, however, I am not anymore. Donnette was always a 'Daddy's girl.' I always held this against them.

"In no way do I mean to imply justification of any of my wrong doing. If I could undo what I've done, I would give my soul to do so. I cannot even fathom what it must have been like for the family all these years, especially Mom and Donette. I thank God for giving them the strength to carry on.

"There is nothing I could ever do or say to express my sorrow for what I have done. This crime will haunt me for the rest of my life as it has done for the past 16 years. I'm not the same person I was back then. I've given my life to the Lord and do my best to live for him each day as a good Christian... not something to do when Sunday rolls around, but rather everyday all day. Too often in this life, circumstances have a way of prevailing over the proper timing of emotional expressions; that is, wishing one could turn back the clock and say what has then become too late to speak. Since beginning hemodialysis four and a half years ago, I have had a few close calls with death and the Lord has rescued me and carried me through each time and protected me from being consumed by the evil I had been living.

"Death cannot be counted on to delay itself for the convenience of those of whom have a scheduled appointment with it. I therefore do not want to further postpone what I should have said years ago and is long overdue."

Dwayne scribbled a postscript on the back of the letter recalling specific fond childhood memories he had of his Uncle Bob. Moved by Dwayne's candor and plea for forgiveness, Bob began corresponding with his nephew. The two continued to write, and on occasion they spoke by phone. Bob even filled out an application to be included on Dwayne's visitors list. He was approved, but it's uncertain if he ever made the trip to visit Two Rivers. Many years later, Bob sent his original letter from Dwayne to Cherie so she could read what Dwayne had written to him and understand why his attitude about Dwayne had changed to the point where he, too, desired reconciliation.

The day after Christmas, Dwayne wrote of more good news. He was ecstatic to report that he'd received money from church members at the Calvary Chapel in Grants Pass. The funds, he wrote, were so he could purchase a guitar, a radio, and a set of headphones. He was excited to buy the items and promised Cherie that he would play music for worship and to encourage others. Dwayne told Cherie that he was looking forward to starting an eight-week Bible study program with several like-minded Christian brothers. Then he enthusiastically described the recent services he'd attended. The program was called Lighthouse ministries. *"It's a wonderful service! Truly amazing! The services are unlike any other I've attended. It's the most fun and joyful event of the week."* Receipt of Dwayne's upbeat letter describing his pursuit of spiritual growth was a welcome respite for Cherie.

New Year's Day of 2003 had come and gone. When Dwayne wrote to Cherie in early February, he was philosophical, wistful for times gone by. *"My greatest regret is that I didn't open up to you years ago. I wanted to follow in Dad's footsteps and try to learn how to do what he did. He taught me some things about welding and how an engine works.*

"Why didn't I pay more attention rather than being so selfish and irrational? When I used to always do the wrong things, it wasn't that I simply disregarded the consequences

at all... the reason was that I never believed I'd get caught, for anything. The more I got away with the more confident and arrogant I became.

"There are times that I tried hard to impress you and Dad but I had so deeply destroyed my credibility with you both that it was only natural that you questioned my sincerity. It wasn't your fault, it wasn't Dad's fault, it wasn't Donette's fault, it was my own doing. I spun my own web and got stuck in it."

CHAPTER 18 – READY TO BE RELEASED ON PAROLE

During 2003, Dwayne wrote Cherie twenty-four letters, attended fifteen church services, and due to continued good behavior, spent no time in the hole. By the first of May, he was still longing to receive a response from Donette to the letter he'd mailed to her seven months earlier. When he initially wrote to her, he'd been anxious to hear back from Donette, hopeful, though not expectant, that she might not be averse to some kind of a relationship with him, but in mid-May when Dwayne wrote to Cherie, he said he'd been disappointed by the content in the letter he'd finally received from his sister. Unbeknownst to Dwayne, Donette had overheard her mom talking about Dwayne studying handwriting analysis, so when she finally decided to write back to Dwayne, she typed her response. She wasn't going to give Dwayne any opportunity to scrutinize her penmanship and formulate an analysis of her personality. The letter was dated March 2003.

"Dear Dwayne,

I originally wrote this letter back in October, so I'll have to edit it a little bit. This is in response to the letter you sent me. You're right. The apology you gave was very overdue and no apology will ever mend my broken heart. I've often wondered how things could have been different if someone else would have been home that night (like me). Would you have killed me too? Maybe, maybe not.

"You'll never know what it was like for me at 10 years old to come home from having a fun time at my friend's house and find my dad dead—murdered! Blood all over the bed, walking over to the other side of the bed to touch his arm, only to find it cold and stiff. I knew he was dead and I knew that obviously someone had killed him, but I never once thought it was you. I didn't find out that you were the one that had killed him until a few days later. I'm not sure even who told me but I remember Mom telling me I had to go to court to testify against you. That alone was probably one of the hardest things I've ever had to do—and at only 11 years old. Do you even realize that every year on my birthday I think about all of this? After all it was only 3 days before my 11th birthday. I don't think you ever really thought about anyone other than yourself.

"You know when I tell people my story about what happened to my dad, the one question they always ask is WHY? Why did your brother do such an awful thing? And you're right again, I don't know. It's been what, almost 17 years and I still don't know why you did it. The excuses you've told Mom I don't believe. The drugs—BULLSHIT. The 'personality disorder'—BULLSHIT. What kind of drugs were they? I've heard you took a combination of marijuana, valium, beer, and maybe crank or something. Those are all downers. They don't give you the nerve to kill. They may have enhanced your warped sense of mind but I'll never believe it was the drugs that you took that night that sent you over the edge. You need to come up with a better answer than that for me. And you probably don't have a better answer at least not one that I'm going to buy.

"I don't know much about your illness that you have now because I don't care to know. Mom tells me that it's some kind of rare kidney disease and you have to have dialysis treatments frequently, but that's about all I know. I truly believe that what goes around comes around and maybe it's

your turn to suffer now. Now it's your turn to feel pain for all the pain you caused so many people.

"Maybe you're right about God allowing you to stay alive for some reason. Maybe I'm one of the people you need to make peace with. But if your letter was an attempt to do that, then maybe you should try again. Because I'm not sure I really have forgiven you yet. Deep down, I have not yet come to peace with the fact that you killed my father.

"I know with God's help and more time I will forgive you someday and come to peace with it, but I'm not ready to do that yet and God hasn't put it on my heart to do so. Your letter didn't give me much insight into what really went on in your head that cold October night, but thanks for trying to apologize and I'll try to forgive you soon. I also don't understand your thoughts regarding Dad and your inferior feelings, bad judgement, poor interpretations, etc. What exactly was it about you or your feelings that were misunderstood? And what prompted you to take Dad's life? From what I understand, Dad was talking to Mom on the phone while you were getting the gun, loading it, and putting it in the bathtub. What was going through your mind while you were waiting in the bathroom? According to the reports and the attorney, this was premeditated. You thought about it, you worked it out in your mind about how and what was going to take place. Sorry to bring all this back to life, but you did open the can of worms and I do have a lot of questions and unanswered issues about that last day.

"In response to the part about taking care of Mom. That hasn't always been easy. I remember days when I would come home from school and I would find Mom still in her pajamas. One day she was sitting on the kitchen floor in tears. There were many days when she just wasn't able to get up and get herself dressed and going for the day. Those were hard days. I felt like I was the mom and I had to take care of her. I had to be strong for her otherwise we would have both fallen apart. I was afraid to cry in front of her for fear she'd start crying again. So then she thought I wasn't dealing with the whole issue of losing Dad. She made me go to some counselor at school that didn't help me at all. I did deal with it in my own way. There were many nights that I cried myself to sleep alone in my bedroom. And I had lots of friends that I talked it through with at school.

"I think Mom told you that I still live at home. That's really not true. The truth is I don't want you to know about my life now. I don't consider myself as having a brother and there is no need for you to know about me. Sorry to be so cold but I don't want to be a part of your life and I don't want you to be a part of mine. I don't know who you really are Dwayne. It's been so long since I've had any contact with you that I just don't really acknowledge that you're my brother. To me, you're just the guy who killed my Daddy. Someday I hope that with God by my side and Dad in my heart that I'll find it in me to forgive you. Keep praying for me and I'll try to do the same for you because we all could use more prayers. With prayer God will mend our hearts, our differences and our souls.

Best Wishes,
Donette
PS If you wish to write me back, you can send the letter to Mom's and she'll see that I get it. Thanks."

Dwayne confessed to Cherie that Donette's letter, "tore me up—not because of me, but for what I put her through. Mom, I don't know how to respond to her. I don't have the answers she seeks, nor do I have the courage to correct where her views are wrong. It would be futile anyway. All I can do is leave it in God's hands. There's a lot of things about this that I've never told anyone and still won't. After all these years, nobody would believe it anyway and it really doesn't change anything at this point." Seventeen years had passed since the killing. Dwayne knew he needed to accept that reconciliation with Donette wouldn't happen anytime soon.

Dwayne put aside his disappointment with Donette's reply, and the following month he invested his efforts in resolving a difficulty that had arisen during his last appearance before the parole board. The February review had been his sixth hearing, and the board had again pointed out that Dwayne hadn't passed a course that was mandatory for his release. Due to Dwayne's history, the board required him to complete a drug and alcohol rehabilitation program and these courses were only offered at minimum security prisons. The seriousness of Dwayne's offense required he be housed only at a maximum or medium security facility. Dwayne decided he would appeal to Judge Neufeld, the judge who had presided over his remand hearing, hoping the judge's intervention could resolve this difficulty.

In May of 1987, Judge Neufeld had sentenced Dwayne to life imprisonment, and the following September the parole board had specified Dwayne's punishment as 240 months. The 240 months wasn't officially considered a firm date for release and, without a firm date, Dwayne was barred from being considered a minimum custody prisoner. Dwayne's completion of the course was of such importance that during his review in 1998, the board cited the fact he hadn't passed the course as the primary reason they denied his release. Frustrated with this circular reasoning, Dwayne appealed to Judge Neufeld to correct this dilemma and allow him to have access to the program. If Judge Neufeld were to set a firm date for his release, Dwayne reasoned, he would be allowed placement in a facility that would give him access to the course.

In his letter, Dwayne advised the judge of the self-improvement programs he'd already finished. Then he offered explanations for events that had occurred during the 1986 trial. *"A variety of factors partook in my going over the edge on the early hours of October 18, 1986. A perceived fear of my dad's anger at me and his frustration at my drug and alcohol abuse, which led to other bad behavioral issues (theft, dishonesty, etc.) in combination with a mixture of drugs prompted me to go over the edge. My being alone with him also was a factor because had there been anyone else around, I would not have been able to do what I did. Sir, it never once occurred to me that my father's life would actually be over, that he would die."* Dwayne continued to explain, hoping the judge would understand his dilemma. He knew the statements he now made weren't consistent with the statements he'd made to the arresting officers and to Dr. Sasser. He was scared, Dwayne said, in a panic, and not really aware of the finality of what he'd done. Adding that no words could ever describe how he felt about this, he wrote:

"I remember seeing my little sister testifying at my remand hearing, crying hysterically. My mother too. This has been a seventeen yearlong nightmare. I would give my life and my soul to undo this tragedy to give my sister back her daddy, to give my mother back her husband." He closed the letter by admitting, *"Nothing I can ever say or do could prove my sincerity to you or guarantee my promise to do well."* He repeated his regret for the crime and appealed to Judge Neufeld to consider his request to set a firm date on his sentence.

But Judge Neufeld didn't change the status of Dwayne's sentence. In spite of the disappointing news, in Dwayne's letter to Cherie six months later he was in good spirits. He started with an apology for not writing sooner. *"The clock seems to leap ahead before I can catch up to it. My life is different, very different. God is so good and full of grace and mercy. Even to me, a pitiful, rebellious sinner. The Lord has rescued me time and time again from my own fate."* Wanting to update her on his health, he gave her details. *"On November 13th I started continuous ambulatory peritoneal. I will begin automated peritoneal in the next three weeks."*

He was feeling better. *"I go to medical four times a day, every six hours to do the CAPD exchanges, 5:00 AM, 11:00 AM, 4:00 PM, and 9:00 PM. Each exchange takes about 40 minutes. I hook myself up to the exchange set, drain the solution out of my body and refill with fresh solution. I always have 2,500 milligrams of dialysis solution in my belly."* He wrote about prayer, then concluded, *"When we love God as we ought, then we want nothing less than to submit ourselves to his perfect will for us. We must do so. We know that on our own, all we do is mess up everything and sometimes it takes a long time for God to undo the mess we've created for ourselves."*

Cherie noted Dwayne's growing acceptance of responsibility for his circumstances. A correlation, she thought, to the growth in his spiritual life. He'd begun to be more honest with himself and with her.

Much of 2004 was fraught with serious health complications for Dwayne. He wrote to Katheryn instead of Cherie, fearful of worrying his mother. He explained, *"Three days after you and my mom left* [from a visit] *I got really sick. I eventually developed an infection in my peritoneum. It came back twice after going away, then I started getting sick again. I had another infection that went undiagnosed until it was too late.*

"I was taken to the hospital in Richland, Washington for an emergency procedure to remove an electrolyte from my blood that was dangerously high. On the day I was to be discharged, the doctor came in with some newly diagnosed bad news. When I first got to the hospital, he ordered a thorough culture panel. The fungal culture showed I had a yeast infection in my peritoneum. It's called a fungal peritonitis. That's bad, yes."

He continued for several paragraphs with details regarding the probable treatment ahead. Then he explained his hesitancy in writing his mother. *"I'm really afraid to give Mom this news because I've put her through so much already. She watched me go from a troublesome inmate with nothing going for me, to a Christian with everything going for me. The only thing—and the most important—that has not faltered is my faith."*

When Dwayne wrote Cherie three months later, he wished her happy birthday and told her of his health complications. Much of his medical crises had stabilized by then and he was no longer reluctant to share details. The following year would bring further health struggles into Dwayne's life. He knew it was inevitable. Most persons affected by Alport syndrome experience end-stage renal disease and complete deafness by age forty. Dwayne had turned thirty-five on his last birthday.

Cherie had been notified by the VINE that Dwayne's deteriorating health had caused him to be transported to Portland and admitted to Oregon Health and Science University (OHSU). Because his prognosis was considered critical, Dwayne was allowed a brief conversation with Cherie on the phone. Several days later, he wrote her a short note. His condition would keep him in the infirmary at TRCI for at least a few months, he told her. Although he reported feeling really weak, he said he was getting better. His spirits appeared high, and he asked about her and encouraged her by sharing the joy he was experiencing in his spiritual life believing that God *"is involved deeply in even the most seemingly trivial things and a large portion of what we take for granted, we do not realize is from God and not our own doing."* He talked about his hopes to be paroled in 2006, adding that he was considering returning to Grants Pass rather than the Portland area. No matter what, he said he was trusting in God in this situation.

Dwayne was in the infirmary when he wrote to Cherie in March. He often sent Cherie handmade cards with short notes, checking on her welfare and passing on news. This envelope contained a card in which Dwayne informed Cherie that he'd taken the MMPI (Minnesota Multiphasic

Personality Inventory) test several weeks ago as a portion of the packet that would be viewed by the parole board at his next hearing in May. He would be scheduled to meet with a psychiatrist soon also due to the review. Optimistic, he wrote, *"I'm sure the results will be good."*

When Dwayne did meet with the psychiatrist, he described that the meeting went pretty well and he thought he'd passed. Then he added, *"The doctor suggested that I ask you to write or call the parole board on my behalf. He said it'd be helpful. Would you please do this for me? It needs to be done soon, like within the next of couple weeks."* He explained that if he were paroled, he would first go to Grants Pass and then, if he still wanted to be transferred, he could ask to relocate. Dwayne explained that standard procedure was to be paroled in the county where the crime was committed, then he promised to send her a copy of the psychological report when it was given to him.

By the end of March, the promised copy of the psychologist's evaluation arrived. The comprehensive report, submitted by Dr. Terrell L. Templeman, was six typed pages divided into categories of background information, psychiatric history, prison adjustment, current adjustment, mental status exam, parole plans, assessment results, and diagnostic impressions. An interesting notation under psychiatric history states, *"Mr. Wier recalls bouts of depression with suicidal ideation during adolescence. Yet he has never attempted suicide."* Dwayne's reported statement to Templeman contradicted Dwayne's account to Cherie early during his incarceration when he claimed he'd attempted suicide more than once and was hospitalized in a mental health ward at OSP.

Under the category of prison adjustment, Dr. Templeman wrote, *"Mr. Wier has a significant history of misconduct dating back to his first year of incarceration, when he incurred five disciplinary reports. These have diminished somewhat over the years, and his last DR was in 2003 for* contraband packets of rubbing alcohol, which he had taken from his dialysis treatment. He has multiple misconduct reports for sexual activity with other inmates and drug use, including drug smuggling in 1999. Mr. Wier indicated, 'I had a sexuality problem for years. I was confused about who I was.' He now considers himself heterosexual and avoids sexual contacts with other inmates. He also admitted a persistent drug problem in prison, especially after he started dialysis in 1998. He developed a strong craving for methamphetamines and relapsed for about four months before regaining abstinence."

Dr. Templeman's assessment of Dwayne's current adjustment was straightforward and positive. "Mr. Wier participates in regular church services and visits privately with the pastor every other week. He indicated that his religious faith has been very helpful to him. He resumed contact with his mother after a lengthy hiatus in 2000, when he went into a coma after kidney failure. He now describes a close relationship with his mother and they correspond every two weeks and she occasionally makes the drive from Grants Pass to visit him."

Regarding Dwayne's plans if he were to be paroled, Dr. Templeman cited options Dwayne had discussed with him about employment and Dwayne's desire to be closer to Portland to have access to good medical care and the possibility of a transplant. Dwayne had admitted that using drugs and alcohol wasn't smart for his health, adding that consuming either would disqualify him from getting a kidney, and this was life or death for him. Dwayne expressed a desire to attend AA and NA meetings and commented that maybe his experiences could help someone else as well. He thought his biggest challenge on parole would be dealing with his medical condition and "fitting in socially." Dwayne also expressed his desire to attend a church regularly and had hopes he could continue to do legal work in a law office.

Dr. Templeman concluded the evaluation, describing Dwayne as having *"a moderately defensive profile, suggesting that Mr. Wier was downplaying symptomatology. The profile is most common for men with antisocial histories who have begun to modify their thinking. Although the profile still reflects an individual who dislikes being told what to do, he clearly has a history of acting out, and may become impatient with others. It also reflects increasing concern about health and feelings of guilt, which are somewhat unusual for this profile type. He certainly does not present himself in a grandiose or glib manner and clearly appears ready to accept responsibility for his actions.*

"To address risk for future violence, Mr. Wier's case was reviewed using the HCR-20 protocol. Historically he shot his father to death at age 16, but has little other history of violence in his record. His history of substance abuse and other early maladjustment also place him at risk. Relationship instability and employment problems seem to have remitted in recent years while in prison, and he does not appear to be suffering any active major mental illness. Clinically he shows some insight into his early acting out, particularly with regard to anger and substance abuse, does not harbor negative attitudes about family, treatment, or being on parole. He does not appear impulsive at present and has been fairly responsive to treatment. His future plans appear feasible, he now has support from his mother, but it is likely to be stressful for him once he is released, particularly with his medical condition. I score him 12 points out of 40, which would indicate a low risk for future violence at this time."

The parole board had required a second psychological evaluation. This assessment was conducted on April 7, nearly thirty days after Dr. Templeman's, and a month before Dwayne's scheduled parole board review. Dwayne wrote to Cherie giving her his impression of how the assessment went. *"I've been pretty preoccupied (and stressed) over getting out. I took my second psych exam and this 'doctor' seemed like he had his mind made up before he even seen me. The board can extend my parole date for two years if I get a bad report. Then after two years, I can go through the process all over again. I'm going to try to get an attorney to represent me pro bono at my exit interview with the parole board next month. It's my only chance, I think. I'm scared of not getting out! I'm ready to be out, Mom."*

When Dwayne wrote Cherie at the end of April, he included a copy of his second evaluation. Before he jumped into his irritation with the report, he had these words for Cherie: *"I've been thinking a lot about my childhood, etc. I want you to know that I'm truly sorry for being so problematic. You and Dad were excellent parents! You were always there for me. It's up to 35 years late, but thank you, Mom!*

"I'm enclosing my second psychological report. The doctor is out of his mind. He's basing most of his crap on my past rather than how I am now. The report is bogus. Anyway, Dr. Templeman did a thorough examination of me. He gave me the MMPI and spent over two hours talking with me."

Dr. H. F. Shellman, also a clinical psychologist, gave Dwayne an unflattering review. His report was half as long as the one submitted by Dr. Templeman and not nearly as comprehensive. Dr. Shellman added these comments in his summary about Dwayne: *"I am concerned about his poor insight, his poorly developed sense of identity, his proneness to impulsivity in an uncontrolled environment, and the indications that he functions best in a familiar and controlled environment. In my clinical judgment, he definitely needs psychotherapy and an intensive substance abuse treatment program. I should not consider him to be a danger to the community if he were to have the recommended therapies and, very importantly, very close supervision. I consider his prognosis to be guarded."* In conclusion, Dr. Shellman noted, *"Mr. Wier presents only a moderate risk for future violent behavior."*

Cherie had received an invitation from the parole board to attend Dwayne's hearing in person, be present by phone, or submit a letter regarding her view about his possible release. Dwayne had also asked her to write to the board in his behalf. She decided to write a letter to the board.

"My name is Cherie Wier. I am the mother of Dwayne D. Wier and also a victim of the crime he committed. I am requesting that you keep this letter strictly confidential and would appreciate a response as well.

"I am writing to express my concern about the possibility of Dwayne being paroled and released in Josephine County. Let me explain a little about my relationship with Dwayne. By the grace of God, I was able to forgive him for the murder of my husband (Dwayne's father). I have since visited Dwayne several times in prison over the past few years and have seen some very significant changes in his life. He has become a Christian and I believe he truly has changed in his heart. I also believe he has repented of his crime and has completed his sentence, having been incarcerated more than half of his life since the age of 16, and deserves a chance to experience life outside of prison.

"Because of the way the system works, I understand that if granted parole, Dwayne will be released in Josephine County. That is my main concern due to the fact that my daughter is also a victim, having lost her dad in such a tragedy, and she has not forgiven her brother nor does she ever want to see him or have him be part of her life again. She is the one who found her father shot to death when she was 10 years old, three days before her 11th birthday. She is now married with two small children and has made a nice life for herself and has moved on after that horrible experience and loss of her father. I have a wonderful relationship with her and her husband and my grandchildren. She does not want Dwayne to know

anything about her life. I honor her wishes and understand her feelings and unwillingness to forgive her brother. She lives close by and we are very close. She's expressed her fear that if Dwayne is released in Josephine County there is the possibility that she and the children might run into him at a store or somewhere in town which would bring back all of that trauma she experienced as a child. She's tried very hard to put the past behind her and would like to keep it that way. If Dwayne were released here, I feel it would jeopardize my daughter and my relationship. Family, friends, and neighbors have also expressed their concerns and fears about his release and feel that he should not be released in Josephine County. From comments I've heard, I know he would not be welcome here, and I would also have concern for his safety. I feel he can never come home because of what he did.

"I will always be his mother and will try to encourage him in his life, spiritually and emotionally; however, I am not in good health and there is no way I can care for him physically or financially. I have lived in the same home for 35 years and do not want my life with my daughter and family, my friends, and neighbors, who are my support, jeopardized by Dwayne being released in Grants Pass.

"If Dwayne is granted parole, I am asking you to seriously consider releasing him in the Portland area. He would have a much better opportunity of getting a kidney transplant, which he desperately needs, and the health care that is offered there. Housing is less expensive, there are more social service agencies and accessible transportation in Portland than in Grants Pass or the surrounding areas.

"Thank you for hearing my concerns and I hope you will seriously consider my request."

Cherie and Katheryn made a trip to Umatilla two weeks before the scheduled parole board review. The visit with Dwayne was a good one, with much of the conversation revolving around the upcoming hearing and speculation about how Dr. Shellman's report would affect the board's decision. Cherie and Katheryn followed their routine of staying in Umatilla for two days so they could avail themselves of three sessions of visits, as well as meeting up with other women visiting inmates who had become friends. Increasingly familiar with the prison's rules and sharing in the camaraderie of this small group of women, who jokingly referred to themselves as "the girls," Cherie moved with less apprehension through the visitation process. For Dwayne, who had been uneasy about his imminent review, Cherie's visit was a welcome reprieve from his brooding.

After he'd received a copy of the psychological evaluation from Dr. Shellman, Dwayne knew the report would weigh heavily against him. He'd done all he could do to prepare for the hearing by putting together a packet of information requested by the board. The board wanted to know of the specific plans Dwayne had prearranged if he were to be released. He was expected to itemize the areas he anticipated would be most difficult for him when getting out and how, exactly, he would deal with any probable obstacles. Dwayne needed to provide names of people he'd contacted who were willing to be of support, the days and hours of local organizations he would rely on for assistance and, if appropriate, a church and church member or leader who would sponsor him. It was incumbent upon Dwayne to have checked out the costs and availability of housing options, and how he would access the services he needed from his place of residence. He'd been working on accumulating the required information for several months, and his hopefulness had motivated him to be thorough in preparing his packet; that is, until he received the copy of Dr. Shellman's report. He'd been praying he would find favor with the board, he told Cherie. He'd done all he could do.

Dwayne was right. Despite the months of good behavior reports and the pages of carefully prepared names, addresses, and phone numbers of willing supporters, Dr. Shellman's evaluation superseded even Dr. Templeman's recommendation for release. The board sent Dwayne back to his cell, telling him he would have another chance at parole in two years. He was devastated.

Cherie knew that Dwayne would be disheartened with the ruling, and in a letter from him a week later he let it all out. *"Mom, nothing's right here. I'm barely coping—back on Prozac and sleeping pills. Haven't been to church in a while, have been backsliding a lot. I'm in the hole again for contraband II. I got caught coming from work with a bunch of colored paper and some new pencils. Stupid choice, regardless of the reasons. So I lost my job, got 14 days segregation, 14 days loss of privileges and lost my housing, my mental health programming. I'll have to do it all over."*

In previous letters Dwayne had wondered if he would have a chance at marriage and family. Now, as he felt his health continuing to slip, it seemed fruitless to dream of a life besides the one he was in. *"I'm not really okay with doing 2 more years (at least) and I'm going to fight it tooth and nail. The board was wrong. I don't mean to ramble on about it. It just has me so damn frustrated. Honestly, the only reason that keeps me going is you. You're all I have, Mom. I know that's my own fault too and that doesn't make it any easier. All my life I've made bad choices that reaped consequences that frustrated and angered me to the point of making more bad choices! About five years ago I started growing up. Two and a half years ago I gave my life to the Lord. Nearly two months ago, everything seemed to fall apart. I feel like the answer has been 'no' most of my life largely my own fault, yet... I really have to question whether I've ever forgiven myself for ruining all our lives. I don't know that I have.*

"If only I could have quit using that dope back then. Maybe I needed Prozac or something like that 25 years ago. I don't know really. I feel very, very fortunate and blessed to have such a loving and forgiving mother that I do. Mom, I want you to know that not a day has ever gone by that I didn't wish I could change the past. The older I get, the more intense these feelings get. It's not even about me—it's about you and Donette. I'm so sorry for all the grief I've caused you both."

Cherie felt the defeat in Dwayne's letter. Hearing from him over the years had always meant sharing his emotional roller coaster, riding the ups and downs. She couldn't shake it. He was her son and, no matter the reason for his emotional swings, she found herself pulled into the chaos. She used to fight the inclination, sometimes successfully distancing herself from his troubles, knowing she had no control over his circumstances or his emotional responses to them yet, despite her efforts, Cherie couldn't help but carry Dwayne's emotional lows in the back of her mind.

Transforming the Applegate property was always a welcome distraction from trials for Cherie. Whenever visitors stopped by, they raved about the beauty of the place. The comments came as no surprise because Don and Cherie had converted acres of brushy land into manicured areas with mature trees surrounded by lawns and seasonal flowers.

After Don's death, Cherie completed what remained to be done on the landscape project by working countless hours in her yard. Capitalizing on the picturesque quality of the property, Donette and Cherie dreamed of marketing a portion of the land near the river as a wedding venue. Michael Wood volunteered to help Cherie complete the work necessary to start the business. Michael funded and oversaw the construction of a small building where a bridal party could dress, in a location that would accommodate an impressive staircase leading to the ceremony site near the water's edge.

Cherie's River Rendezvous officially launched as a wedding venue in the spring of 2005. Maintenance of the grounds fell to Cherie and Donette, who worked another job full time, took care of the marketing and meeting with prospective couples. The business required more effort than either had imagined and the profit margin was narrow, but the work was gratifying, and the extra income helped.

Dwayne initially responded to the news of using the property as a wedding venue by encouraging Cherie in her new enterprise, but as he considered it further, he realized how his actions had brought a financial burden to Cherie that had forced her to seek ways to supplement her income. The reality of how his choice had impacted the lives of his mother and sister weighed heavily on him. *"There's no acceptable way to say it Mom. The fact is I fucked our lives up and I can't do a damn thing to fix it and it's ripping me apart inside. I'm really having a hard time with this. What do I do? Every time I start thinking about this shit it devastates me inside! Over the years, I've just learned to keep a straight face, it just seems easier to deal with because I'd be a wreck if I started letting my emotions flow out. It's difficult enough just dealing with the daily ration of BS in this place, let alone come to terms with what a horrible thing I did almost 19 years ago. I can't even really make peace with myself over taking Dad's life. This is eating away at me and I cannot seem to shake it or bury it. My life is an utter disaster! I'm trying hard to cope, but I'm at a loss. There's unfortunately, no procedural remedy for this type of thing. Every time I go to dialysis, I ask myself why I keep hanging on and I don't even have a good answer to that. I'm just so sick of all of this. Pray for me, Mom. I really need it right now."*

When Dwayne realized his prolonged sense of depression was a result of his recurring thoughts of the past and the inability to change what was already done, he tried to refocus his mind on current matters that he could alter. Despite weakness and secondary problems from his Alport syndrome, Dwayne had taken an active interest in his physical well-being. In elementary school, he'd been self-conscious of his awkwardness and embarrassed by his small frame. Dwayne wrote to Cherie about his renewed desire to develop muscle mass and thus build a more powerful appearance. He mentioned several photos he'd sent to Cherie eight years ago and asked her if she could try to locate them. He wanted to prove to other inmates that he'd once been big, and he said he thought the photos would give him inspiration to seriously begin training again.

Speaking of the images, he said, *"Man, I wish Dad could've seen me then—he'd have been proud. I wish I could get like that again."* Dwayne followed up concerns about his physique with questions that had been plaguing him regarding spiritual matters. Disillusioned, he looked to Cherie for insight. He asked about the scripture in John 14:13 that promises *"whatsoever ye ask in the Lord's name…"* Saying the promise didn't seem to be working out as he thought it should, telling her, *"In every area of my life I feel discouraged. I simply don't understand. I call on the Lord and it's as though He doesn't hear me. What am I doing that's so wrong?"*

Dwayne's musings took him to thoughts of Don. *"The truth was I was more at ease with you—much more comfortable with you than Dad! Dad was hardly ever there and when he was there, I was afraid of him. Yet I wanted to be like him. He was my hero, but I couldn't relate or open up to him on an emotional level. With you, I could, but I was usually embarrassed by my feelings, as though they were somehow inappropriate. I never thought the real me was good enough. I wished I was like Dad."*

Writing of his dad led Dwayne to more thoughts about his childhood. *"I'm quite ashamed of the number of skeletons in my closet. Maybe you can help me with this? I've always felt as though I was a burden to you and Dad. I was a sorry excuse for a brother to Donette. I wanted to be the good son, but I was more of an embarrassment to you and Dad. I just did what I thought I had to do in order to fit in with my peers. I was an oddball as it was—I really didn't fit in with anyone, so I always tried to invent a character who'd be liked and accepted rather than the loner I was. Of course, I failed miserably, but tried my best. Finally, I was content to be a 'stoner'—after all, I was accepted by that crowd; or, rather, used by that crowd, which, in turn, made me feel needed. I guess I pretended that they were my friends. They really weren't. Mom, I've made so damn many bad judgment calls that I've permanently scarred myself for life. I'll never be able to amount to much—I know this deep down, and it really pains me to face the reality of this. I don't give up and I keep on fighting because I believe that if I didn't continue on then I'd be letting you down."*

Before closing, Dwayne told Cherie he'd sent a card to Donette several weeks before and was hoping for a reply. He was disappointed but not surprised he hadn't yet heard from her. *"I'll keep writing to her occasionally. I feel as though I'm intruding into forbidden territory with her, you know what I mean? I don't know her and I suspect she'd rather not know me."*

Donette didn't respond to letters and cards she received from Dwayne. She hadn't accepted his apology, though she knew her mother was right when she told her, "Donette, you need to forgive Dwayne. Not for him, but for you." Cherie realized for herself that she couldn't fully heal from the trauma, bitterness, and grief, unless she was able to let go of her anger toward Dwayne. She knew that truth was the same for her daughter. Donette didn't really want to forgive Dwayne, and she certainly wasn't in any hurry to do so.

When Dwayne mailed his next letter a week later, he didn't mention Donette. Instead, he focused on answering questions Cherie still had in her mind, ones she'd asked him about soon after the murder. *"If there is any one thing that you and Dad perhaps could have done differently, is you guys should have disallowed me to have any involvement with the guys from the band on Humbug. Hell, even the parents were dopeheads too! They just did a good job of hiding it. A good move would have been to encourage me to spend more time with people we knew who were never into any of the garbage that I was into."*

Dwayne had several more thoughts about what might have influenced his path. *"Another good move would have been to insist that I attend Calvary Chapel with you guys rather than to allow me to go to the Four-Square church. The youth group there was a joke."* Cherie flinched when she read these words. She and Don had agonized over the decision to change churches. They'd wanted Dwayne to have friends and choose to go to church. Despite their efforts to do the best thing for Dwayne and the family, maybe they should have required Dwayne to accompany them to Calvary.

Lastly, Dwayne brought up family activities, suggesting, *"We should have made a point to do more things as a family, without having other families involved. I probably would have protested at first, but if the other bad influences in my life would have been removed, I believe things would have been okay. Of course,"* he added, *"it's easy to speculate about such things nearly 20 years after the fact, but they are just thoughts."* Making it clear he didn't intend to sound critical, he clarified, *"I'm not blaming you or Dad at all— that's the very last thing I want to do. I'm merely making suggestions, which may or may not have made a difference. It doesn't matter at this point, but I know there are still a lot of unanswered questions in your mind. I am always asking myself what is to be learned from my past experiences and*

I find it to be quite helpful. Life is a big learning experience and if there is nothing to be learned and therefore, gained from these experiences then there would be little point in living."

Dwayne left the lower half of the last page empty and then, as if in afterthought, he wrote more on the backside of the paper where he jotted brief thoughts. *"You've asked a few times about my past gender identity issues. I was thoroughly in a state of confusion. When I got transferred to TRCI in 2002 I decided that it was a chance for a fresh start. Around the end of 2002, I gave my life to the Lord and asked Him to make me as He intended for me to be, to take away my confusion of who and what I was. He did. Did I have these types of thoughts before I went to prison? Yes, but I just kept it buried. I was never really comfortable around girls, but I managed because, deep down, I knew that what I was feeling was wrong. Nobody ever knew because I didn't want anyone to know. I was ashamed of it, so I kept it hidden from everyone."*

Changing subjects, Dwayne brought up his health. *"By the beginning of 1998, I was starting to become ill but I didn't really know what was happening. I lost an incredible amount of weight and always felt fatigued. In May 1998, I received a letter from Dr. Stor telling me that if I didn't get dialysis treatment then I'd die and to at least keep the appointment with him to discuss my options before making a decision to die."*

Dwayne shifted again, writing of his poor character traits during his adolescence and how his inner flaws had affected his behavior. *"I possessed very little integrity, during my youth. Again, I'm just sharing stuff with you. I want for you to know your son because I love you and because I feel that you have a right to know these things, so I share both the good and the not-so-good feelings and thoughts I have. If I only shared the good and kept the bad to myself, then I'd be a liar and a phony—and that simply isn't what I'm about.*

But, like I said, you have the right to know. And I want you to know this stuff because I know you want to try and understand what all was going on in my mind at that age.

"When I started working at the Chevron station was when I really started getting heavily into the drug scene. That was in 1986. Prior to that, it was mostly a little here and a little there and mostly alcohol and weed, but some other stuff too. When I got fired at the Chevron station it was because I overdrew against my paycheck—a little bit over $150. Every cent of that money, plus some, went into my drug habit. That's why I never had anything to show for it. And almost everyone I hung out with was there only because I always had the dope bag—they certainly weren't my friends. The reason I started doing crank all the time was because the first time I tried it the Chevron manager told me how great of a job I was doing and that he'd gotten good reports from customers. Anyway, enough about that."

Wanting to end his letter on a positive note, Dwayne reassured Cherie that he wasn't giving up. In the letters Dwayne wrote, he sometimes just needed to vent and have someone who would listen and encourage him. He felt he was at liberty to talk to her about anything at all. He wrote that he went through phases of despair and depression, but that he always got back up.

CHAPTER 19 – A MOTHER'S INFLUENCE

On July 22, Dwayne painstakingly wrote his letter to Cherie on toilet paper and carefully folded the connected squares, placing them inside the envelope. The guards had given him a pen and envelope, but no paper. He was in the hole. He said he'd *"been having a lot of problems these past several months—some nearly unbearable tribulations and persecutions, all from staff."* He wrote that one of the nurses reported that he was making himself throw up. He said he'd been written up for various false reasons. He told Cherie he was *"doing all that I can to stay close to the Lord and I still fail so miserably, but the Lord is the most important priority to me. At times, though, I feel like He just doesn't hear me or doesn't answer. Is this stuff supposed to build my faith? It ain't—it's tearing me apart. I cannot take it anymore!"*

He apologized for burdening her with his troubles but said he felt like she was the only one he could come to. *"Now, because of all these petty bullshit write ups I've gotten over the last several months, I am not only not likely to get out in January 2008, but I'm also disqualified for a kidney transplant because my custody level is too high (every time you get a write up, your custody level goes up). I'm not even going to try to explain everything that's going on because I know you probably wouldn't believe it anyway! Besides that, I'm the one who put myself here so I guess I've got coming whatever goes with the territory.*

Nonetheless, I feel betrayed, let down, lied to, lied about, unjustly treated—where is God in all this? I am very much on the verge of either quitting dialysis or simply taking the caps off my catheter (that they use for my dialysis) and opening the clamps and just lie back till everything fades away. I'm trying to work up the courage to do this. It's what I deserve anyway. I'm not mad about what's been happening. I'm hurt and full of sorrow and drained of energy. I don't want to live like this anymore—I can't glorify the Lord being a physical wreck as I am anyway. Mom, you have been the main factor in the past that kept me from going to the point I am at now. But I'm at the end of my rope. I pray that God will have mercy on my soul and forgive me." He pleaded with her to believe him regarding the injustice he was experiencing. *"I'm telling you the truth!"*

In his next letter, two days later, Dwayne wrote that he was in a renewed place mentally, emotionally, and spiritually. He apologized for his previous letter, calling it hastily written. *"I felt desperate and needed to cry out to someone and it felt as though God wasn't paying attention, though He surely was. And He gave me the strength to endure. After all there can be no triumphant victory without harsh tribulation."* He was still in the hole but had been allowed to attend the Dayspring Chapel services, where he played drums.

Dwayne immersed himself in church services again, reading the Bible and studying supplemental Christian commentaries. He was encouraged when he wrote to Cherie in September, so much so that he quickly filled ten pages front and back with writing. He quoted insights from the Biblical story of the prodigal son and how that story relates to modern day parents who have seen their kids walk away from the Christian life.

"I feel compelled to share this with you: The scripture is in Jeremiah 31: 'There is hope in your future. That your children shall come back to their own border.' The

commentary reads as follows: One of the greatest heartaches of any believing parent occurs when one of their children has rebelled against the ways of the Lord. The Bible offers comfort and hope in this situation. He understands. Much of the Old Testament is the story of God's children straying. He knows our heartaches. And He promises to bring our children back! He promises that ultimately, they will come back to the ways they were taught as children. That peace will be their portion as they encounter Him. Therefore, 'Hope in God for your children's future.'"

Dwayne admitted he'd slipped into old habits. *"Mom, I know I fell on my face recently, but I had other Christians praying on my behalf and God was merciful to me and set me back on my feet even stronger than before. So much is happening in my life as a result of God's amazing grace and mercy. I don't even know where to begin! I'm sorry if I stressed you out with my last letters when I was in the hole. I'm quite ashamed of stooping so low that I lost sight of Jesus for a brief time. Without the fiery trial to endure, there could be no victory.*

"I've been having some bad experiences health-wise. There is no apparent hope for getting a transplant as long as I'm incarcerated. But I always suspected it would come down to that otherwise, it would have occurred years ago when first requested by the doctors."

Eager to switch topics, Dwayne shared insights about his past. *"The one thing I'll never understand is where I went wrong. You and Dad put me in a Christian school in kindergarten. I always went to 'release time' in elementary school across the street at Murphy Chapel. I still remember a lot of the songs we sang and the lessons we were taught! Even Donette quoted scripture when she was 8, 9, and 10 years old! All those experiences, should have prompted me to build a relationship with God. But, and even to this day though I have a much different attitude about it, I'd see people who went to church and they'd put on their innocent* masks at church and as soon as church was over, they'd be smoking, cussing, and not edifying anyone. Of course, I was critical about it all at that age because I never saw any real difference between me and everyone else. The kids in the youth groups were doing the same things I was doing—being hypocritical. Maybe I should have set myself apart and took the initiative and made the decision to do the right thing. Please don't misunderstand what I'm talking about here. I'm trying to learn from the past. I want to be able to identify where I went wrong so I know what my weaknesses are and can identify those same traits in others and be an encouragement to them. It's quite difficult to encourage people when you yourself lack insight into the root of your own problems."

Because Cherie's birthday was approaching soon, Dwayne wanted to do something personal for her that she would appreciate and searched for a scripture that might reflect their relationship or his affection for her. Finding a story in the New Testament about a widowed mother and her son, Dwayne quoted the story, then gave an explanation as to why he'd sent it to her.

"And when He came near the gate of the city, behold, a dead man was being carried out, the only son of his mother, and she was a widow. And a large crowd from the city was with her. When Jesus saw her, He had compassion on her and said to her, 'Do not weep.' Then He came and touched the coffin, and those who carried him stood still. And Jesus said, 'Young man, I say to you, arise!' So he who was dead sat up and began to speak. And He presented him to his mother."

Dwayne explained his personal connection to this story. "I was the dead man—lost and without hope. When you prayed for me and wept over me all those years, the Lord heard you and had compassion on you, a widow who's only son was heading straight to eternal damnation. My corrupt nature enclosed about me as though it were a coffin. And, *indeed, God touched me and made me alive and no longer dead in my rebellion, presenting to you your only son who had been restored to life. A new creation. You stood in the gap for me, pleading with God to save me; indeed, for many years! Be assured, Mom, your prayers, which you prayed for over 2 decades, have been answered! Thank you for not giving up on me. As long as I live, I shall be a debtor to you because you brought me into this world, you cared for me and preserved me when I was a child. The pains, fears, sorrow and afflictions that you and Dad endured while bringing me up. I have no clue what it must have been like and, unless I one day have children of my own, I won't know. When I begged to be out on my own at 16 years of age, you and Dad wisely forbade that idea, to my own good. When I look back 20 or 25 years ago and recollect the way I treated you and Dad, I am saddened, my heart is grieved intensely. I disobeyed and dishonored you both. We all need to be willing to stand in the gap on behalf of others—We may trust Him to carry us through that dark night of the soul and on into the dawning light. When we have nothing left but God, we'll find that God is enough."*

Dwayne was expecting a visit from Cherie at the end of October, but that didn't stop him from writing to her in the interim. He anxiously shared his recent perceptions that had been prompted by a conversation with an inmate. *"I often hear of the horror stories of the type of home and parents many people in here have had and yet never did they go to the extremes I did. Of course, this makes me feel horrible, like a little worm. Reflecting back, I can't make sense out of the 'why' I was the way I was. Twenty plus years later, it still doesn't satisfy my own inquiry because I wasn't that way because I wanted to be. My reasoning was certainly impaired. Maybe some things are inherited in the genes, this I don't know. But I do know that I never **wanted** to be a rotten kid and I'm sorry that I was. Now I aim to do all I can do to encourage others and perhaps cause them* to make a detour before they make the same bad choices I made."

After Cherie's trip to Umatilla, Dwayne dropped her a note thanking her for the visit. He knew the drive was a long one and that it was a financial sacrifice for her to come so far. During Dwayne's time in Two Rivers, Cherie had travelled the 800-mile round trip infrequently at first, but as the two grew closer she visited him more often. Almost as an afterthought, Dwayne wrote, *"Another thing—you called me 'son' in your last letter! That really made me feel good, Mom. You haven't referred to me as 'son' in many years. That means a lot to me. My thanks is abundant."*

Dwayne's words took Cherie by surprise. She hadn't consciously thought about calling Dwayne "son." She wondered whether their relationship had taken a turn she hadn't noticed. Had she used the endearment naturally because true forgiveness was transforming her heart in those deep wounded places she thought couldn't change? She wasn't sure why she'd called him "son" in her last letter and wasn't going to over think it, but she made a mental note to use the word in future letters to Dwayne since it seemed to mean so much to him.

Acting on his desire for reconciliation, Dwayne solicited relatives hoping to reestablish relationships. After twenty years of no contact with his family, he'd been pleased to reconnect with his Uncle Bob, and he'd recently responded to a letter sent to him by his Uncle Gary, Cherie's younger brother. Gary was a Christian and Dwayne wrote to him knowing Uncle Gary would understand references to scripture verses and descriptions of his spiritual transformation and change of heart.

Dwayne began by answering questions that his uncle had asked him in his letter. *"I sincerely apologize for taking so long to respond. Your letter was deeply appreciated. It challenged me to take a step back and re-examine myself from a different perspective. One thing that many people have questioned over the years is whether or not drugs and alcohol could put a person over the edge to the point of taking another's life. The answer is no. Drugs and alcohol will not, by themselves, cause this. They do, however, distort one's perspective of events, misinterpreting things radically and will provide the nerve to follow through with such a heinous act. Drugs didn't pull the trigger though, I did. Though difficult to accept, I am responsible. I had no idea how much my dad wanted to help me, no clue. I thought he was trying to make my life miserable.*

"It's taken years to truly realize how wrong I was. One of the psychiatric evaluations I had in mid-2005 said no access to diagnosis, meaning no active personality disorder. A second one said, I do have an antisocial disorder. Either way, both said I do not pose a threat to the community. I've stumbled and fallen on my face many times, but in God's mercy and grace, I find the determination to get up and march on. My past can and does haunt me, but it cannot take a stronghold upon me.

"I've been blessed in being a musician on two teams for a bit over a year. I also attend a Baptist service that I really enjoy. I do have a long journey ahead and I aim to finish the race. As Paul says, 'I am confident of this very thing, that He who has begun a good work in, you will complete it.' We are told that we ought to be reconciled to each other. This is easier said than done, but what is impossible for man is possible with God. Nothing is too difficult for Him. Our past must not be permitted to determine our future.

"I have a large picture of a lighthouse sitting upon a hill next to the vastness of the sea with the verses of Proverbs 3:5-6 inscribed across it. It is one of the first things I see upon waking up. 'Trust in the Lord with all your heart and lean not on your own understanding. In all your ways acknowledge Him and He shall direct your paths.' This really starts off my days well.

"The biggest drawback here is letting other people's circumstances sabotage my thinking. I read this in a book called <u>Living Above the Level of Mediocrity</u>, A Commitment to Excellence, by Charles Swindoll. He puts it best as follows, 'Monkey see, monkey do. When you spend enough time around those in a particular scene, our actions usually become similar. All things being equal, if you run with bad company, you'll be corrupted. The good won't rub off on them, their bad will rub off on you.'

"Uncle Gary, I deeply appreciate that you reached out to me to begin reconciliation. Thank you for forgiving me. There was no way I could ever right my wrong, but what I can do, and make an attempt to do, is make a difference by serving others. After all, we are to be salt and light. I had been praying for reconciliation between me and the rest of the family. Your contact with me is an answered prayer."

CHAPTER 20 – CONFLICTING PSYCH EVALUATIONS

In late March, Dwayne wrote to Cherie about his upcoming parole board review scheduled for May 15. This would be his tenth appearance before the board, and he was all too familiar with the drill. He'd known since his last review in 2005 that he would be up for a hearing in May of 2007. He'd begun his preparations long before he received official notice of the hearing in March. Dwayne had been thinking about what he needed to do to improve his chances for a favorable ruling. As usual, the board expected a specific plan from him detailing his intentions for life if he were to be released and before each hearing, he put effort into contacting people on the outside and establishing a support system to show the board he was prepared for any situation. Each time, he hoped against hope that the three members would believe he was a good candidate to be safely released into the community. Remembering what had happened at the last hearing, he tried not to think about the psychological evaluations the board was certain to require, telling himself that he would do whatever was necessary to meet the board's expectations, then trust God for the decision that would come.

While Cherie and Dwayne anticipated the scheduled parole board review, the letters between them continued. Dwayne's correspondence that arrived in early May surprised her. He announced to Cherie that he'd converted to Catholicism. Initially, Cherie was quite concerned with the news, though she didn't know exactly how Catholic and Protestant beliefs differed, and it prompted much discussion between them. Cherie wasn't supportive of Dwayne's decision, but she was pleased to know he continued to read his Bible, and she reluctantly accepted the fact that he'd been baptized and confirmed into the Catholic Church. Dwayne was excited with this new perspective and committed much of his time to studying specific teachings of the Catholic Church.

While Dwayne immersed himself in his chosen faith and fought his inclination to worry about his review, Cherie and Donette geared up for the approaching wedding season, leaving Cherie little time to think about Dwayne's hearing. She was consumed with strategically planting varieties of flowers around the bridal cottage, wanting to keep their wedding customers happy. Donette had scheduled a full season. They would host twelve weddings this year. On weekends when there was no wedding on the property, Cherie and Donette were either cleaning up from the previous one or preparing for the next. By the time Cherie received another letter from Dwayne, he wrote again about the hearing, specifically addressing confusion regard his hearing date.

The original day for Dwayne's hearing had passed, and two weeks later there was still no indication when the postponed review would be held. Dwayne's letter at the end of May expressed frustration. He'd received copies of his two recently conducted psychological evaluations. One of the reports, conducted in late March by psychologist Dr. Frank P. Colistro, was very favorable. The doctor had administered the Hare Psychopathy Checklist, which uses twenty items to measure traits such as lack of empathy, pathological lying, and impulsivity, to determine whether an individual might be a psychopath. Dwayne scored a very low ten percent, when any score under a thirty indicates no psychopathy. Dr. Colistro identified amphetamine relapse as the most significant risk factor for Dwayne if paroled, stating that his current confinement in the infirmary had, in essence, been a protective factor; and that there had been no indications of drug use for nearly a decade. The report highlighted Dwayne's efforts in recent years, listing the many programs Dwayne had participated in during the past two years and stating that he'd had no major rule violations in the prior four years. Dwayne asserted to the doctor that his biggest support group was the church, and indicated that involvement in religious activities while in prison had helped him maintain emotional and behavioral stability. Dr. Colistro concluded that Dwayne's antisocial personality disorder was largely in remission, rendering him amenable to community-based treatment and unlikely to recidivate violently. Under "Recommendations" Dr. Colistro wrote, "If allowed to return to the community, he should participate in a 12-step-type substance abuse relapse prevention program and should adhere to his expressed intention to connect with a religious congregation and become an active member of it. He is capable of adhering to these program directives."

The second evaluation was conducted on May 11 and not transcribed until May 23, days after the review was to have taken place. Dr. F. Robert Stuckey, also a psychologist, didn't speak to Dwayne in person, but conducted his hour-long interview by live video from the parole board room at OSP. When he completed his assessment, he reportedly told Dwayne, "I'm inclined to give you a favorable diagnosis." This remark had encouraged Dwayne and served to heighten his disappointment when he received a copy of the report and found the doctor's recommendation anything but favorable. In his written assessment, the doctor stated, "In my opinion, the results of the present psychological evaluation indicate that Mr. Wier has a present severe emotional disturbance such as to constitute a danger to the health and safety of the community."

Other adverse comments included reference to Dwayne's sexual identity, describing him as an "extremely immature and sexually inadequate individual who has inner conflict between suppressing his homoerotic impulses and acting out in a homosexual manner." Dr. Stuckey continued, "And also, of even more concern, is the underlying potential for episodic aggressive acting out." The report went on in this vein. Dwayne said he was shocked, hurt, and saddened by the contents. A report that concluded that an inmate presently had a severe emotional disturbance and was a danger to the community would prevent any parole board from releasing said inmate. The board would have to ask the question, how could two equally accredited doctors arrive at opposite conclusions about Dwayne's mental state and his likelihood to reoffend? After all of the effort he'd put into compiling the fifteen-page packet of information for the board's review, Dwayne feared that the single adverse report from Dr. Stuckey would supersede everything else.

By June 7, the much-anticipated parole hearing still hadn't convened. Dwayne wrote a lengthy letter to Cherie, quoting excerpts from the conflicting doctors' reports. Attempting to be positive, he briefly discussed his release plans *"I'm trying to be optimistic and expect a miracle. I could have made several other off the wall quotes from Dr. Stuckey's report, but you wouldn't believe it. I think, all the fancy jargon they use to try to sound intelligent in their reports (in my opinion) says more about themselves than me!"*

As Dwayne sought out understanding about the Catholic faith, he met Paul Fischer, a lay pastor whose kindness profoundly affected him.

Amid the uncertainty of when his review would take place and the anxiety caused by Stuckey's assessment, Dwayne received much needed encouragement from an unexpected source. Dwayne had met Paul Fischer at the Catholic chapel services where Paul volunteered as a lay pastor for the Catholic Church. For the past year and a half, Paul had acted as a mentor to Dwayne. The two had become close, and Paul became a father figure to Dwayne as well as a spiritual teacher and friend. Knowing Dwayne was to appear before the parole board, Paul had, without his solicitation, drafted a letter to the board on Dwayne's behalf. Dwayne told Cherie he'd just received a copy of Paul's letter and shared a portion of it with her. "[Dwayne] *has impressed me as a man of faith and conviction. He is intelligent and has read and studied his faith to a considerable extent. This is obvious in our discussions during my visits.*

"*He seems to have a very calm and even temperament, has contacted persons in his home area so that at such time as he is released, a base has been established for support for his new life. And he has received their promise of support. I feel Dwayne would be an asset to the community."*

Dwayne was humbled by Paul's favorable endorsement and moved by his friend's effort to help him. While he hoped the board would consider Paul's recommendation credible, Dwayne knew how the system worked.

Paul's letter had at least helped calm Dwayne's worries. *"Whatever happens,"* he wrote Cherie, *"I'm not going to get all stressed out like I did last time, in 2005. Whether I get out or don't get out—I'm still living out God's will and this life is only temporal. I've got to keep an eternal perspective in all things. God's way is not always my way."*

When Cherie had originally been notified of Dwayne's parole hearing scheduled for May, she'd made arrangements to be called during the hearing and drafted a statement she would read. But it wasn't until mid-June that she appeared by phone at the hearing. In her presentation, she told of the change she'd witnessed in Dwayne, particularly since his conversion in 2002. She stated frankly that she was aware of the trouble he'd been in over the years, but said she felt he was showing improvement in this area and had been helped by classes he'd taken on anger management and by his desire to serve God. She said she believed that Dwayne was sincerely remorseful and deeply regretted killing his father and that Dwayne spoke of his dad often at visits or in letters. She said Dwayne's health was poor and that it was necessary for him to have a kidney transplant soon to save his life and that, unless he was released, it was doubtful he would be put on the transplant list. Dwayne could live a productive life, Cherie stated, and she said that he expressed a desire to make a difference in the lives of troubled youth who might be inclined to listen to someone like him who could relate to their situations.

On June 13, Dwayne returned to his cell and wrote a letter that took him three days to compose and covered eight pages front and back. He started the letter right after he returned from his hearing. The parole board had denied his release. Dwayne thanked Cherie profusely for testifying before the board. He wrote that he'd been *"deeply moved by the statement you made on my behalf. Thank you, Mom, for speaking up for me."* He believed he'd been treated unfairly, specifying that the board had put undue emphasis on the one psychological evaluation and had minimized the many classes he'd taken and the efforts he'd made to demonstrate he was taking advantage of all resources available to him. The write ups he'd received were petty in nature, he explained, and he gave details to Cherie regarding each one. Tired and forlorn, Dwayne had been encouraged by fellow inmates and correctional staff when he'd returned from the hearing, and he was pleased to find a fellow Catholic, whom he knew, would now be sharing his cell. This was an unanticipated surprise.

"I'm not really mad," he said to Cherie. *"I'm saddened and frustrated. I prayed for God's blessings and forgiveness upon each of the parole board members. I feel I was treated unfairly and I forgive them for that. I prayed earnestly prior to my hearing that I'd find favor with the parole board and I also prayed that I'd get a cell move today because I knew I'd need a friend close by regardless of the outcome of my hearing. This time I'm not throwing a pity party—I thanked the Lord for His great wisdom and His Divine Mercy."* Dwayne said he would *"do all possible to not get any write ups and have a clear report in two years when I would again have a hearing. If I were not paroled at that time, I would devote myself to the Lord in whatever capacity that meant in the prison and not subject myself to the scrutiny of another board hearing."*

A month later Dwayne wrote to Cherie, giving her an update on the classes he was taking and those he planned to take. *"I'm doing everything I possibly can do—I'm not giving up hope, no matter what! They will eventually let me out; and, if not, I'll just find God's will for me in my circumstances."* He updated her on his physical condition. *"What I really fear is my health going from bad to worse. I don't want to die in this place and I can't keep hanging on with dialysis indefinitely—my number is not all that far away. My kidney doctor says nobody lives 30 years on dialysis, some people live up to 20 years. The mortality rate is about 60%. I've been on dialysis for almost 10 years... when I do the math my future is not really very promising. I realize I must maintain an eternal perspective and this is difficult at times! But I also know I have a purpose which I've not yet fulfilled."*

By mid-August, Dwayne was anxiously looking forward to a planned visit with Cherie the following weekend. After casually writing regarding his personal devotional time and growth, he carefully approached the topic of his health. He wrote of his recent conversation with his kidney doctor regarding long-term expectations. *"I sense, the Lord is calling me home soon. I do not believe I will live long enough to make it out of here. But, as a certain king in the Old Testament was told by the Lord to set his things in order because he was going to die, this king prayed earnestly and God heard him and granted him another 15 years... Perhaps the Lord will bless me with a few more years of life... please pray about this, okay? I, of course, do not deserve this."* Soberly he brought up his end of life wishes, telling Cherie. *"I do not like discussing death, but it is the one thing we are guaranteed to most certainly face in this life. My wishes are that I be cremated and my ashes scattered beside Dad's grave site. If this is not possible, for whatever reason, I would like for my ashes to be scattered over your yard, for that is where you and Dad made my home and a wonderful home it was! And I want Psalm 130 read and that the Lord will have mercy on my soul and that I rest in peace."* He ended the letter by recounting childhood memories of good times and reaffirmed how much he was looking forward to her upcoming visit.

Dwayne addressed a reoccurring topic when he wrote his letter to Cherie a month later. He and Cherie had often talked about him writing a book that would be of help to rebellious teens or those struggling with drug use. *"Mom, do you believe that it would maybe help somebody if I wrote out my brief testimony and sent it to someone like Pastor Ron for their youth group or maybe even Father Peter at St. Anne Catholic Church? I feel the deep urge to reach out to people with my experiences, what I've been through and why, what caused the circumstances that led up to what occurred in my life, how I've resolved it, and how I maintain my new life in Christ. Somebody, somewhere has a need to hear this information—and to be able to diligently read and reflect on my story. It could actually save a life or lives. Do you agree? I feel quite passionately about this! I really feel driven to take on this project."* He said he lacked confidence in his writing skills, which was the primary reason he hadn't begun writing the book.

Another subject that Dwayne highlighted in this letter was his appreciation for Paul Fischer, who had continued to meet with him from the outside. Cherie had met Paul on her last visit to see Dwayne. The seventy-seven-year-old man visited Dwayne regularly in hopes of being an encouragement to him. Dwayne enthusiastically wrote, *"Paul has been up to see me twice since you left. Every visit has been a continuous dialogue and we discuss a wide array of topics! It's great! I asked him to be my 'godfather.' His response was, 'Well, it looks like I just adopted another son!' There were tears and a strong embrace. I told him I screwed up my first chance to have a father figure in my life and I believe the Lord has given me a second chance."*

Paul Fischer wasn't the only support Dwayne could count on. He'd become good friends with his new cellmate, Justin, and Justin's help had possibly saved Dwayne's life.

The November letter from Dwayne explained the alarming incident. Dialysis had gone poorly the day before, and Dwayne's blood pressure dropped significantly. *"I got to feeling dizzy so I got up to get a salt packet off the table. That's about as far as I got and I went out like a light; smashed the crown of my head into the wall between the sink and toilet and kinked my neck kind of and bruised my tail bone badly. If it wasn't for Justin, I would have been in worse shape. I was bleeding profusely from my head, sustained a possible neck injury, and fallen unconscious. Justin literally begged an officer to call medical and bring me a wheelchair because I can't stand up, let alone walk!"* But no medical staff responded to Justin's call.

Desperate, Justin finally got the attention of two inmates willing to help him carry Dwayne to medical. *"I look like a purple chipmunk at the moment,"* he wrote in his letter. *"I'm still having dizzy spells but Justin sticks by me as much as possible to make sure I don't fall again."* Dwayne explained that he *"had a new dialysis catheter put in the previous day and the newness of that and the head trauma caused internal bleeding. They're supposed to take me to the hospital tomorrow to change the catheter to stop the internal bleeding."*

The following day, Dwayne continued writing. *"I just got off the phone with you earlier. I regret having to call you with bad news, but you needed to know what exactly was going on. I only knew bits and pieces until today. Partially blocked superior Vena Cava (the Vena Cava is 'either of two large veins that empty into the right atrium of the heart'). It's not a good thing, but my hope is in God no matter what! I don't know what'll happen, but I know it will be God's will. I don't want to die and who really does? But I accept that reality. I just pray that I'm ready, in right standing with God."*

Dwayne added more health complications. *"I'm being pressured to make a major decision regarding my dialysis treatment, and I don't feel at ease about it at all! I'm basically out of options. The catheters have begun to not work well—just because I've been using them for so long. Now my only option is to get a leg graft put in my left leg, the last place I have to put an access. I don't know what to do. The last graft I had done at OHSU worked for three months and failed. I need wisdom and grace. Wisdom to make the right decision and the grace to endure it."*

A very sick Dwayne would be transported to OHSU the following day.

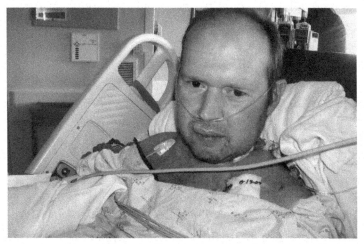

One of Dwayne's many hospital stays at OHSU. This photo is from 2009.

CHAPTER 21 – CAN PEACE AND RECONCILIATION BE FOUND?

The letter postmarked January 11 was the first one Cherie received after Dwayne's emergency transport to OHSU. Dwayne's penmanship was noticeably messy, with words written awkwardly between the lines. The note was brief and the tone hopeful.

"Praise God for every breath of life He's given me! This has all been quite an experience –an opportunity to grow and become more mature and gain insight about life. Even when I feel so over-whelmed that I want to give up, He reminds me that His strength is made perfect in my weakness. My writing is getting better, I think. I've lost a lot of sensation and coordination in my hands and feet. It's an effort to hold on to stuff. I can't believe how weak I've gotten. Keep praying that I recover fully, please. I'm going to stop here. I'm losing my endurance. Pray always for me, please. I love you! Your son." He told her he was housed at OSP, recovering from his surgery at OHSU, and at some point, he would be transported back to Two Rivers.

Three months later, when Dwayne was transferred back to Umatilla, he was perplexed about the timing because he'd been told he still required several surgeries at OHSU. In the meantime, though, he enthusiastically reported that an unknown sponsor had purchased him a Catholic prayer program titled *Liturgy of the Hours*. Dwayne had been encouraged by the materials, explaining to Cherie, *"At the conclusion of each prayer time (4 times daily) I am somewhat saddened that the prayer time is over and I long for the next prayer time to arrive and I get excited when it does come! I really needed this in my life—I'm so grateful for it!"* He wrote that his current doctor was working to get his meds adjusted and his diet back in order. *"He's a Christian too— we've had some good talks together."* Gingerly, he updated her on his medical condition, trying to maintain a positive spin. *"I weigh 120 pounds—way underweight and am still pretty weak and feel sick and fatigued most of the time. The important thing is that I share my faith with others every chance I get! I shall continue to do the Lord's work for all of the days He's given me, until He finally calls me home. And I do long anxiously for this day!"*

In the same letter, Dwayne told Cherie that one of the dialysis nurses had made a quilt for him. Overcome with gratitude, Dwayne responded this way: *"I expressed my warm thanks and appreciation. I gave her my promise to always intercede for her in prayer. I've never experienced such a kindness and love—I started crying when the nurse handed it to me. I just embraced it and prayed for her."* Prisoners weren't allowed to accept gifts from staff, so Dwayne requested that the quilt be sent to Cherie.

Only a month later, Dwayne's health report to Cherie brought news that he had a bone disease and was getting painful shots in the shoulder for it. Some symptoms had improved due to his revised medication regimen, but he was often frustrated with his muscle weakness that wasn't getting better. Dwayne struggled to tie his shoes, pick up small objects, or zip zippers. However, after the brief overview of his current setbacks, he shifted the focus of his letter onto those less fortunate than himself, telling Cherie he was praying for people he knew, particularly other patients he met in the infirmary. He enclosed printed lyrics from his favorite hymns, saying that the words had given him encouragement and he hoped they would encourage her too.

Dwayne worked hard to adjust to his physical limitations. Two months later, he explained his progress to Cherie. *"I can tie my shoes and fasten buttons now, but it is very difficult and time consuming. I can walk short distances with a cane, but I always have someone with me in case I lose my balance (which is more often than not.)"* He had two Christian brothers who sat on either side of him during mass. *"They both help me stand up, genuflect, and walk over to receive communion from the priest. They are a great couple of guys."* He reported on a new corrections officer who was working in his area on the graveyard shift. *"He and another of my non-Christian friends, who works the night shift always come by about midnight when I'm done praying for that evening. I always pray on my knees when I'm in my cell. These guys come by and lift me up and help me get back into my chair."*

A week later, Katheryn received a letter from Dwayne. It started off with unwelcome news:

"As for me, my health isn't really getting any better. Every time one ailment is mended, another occurs. Right now, I have a staph infection in my dialysis catheter, an infection that the doctor thinks might be MERSA, on my lower abdomen and another infection starting on my lower chest. I'm on Vancomycin the strongest antibiotic there is— it's known as "the end of the road" as far as antibiotics go. The doctor told me a few days ago that if I keep getting these various infections, then I will eventually die from one of them.

"I'll be honest—it's a really rough road. Last weekend when Mom was here, I was getting ready for my visit on Sunday morning, and I was fumbling around with the buttons on my shirt trying to fasten them for a good 15 or 20 minutes. I just broke down and started bawling like a baby. The little things I once took for granted are very difficult for me now. It's very disheartening. I can't even

hardly move my fingers very much to even write, let alone play the guitar. I can't even get a grip on the pick.

"Please don't get me wrong. I'm not giving an invitation to a pity-party. I'm merely filling in some unanswered questions. On behalf of the less fortunate people in this world who lack clean water, food, hygienic items, medical care—I, a convicted felon, have all these things and more! That is very much unfair!"

As a postscript, he added, *"For every breath I take I thank and praise God! I know not how many pages are left, but I do know I'm in this life's final chapter and I, therefore, want to leave a legacy behind. It doesn't appear that it will be with music, but perhaps my writings... All in the Lord's good timing and in harmony with His will."*

Summer had passed and it was fall when Dwayne wrote to Cherie that the morphine he'd been taking for chronic pain for seven months had been abruptly discontinued. *"I got very sick—horrible feeling! It's beginning to subside a bit now, but it was not at all pleasant. I never thought anything of it, but I became physically dependent on it. Night sweats, chills, headache, stiffness and fatigue, nauseous, vomiting, dizziness, not able to concentrate. Horrible!"* Because Dwayne had been moved back into the general population, that meant he had farther to go to get to any services he regularly took advantage of, including the infirmary, church meetings, or the cafeteria. Due to his general weakness and the swelling in his ankles, he found it necessary to use a wheelchair.

He brought up another pressing matter: his next parole board hearing, scheduled in seven months. The stress of thinking about attending the hearing, enduring the required assessments prior to the review and the inevitable self-reflection that the evaluations provoked in him, had stirred up his emotions. *"I want so deeply, to learn what exactly is wrong with me, so I can work to correct it. There are 2 books that might help me in this."* He included the names of the books in the letter, hoping that Cherie might order them for him. *"I have taken every program they have to offer (at the prison) some of them I've taken more than once. Now I feel I need to indulge in self-discovery and modify my thinking and behavior accordingly, rather than listen to someone (psychiatrist hired to evaluate for the Parole Board) who's known me for a mere 60 minutes tell me what's wrong with me."* Enclosing several articles in his letter from Catholic publications for Cherie's information, Dwayne always reminded Cherie that his objective wasn't to convert her or criticize her personal spiritual convictions, but to share with her what he was learning.

Two weeks later brought more discouraging news about Dwayne's health. Ever since his fall a year before, his condition had steadily declined. He couldn't hide his tendency to slip into discouragement. *"As long as the Lord gives me on this earth, I have to always try to do all I can to make a difference. I stumble and fall, get discouraged at times, like we all do; but the Lord takes me by the hand and lifts me back up and tells me 'I'm with you, Dwayne; fear not.' It's been very stressful! A dialysis catheter hanging several inches out of my upper left chest near the clavicle bone, a colostomy bag on the right side of my waistline near a belly wound from my surgery last year that still hasn't completely healed, hyperthyroidism, hyperparathyroidism, osteoporosis, liver disease, calcium deposits in my lungs, very low blood pressure always between 70 and 90 and 40 and 60. I'm always fatigued and sometimes so dizzy my vision goes blank (as if I were blind). It takes nearly all of my energy just to stand up, but even though the list could go on, I don't feel self-pity; but rather, I thank the Lord for keeping me humble and dependent on His grace. My every breath is a gift from God. They gave me a part time caretaker because there's some things I just can't do anymore. I can't clean my cell properly or push myself outside the unit in my wheelchair. Can only walk very short* distances with a cane. *Pray for my strength, Mom. But, all the same, it is a very, very small price to pay for sound spirituality. I know the Lord is with me and, if He weren't, then I'd not even be able to do those things I can do! For which I am most grateful!"*

Dwayne was relieved to finally be able to bring Cherie good news a month later. He'd been assigned *"a permanent single cell in a rather mellow unit thanks to Dr. Lytle. It was very kind of him to arrange it,"* acknowledged Dwayne, who then added that Dr. Lytle, *"is a Christian too—quite devout, very compassionate."*

Dwayne's prognosis hadn't improved. *"I haven't made much progress with my recovery. My hands are still numb and tingly, but I can differentiate hot and cold. My legs and feet are weak so I'm still in a wheelchair. No plans yet to reconnect my 'plumbing' so I can have normal bowel movements—that deal really freaks me out still. I have a difficult time with that and the huge scar and abdominal disfigurement. Only by the grace of our Lord! He indeed keeps me together, otherwise, I'd fall apart emotionally. Anyway, I just wanted to write and say 'hi' and let you know you're in my prayers daily.*

"PS I'll write again soon. I'm quite under the weather lately so I feel pretty miserable. Pray for me."

Cherie faithfully prayed for Dwayne, as she always had, understanding that the prolonged downturn in his health threatened to depress his spirit. The progression of his Alport syndrome steadily depleted his well-being as he gradually lost kidney function. In March of 2009, despite Dwayne's extended and in-depth commitment to the Catholic Church, he announced his intentions to turn his back on Catholicism and return to his Protestant teaching. After fellowship with a trusted Christian inmate and his own personal study, Dwayne believed that some creeds taught by the Catholic church conflicted with biblical thought. As much of his support system from inside and outside the prison came from Catholic brothers, he inquired of Cherie what she thought of how he should move forward since this personal revelation. He also reported that soon he expected to be taken to Walla Walla, Washington, where he would have surgery to place a new access in his left leg. The doctors had told him this was a last resort.

When Dwayne wrote to Cherie later that month, his foremost thought was to thank her for her visit to Two Rivers the previous weekend. *"Mom, I feel like every time we meet, we become a little closer and I thank our Lord for this! I have a wonderful and blessed time at our visits! I am so happy that you came up; it was a great surprise! Thank you!"* He wrote of his continued uncertainty regarding particular teachings of the Catholic Church. His parole board hearing scheduled for May was rapidly approaching and he'd stayed in close contact with a representative of St. Anne's Catholic Church in Grants Pass (in Josephine County, where he would be released if paroled). Rick Nelson, from St. Anne's, had corresponded consistently with him during the past year. Mr. Nelson offered support and had even talked with the local parole officer who would be assigned Dwayne's case, should he be released to Josephine County.

Although Dwayne felt an inner conviction that he needed to extract himself from Catholicism, there was much about the Church he respected and still agreed with. He wondered if he was being deceitful by not divulging his reservations about his faith to Mr. Nelson. After all, his Catholic brothers had agreed to vouch for him at the upcoming hearing. The situation had produced an unsettling predicament for him.

When Dwayne discussed with Cherie his possible release, he often brought up how he yearned to share the act of communion with her. Through the years, he'd detailed to his mom his spiritual journey, sharing his search for truth, his questions, and the answers God had provided through the Bible or in the teachings he'd heard from the chaplains.

Dwayne admitted his disappointment when God didn't answer his prayers in the way he hoped He would, and he told Cherie when he felt discouraged.

When Cherie opened Dwayne's next letter, she was surprised to read that he'd included an invitation for her to take communion with him. Wanting to give the correspondence her full attention, she waited until her day's chores were completed before sitting down with the letter. In the absence of the opportunity to physically take communion with her, Dwayne used the only means available to him: he invited her to share in communion by letter. He'd outlined his left hand on the back of page one, then carefully written instructions for Cherie to get bread and wine and bring it to the table. As she read and followed his instructions, Cherie placed her own hand on the outline of his.

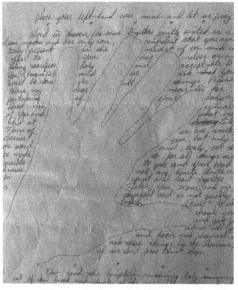

Dwayne wrote to Cherie repeatedly about his desire to share communion with his mother, hoping he would be released on parole one day and that they could participate in communion at a church together.

"Place your left hand over mine and let us pray together, 'Lord in Heaven, we come together jointly united as a dear mother and her only son, confident that You are truly present in the midst of us and we offer ourselves to you. We ask that Your will be done in all things. Please bless my dear mom in her partaking of Your body and blood in remembrance of You and as we remember and give thanks for all that you have done for us.'"

Cherie was deeply moved by Dwayne's novel solution to find a way to share communion with her. This letter, she thought, demonstrated a growing spiritual understanding on Dwayne's part, and a noticeable lessening of a focus on himself.

On the next page of the letter, Dwayne added, *"In reflecting back upon the past 25 years or so, I made a whole lot of bad choices, stupid decisions, was blatantly hypocritical, among many other things. But one thing I clearly see is that there was no other way (how I wish there were!) to learn what I know today. Nothing else could have given me the treasures I now have! Even Donette said she would not be the woman she is today had she not experienced what she did! I say, though sadly, nor would I and nor would you, Mom. Please, please do not misunderstand what I'm saying—I am certainly not trying to pin some type of justification for my many sins, tragic they were. The difficulty I have in saying so, I say in spite of it, Dad's death was not in vain. And, I believe, Dad knows this too and has forgiven me. What do you think?"*

The vicarious connection of sharing communion with Dwayne had boosted Cherie's spirits, and on the following day it was with renewed enthusiasm that she prepared for an afternoon wedding. Donette had scheduled three parties on consecutive weekends and today was the last of the three. She and Donette were busy from dawn until midnight. Despite the non-stop activities during the day, Cherie found her thoughts wandering back to the communion letter and onto Dwayne's present situation, preparing for yet another parole hearing.

In August, Dwayne wrote to the Bethel Assembly of God church in Medford. The three and a half pages were a synopsis of his time in prison and the crime that had gotten him there. He described his spiritual life and his declining physical condition. He mentioned that he'd been denied release by the parole board again in August of 2009 because of two misconduct reports. He said he was likely to be released in 2011 and desired to connect with a member of their congregation who would be willing to mentor him by mail, suggesting an exchange of letters once or twice each month. He wrote, *"I am only interested in learning about living the Christian life. I want a prayer partner, someone who can help me strengthen my walk with God. I would appreciate this beyond words and I hope and pray that it can be arranged. I really need help. I'm in a very weak and vulnerable state, living in the midst of much evil. I have determination, but no encouragement. Please help me, if you are able."*

When Cherie heard from Dwayne in late September, he expressed his wishes for Christmas. *"I am not able to play my guitar anymore because I have no feeling in my left hand. I keep trying, but I can't do it! A CD player would be a great thing for me for a lot of reasons."* He asked for three Christian CDs, writing that he also wanted a CD adapter and batteries. He apologized, as he usually did when asking for money, but he felt the need to express his desires so they would be known. He ended with, *"I only want what God wants me to have. Period."*

In the letter that arrived shortly before Thanksgiving, Dwayne pointed out that he was thirty-nine years old and Cherie sixty-nine. He wrote about his frustration, knowing that at this time in his life he should be helping Cherie with physical chores and the upkeep on her place. He slipped into related thoughts involving his life prior to his imprisonment. *"There are certainly a good number of ways in which I went astray, but, Mom, I need you to know that you and Dad raised me very well and, even though I greatly strayed, what you both taught me has never left me. I was just stubborn, hard-headed, and bitter for most of my life. About the first 30 years or so anyway. I could say easily 'what a waste,' but I don't think that would be correct because it was all part of God's plan."*

Physically, Dwayne felt better. He was able to walk with a walker for up to sixty-one feet without support. *"It's challenging, but I do know how to push myself... it's just been a lot of years since I did! And, funny I find myself saying this, but I was a lot younger too!"* Other good news was that most of his blood levels were improved. He enclosed an article titled "12 Tips for Teaching Thankfulness." Dwayne had written across the top, *"I thought this was a great article for the week of Thanksgiving and wanted to share it with you. Mom. I have so very much to be thankful for, it would take a lifetime to name every single thing!"*

After bringing Cherie up to date on his medical condition, Dwayne reported on the content of his recent introspection. He'd been thinking of his middle school years. He remembered how his slight frame and the early onset of asthma had prevented him from participating in sports, but he told her he'd always taken a special interest in football. *"I'd always loved to play, but I was always not good enough, fast enough, big enough, tough enough, or strong enough. But I damn sure tried."* He admitted to Cherie that when he got into drugs, he didn't want to do anything that required expending any energy. *"I know you remember those days. I remember them vividly and with very deep regret! I had so much potential for so many different things."*

During his imprisonment, Dwayne had continued to watch professional ball whenever he could, even referring to the sport as his *"secret love."* His letter to Katheryn in

December that same year began with a reference to how one of his favorite players illustrated that determination and hard work were critical to achievement. *"One of the people I've been inspired by is quarterback Brett Favre. He played 15 seasons for the Green Bay Packers, then went to the New York Jets for one season, and now plays for the Minnesota Vikings. Making his mark everywhere he goes. He holds all the records for passing, touchdowns, etc. and is rated the 4th greatest of all time. But what got me is he is my age (3 months older) and he is still going strong. In the NFL, 40 years old is an old man! 'If he can do it, I told myself, then so can I.' And that's when I started getting better. I'd watch him play every week, then I'd set new goals for myself.*

"I've gone from barely being able to get out of bed on my own and getting winded doing so, to walking 984 feet with a cane! Next week my distance will increase to 1107 feet (that's the distance of the infirmary hallway 9 times). My blood labs are better than they have been in probably 10 years. I'm not using a catheter for dialysis anymore (I have a functional fistula in my left arm—a miracle in itself that it could even be done!) and the order was written by my outside kidney doctor today to have my bowels reconnected so I can get rid of the colostomy bag. The doctor approved it last month, but I asked to wait until after the holidays. I am hoping I can regain about 50 pounds and get back into shape. I weigh 123 right now up from 107.

"God has indeed blessed me in many ways and kept me through all that has transpired these past couple years. There were times when I was quite angry with God and wondered if He was still there. It was frustrating, scary, and provoked feelings of despair sometimes. But in the end, He always proved Himself and opened doors for me, probably many more than I've even realized! I guess I was looking for the miraculous and He was giving me the practical that was well within my reach.

"Remember the story of the man who was stranded on the roof of his house because of a bad flood? After 2 boats and a helicopter came to his rescue, he turned them all away saying, 'No, thanks. God will save me.' Well, after he drowned and went to heaven, he asked God why He hadn't answered his prayers and God said, 'I did. I sent you 2 boats and a helicopter.' Well, I sort of feel like that man.

"I was reminded of my old workout philosophy: with weightlifting—if you don't give your muscles a reason to grow, they won't. With martial arts—repetition is the mother of all skill. With things in general—if you don't pursue your goals relentlessly, you'll never get them.

"My music talent is still sleeping, however. I have limited control and coordination with my left hand. When I try to play my guitar, it sounds as if I've never played before. It's distressing! But I believe it'll come back—our Lord gave me that talent for a reason.

"Spiritually I've been really struggling. I've left the Catholic Church for the most part, and I was on fire for a while going back into the Pentecostal church. But I feel like I'm starting to grow cold and I don't know why. I've been angry with people, and can't seem to focus. It seems like every time I try a new service, I hear blatant contradictions between the preacher's words and scripture. I don't know what to do. I need prayer for sure. I don't want to tell Mom and give her reason for alarm... she has enough to deal with where I'm concerned. I'm going to write Pastor Ron though and open up to him.

"Well, I wish a great new year to you and a wonderful, merry Christmas. May we all remember the reason we celebrate this Day! 'For there is born to you this day in the city of David a Savior, who is Christ the Lord.' "

Until Cherie visited Dwayne in early December, she didn't realize he was so sick that he'd been moved to the prison infirmary. Visitors were prohibited from seeing inmates confined to the medical unit, but because Dwayne had been on good behavior, the decision was made to allow Cherie in to see him, which was a privilege that she was told "they never do."

When Cherie entered his room, she found Dwayne confined to bed and guarded by two corrections officers. She sat in the chair next to his bed, clasped his hand between both of hers, and kissed him, ignoring the rules that prohibited touching during a visit. For the first time since his incarceration, Cherie and Dwayne had time together without the distraction of others. Dwayne's medical condition necessitated he be housed in the infirmary, but he was clear of mind and wasn't going to let the opportunity of his mother's visit be wasted. Intent upon having communion with Cherie, he asked the two guards if he and his mom could have crackers and juice. One of the men returned moments later with apple juice and crackers, which Dwayne divided between himself and Cherie.

Cherie recalled the years she'd prayed that Dwayne would truly be sorry for what he'd done. For so long, she hadn't seen signs of empathy or remorse. In fact, for years his letters indicated that his heart was hard, and her prayers appeared to go unanswered. But today she saw a totally different person in the hospital bed taking communion with her. She marveled at the change God had brought about in her son, a change that seemed to have followed Dwayne's search for spiritual understanding. As Dwayne led the two of them in communion, Cherie started to cry, and so did he. They both knew that change had come about in themselves and their relationship with each other.

When Cherie wrote a Christmas card to Dwayne a week later, she told him she was sending some money and regretted that she didn't have more to offer. *"Merry Christmas to my son Dwayne. May 2010 be a wonderful year for all of us."* On the back of the card, she reminded him that she was almost seventy. She'd been thinking of who would be there for him if she were to pass away. *"I* want you to know, if anything happens to me, you continue to study the Word, stay close to Christians that love the Lord, and ask for pen pals that are Christian. Keep connected to Christian people that have the love of God in them. Promise me that and I know you'll be okay. I love you son and want the best for you."

Dwayne penned his first letter of 2010 the day before his fortieth birthday. Although he still needed to live in the infirmary, his blood levels had continued to improve. The dialysis fistula in his left arm was working well, and since the dialysis was going better, he was feeling better too. "I plan to start working out as hard as I can as soon as I get my bowels hooked back up. I'm going to be 40 tomorrow so I better get myself as healthy as I can while I can, right? I was talking to the dialysis nurse yesterday about seeing if they could speed things up on my getting that surgery and told her why. She said, 'So you're having a mid-life crisis? Is that what you're telling me?' I laughed so hard I nearly cried. 'Maybe I am.' I just told her. 'Well, yeah, I guess I am.' She just laughed."

On Thursday, February 11, 2010, Cherie wrote the last letter she would send to Dwayne. She began by thanking God for the good report on his health, then wrote news of people they both knew. She apologized for not writing sooner, talking of the endless chores involved in taking care of the property and managing the household.

Cherie carried on with the letter by returning to a familiar matter. As the years passed and she'd witnessed positive changes in her son, she again pressed Dwayne to document his life story. She was convinced that parents with a wayward son or daughter would be encouraged to read that Dwayne had changed and believe in the possibility that their son or daughter could transform too. Cherie was certain that an account of Dwayne's conversion would offer hopefulness to discouraged and frustrated parents.

But Dwayne viewed the idea of a written testimony differently. He wished that his story would persuade young people to redirect their lives away from making bad choices like rebelling against their parents and experimenting with drugs, but he worried that others might think he was exploiting his story for personal gain. The passage of time had dulled the memory of Don's murder. Dwayne feared that Donette would be hurt if he recounted events that were painful for her. So, whenever Cherie mentioned the idea, Dwayne agreed that the objective and intentions were good but always made excuses for not pursuing the project.

When Dwayne wrote his letter dated March 15, he didn't respond to Cherie's queries about writing his testimony, but he was in good spirits, delighted to have received a letter from his mom. *"I was happy to get your letter as I've been wondering how you're doing and a bit worried."* He thanked her for the birthday card, joking about turning forty. *"It's not so bad being 40, but I'll tell you this—it was a hell of a lot easier to bounce back into good health at 30 than it is at 40! ha-ha."*

He was ecstatic to report that he'd seen the gastrointestinal surgeon at OHSU for a consultation. *"They have me scheduled to get the reconnective surgery done within the next two weeks. Then I won't have to have this colostomy bag anymore! No more accessories hanging out of me— no more dialysis catheters or poop bags! That means I can exert myself to a greater intensity so I can get some muscle back, get back into the martial arts, and live with more purpose than I have been these past several years. Maybe I can pass all the knowledge and wisdom I've acquired on to someone else. That would really be great!"*

As Dwayne entertained the idea of renewed physical strength, accompanied by the desire to be of help to others, he recalled an incident that he'd meant to share with his mom. *"There was a Hispanic man here in the infirmary not too long ago who had a colostomy bag put in. It was all* new to him. One day, one of the nurses had to change it and she sent one of the orderlies down to ask me to come look at it to make sure she did it right. I checked; she did. I offered to help if it was needed. There was a language barrier so we had one of the bilingual orderlies translating (made me wish I'd put more effort into learning Spanish!)

"A few hours later the guy with the bag came up to me gesturing that his bag was full and he didn't know how to empty it. So the nurse and an officer had him come into my room and watch me empty mine since I needed to empty as well (although I had to improvise and alter the way I normally empty mine to fit his needs, since his was in a different position than mine—difficult for me, but an easier way for him, given the position of his bag.) Then I went into his room with him and coached him while he emptied his, passing on my 2 years of learned wisdom on how to keep it meticulously clean, comfortable, and odor free. I didn't give it much thought at the time, it just seemed like the right thing to do. But afterward it seemed sort of weird because it's a pretty private thing. But it really felt good to be able to help someone whom I was in a unique position to help. Having the opportunity—and uniquely so, to help someone is beyond what words can express!"

During his years in prison, Dwayne had immersed himself in various churches from Pentecostal to Catholic. He'd made friends, had mentors, learned scriptures and doctrinal differences. He'd experienced the benefits of various denominations and seen hypocrisy in people no matter what their affiliation. He told Cherie, "Something I have come to understand is that when our Lord leads us to something, we ought to do our best to see it through to fulfillment, NOT look for a reason to run from it and certainly not follow 'public opinion' or 'selfish desire,' or 'political correctness!' I have turned my back on the Catholic Church twice in the past year or so, only to find myself again faced with the same inconsistencies, hypocrisy, and heresies that prompted me to join the Catholic Church to begin with back in May of 2007! I could apply a legal analysis and become extremely critical of both the Catholic and Protestant Churches, but that isn't what Christianity is all about. It's about loving the Lord your God with all your being and loving our neighbor as our-self, even as He had loved us."

Dwayne expounded further on his observations. "Some people are critical of this church, others are critical of that church, but who are we to judge our master's servants? We need to search within and evaluate ourselves; are we loving the Lord? Are we loving our neighbor? If we were, would we be so critical? I think not. But enough about that. I really didn't intend to go on and on about this, but I thought it was important to explain why I make the choices I do. I'm your son, you have every right to know and I believe you want to know these things." He added another consideration regarding the differences in peoples' searches for spiritual truth. "There are basically 3 types of people: those who have searched and found, those who are searching and have not yet found, and those who are not searching and will therefore not find."

Returning to the subject of his health, Dwayne couldn't have been happier to finally be able to tell Cherie that he seemed to be improving. "Maybe a good thing for me to consider is this: get myself into a good state of health and then work with dialysis patients to help them maintain a good state of health, which could very reasonably translate into a longer, better quality of life. Perhaps become a personal trainer. I've done it in here many times and I love doing it. What a model that would be for someone in naturally good health! A man on dialysis for well more than a decade to be raising the bar, setting an example, would be remarkable! Would you agree? I'm up for the challenge! And why not leave a legacy?" He wrote in large cursive letters beneath his signature: "I love you very much, Mom!

You are the World's Greatest Mom still, and that won't ever change no matter how old we get!" (He drew a happy face.)

Dwayne's next letter, written two weeks later, began with answers to questions Cherie had asked him. Yes, he remembered Mr. Mackey, the middle school teacher she'd asked him about, telling Cherie how he recalled the creative activities the teacher had organized and the positive impact the man had on him. He told her he was perplexed about her tax return and wondered why she wasn't entitled to get any money back, questioning whether she needed another accountant. He said he thought her yard worker was charging her too much, speculating that maybe the worker was taking advantage of her.

Having exhausted his worries about her, Dwayne updated Cherie on his health. For years he'd been having problems with his teeth, another consequence of his Alport syndrome. *"The dentist has been preparing me for upper dentures since December. So far, he's taken out 5 on the upper right and 4 on the upper left. The bottoms are okay. I'll be glad when it's done and I won't be so self-conscious and embarrassed to smile big again. I miss that!"* He encouraged Cherie in her plans to join the YMCA, agreeing that getting in shape was a worthy goal. Then he wrote of his own strategy to improve his fitness. *"I've been easing into an exercise regimen myself. I'm up to doing it every other day now. I do 2 sets of pushups, down under pull ups, squats and one arm power cleans with an overhead press added. Next week I'll add chair dips and maybe increase the number of sets to 3. I'm also doing some basic punches and blocks and stretching. I'm definitely starting to feel better. Here's a new goal—to be in the best shape as I possibly can be when you visit."* He mentioned the world news, remarking, *"I really didn't care much about what was going on in the world when I was younger, but the older I get, the more I care... and worry. But rather than turn grey, my hair just falls out! I love you, Mom, Your son, Dwayne"*

In Cherie's next letter she filled several pages, front and back. The letter was incomplete, trailing off in the middle of a paragraph. Maybe she'd started it, then set it aside to finish later. The date at the top was March 27, 2010. Part of what she wrote reads as follows:

"Dear Son, I just received your letters and got notification you were in the hospital for the procedure you were telling me about so I called the hospital [today] and they said everything went well and because it wasn't life-threatening, they wouldn't let me talk to you. It was against the RULES. I was really happy to hear from you. We're going to try a trip the end of April to see you. Money is tight right now. We only have three weddings booked which is very bad for us. Please keep us in prayer, it's so needful. I don't know why things are bad. Maybe the Lord is trying to tell us something. Palm Sunday is tomorrow and Easter is next Sunday. In case I don't get any cards mailed, please know my thoughts and my heart is with you. Have a truly great Easter! It will be great to have your body back almost to normal. Yes, Son you should write Mr. Mackey and tell him all those things you told me in your letter and more. He would love hearing from you and I would love hearing what he has to say to you. Tell him how you felt about him, and all about the things you remember. You'll make his day. Mr. Mackey was a great teacher. I thought also."

Cherie had mentioned Palm Sunday and Easter in her letter to Dwayne. The week between the two Sundays is considered Holy Week by the Christian church and Cherie, like most Christians, believed the week to be a time of solemn reflection. But she found herself distracted, thinking of Dwayne in the Portland hospital. It had been nearly a week since he'd undergone surgery, and she was anxious to have an update on his condition. The procedure was straight-forward and, unlike most of his visits to the hospital, this time Dwayne had been looking forward to the surgery. After her conversation with the corrections officer guarding Dwayne the previous week, Cherie had known that she wasn't likely to get to talk with Dwayne, but at least she might get information about his status.

When Cherie did call Dwayne's hospital room on April 1, the guard said, "Dwayne will be taken back to prison tomorrow. He's in really good shape. He's happy and laughing and talking with the nurses. Everything with the surgery went great!"

Cherie told him, "Good! I'm glad he's doing better!" She thanked the guard and asked if he would tell Dwayne she loved him and that she was praying for him and he said he would.

***

Cherie received a phone call at four o'clock on the morning of April 2. The caller told her that something had happened with Dwayne during the night, although he wasn't sure exactly what. He said that Dwayne was still alive, but he was mentally dead. He was on life support.

The shock of the phone call startled Cherie out of sleep, and her mind was foggy. She tried to focus on the words coming over the phone. The caller identified himself as Dwayne's doctor and said he was phoning to notify her of a sudden change in her son's condition. The doctor knew she lived five hours away and said that if she wanted to come up to the hospital, they would keep Dwayne alive on life support. He realized the news of Dwayne's condition was very hard to hear and that at this early hour she might need to give the decision some thought. He told her the staff would keep her son comfortable and wait to hear back from her. He expressed his condolences and encouraged her to call him back if she had further questions. Cherie sat propped up in her bed, stunned by the call.

Sometime later, Cherie dressed and drove the short distance to Marilyn's house to tell her the news. "We called the doctor back, talked to him on the phone, and he said, 'You know, really, he's already gone.'"

Cherie debated whether to go up to OHSU or not. Would she regret not making the ten-hour round trip to the hospital to say goodbye to Dwayne? she wondered. The doctor had said Dwayne was already gone. Marilyn kindly refused to offer her opinion, telling Cherie the decision was hers, and no one else's. She reassured Cherie that she would be there whatever Cherie chose to do and that she was willing to make the drive with her to Portland if that was what Cherie wanted.

Cherie wrestled with the decision, heartbroken. "I knew what I was supposed to do. Dwayne had sent me papers explaining his wishes. He told me he didn't want to be kept alive if it meant the doctors had him on a machine. But it was hard for me to let him go. I'd never had to do that for anybody and to do it for my own son was very, very hard."

There had been so many horrible years: years of concern about Dwayne's disturbing childhood behaviors, years of desperate parenting as she and Don had tried to control Dwayne's destructive tendencies, years of devastation after Don's death, and years of being blamed by Dwayne for all of the troubles that had befallen him.

After so many awful years, it seemed to Cherie that she and Dwayne had just started building a relationship with each other, finding peace and reconciliation. She'd lost her son twice before, once to drugs and then to prison. Now she was losing him for a final time. How could she make a decision to end his life? She spent the greater part of the day with Marilyn, tortured by having to choose.

"I knew what Dwayne's wishes were. I knew what I had to do. But it was terribly hard to let him go. I was just getting to know a better person." Cherie was painfully aware that to honor Dwayne's request would mean to spare his spirit from being trapped in a body that was only sustained by a machine. To let him go would be the last gesture of love she could show him, acting on his wishes and not hers. The doctor had told her Dwayne was brain dead. There was no chance of revival. Thinking of her son's wishes, Cherie remembered how he'd told her he hoped he wouldn't die in prison. He'd meant that he hoped to be paroled one day and have a chance to live on the outside. She was comforted knowing that Dwayne wouldn't die in prison. He'd been incarcerated for twenty-four years, but he would die in a hospital, not behind prison walls. It was mid-afternoon before she called the hospital and told them they could remove Dwayne's life support and let him go.

Later that same day, Dwayne's doctor telephoned to tell Cherie her son had passed away at 5:07 p.m. on April 2. It was Good Friday.

Dwayne was cremated and his remains were sent to Cherie. There would be no autopsy, and the cause of his death was never specified. No longer locked behind bars or plagued by physical or psychological demons, Dwayne had entered into eternal peace.

EPILOGUE

Cherie had been told that she had bile duct cancer in November of 2017 and for the next two years, she'd courageously endured all that follows a cancer diagnosis. In May of 2019, she was discharged from her last hospital stay and put on hospice. She knew she couldn't vacillate in deciding what to do with her son's ashes. For almost eight years, she'd kept Dwayne's ashes inconspicuously stored in the pale green box sent by the prison. On this particular afternoon, while Marilyn and I met with her to discuss her life story, Cherie unexpectedly announced to us that she "needed to do something with Dwayne" and told us about the green box. I remember in that moment, wondering why she hadn't buried his ashes sooner, though I knew that some people chose to keep their loved one's remains. Cherie told us she was bringing up the subject now because of her declining health and, in her words, she "didn't want Donette to have to deal with Dwayne."

On Saturday afternoon a week later, Marilyn and I were visiting and Cherie asked us if we would bury Dwayne's ashes that afternoon. She told us she would like his remains buried under the myrtle wood tree in her yard, the one Dwayne had brought home as a seedling from Boy Scouts. Of course we would, we told her. We offered to bring a chair outdoors so she could sit nearby but she declined, satisfied that we would carry out her wishes. Marilyn and I dug a small trench in the flowerbed under the flourishing tree, now twenty-five feet high, and carefully removed and buried the contents from the box labeled:

DWAYNE DEAN WIER

January 10, 1970 – April 2, 2010

We cobbled together a makeshift service, asking for God's blessing on Dwayne, reciting the Lord's Prayer and Psalms 23, then praying that he rest in everlasting peace. During the next week, Donette opened the house to visitors, letting Cherie's friends know her mom was on hospice and inviting anyone who wanted to, to visit. The following two weeks, Cherie slept more and ate less as her life in this world faded. Nine years after Dwayne died and three weeks after his ashes were buried, Cherie completed her life's journey and quietly passed away in her home on her Little Bit of Heaven. The date was June 15, 2019. She was buried next to her beloved Don in a cemetery near Grants Pass.

These months later, in 2021, after reading all of Dwayne's letters and relistening to Cherie's interviews, I think I understand more than I did when I first learned of the existence of the pale green box and its contents. I think Cherie kept Dwayne's remains because the ashes were all she had left of him, the Dwayne she'd come to know at the end of his life.

The Applegate River has shifted over the years and although the crying rock no longer rests near the fishing hole where Don caught his first steelhead, it remains a lasting monument to one young couple who moved from California with the simple hope of finding a place to fish and raise their family peacefully in the Pacific Northwest.

For More News About Leslie Ghiglieri,
Signup For Our Newsletter:

http://wbp.bz/newsletter

Word-of-mouth is critical to an author's long-
term success. If you appreciated this book please
leave a review on the Amazon sales page:

http://wbp.bz/tdtka

\

Recovery Center
"Building New Life Upon the ROC"
541-200-3000

MISSION STATEMENT
The ROC is a faith-based charitable organization whose purpose is to empower, inspire, and provide restoration to the brokenhearted as they overcome addiction, rebuild lives, and restore families through God's love.

ABOUT "THE ROC"
The ROC is a faith-based charitable organization that is committed to meet the needs of those struggling with addiction behavior, mental illness, domestic violence, homelessness or emotional trauma in our community. It is our desire to provide healing through one-on-one peer support services and to connect the brokenhearted to the resources within our community. The ROC not only desires to provide HOPE but is committed to the transformation of building new lives.

WE ARE HERE TO SERVE
Counseling and Peer Support services are duly credentialed and certified addiction professionals who have common life experiences with the people they are serving. People with mental and/or substance use disorders have a unique capacity to help each other based on a shared affiliation and a deep understanding of this experience. In self-help and mutual support, people offer this support, strength, and hope to their peers, which allows for personal growth, wellness promotion, and recovery. (SAMSHA)